"Best-selling writer Piercy and novelist/publisher Wood have been co-teaching writers workshops for years and have reproduced their master course in this useful manual. The two authors encourage would-be writers to read as much as possible (included is a list of recommended books) as reading plays the key role in the process of learning how to write. Their exercises are short and to the point, just enough to get the juices flowing. This book, although joining an already saturated market is worth the shelf space."
—*Library Journal*

"Seamless and exceptionally engaging ... a valuable tool for the apprentice in search of practical advice on the craft of fiction and memoir writing from accomplished novelists."
— *ForeWord*

"This new column, The Writing Life, helps to choose the best [of the how-to-write books] ... Writers seriously looking to have their work published should pick up *So You Want to Write*. Wood's advice on getting your work published is extremely helpful and worth the cost of the book alone."
—*The St. Petersburg Times*

To Taylor,

So You Want To Write

For the writer in our family. May this book help you along your journey.

Love,
Grandma and Grandpa
2008

So You Want To Write

How to Master the Craft of Writing Fiction and Memoir
(Second Edition)

Marge Piercy

and

Ira Wood

Leapfrog Press
Wellfleet, Massachusetts

Originally Published in 2001 in the United States by
The Leapfrog Press
P.O. Box 1495   95 Commercial Street
Wellfleet, MA 02667-1495, USA
www.leapfrogpress.com

Distributed in the United States and Canada by
Consortium Book Sales and Distribution
St. Paul, Minnesota 55114

Second Edition

The Library of Congress has cataloged the first edition as follows:

Piercy, Marge.
    So you want to write: how to master the craft of fiction and the per-
sonal narrative / by
  Marge Piercy & Ira Wood.
      p. cm.
  Includes bibliographical references.
  ISBN 0-9679520-2-6 (alk. paper)
    1. Fiction—Authorship. 2. Autobiography—Authorship. I. Wood, Ira.
II. Title.

  PN3355 .P54 2001
  808.3—dc21

                                                              00-069009

ISBN-13: 978-0-9728984-5-4 (pbk., second edition)
ISBN-10: 0-9728984-5-X (pbk., second edition)

10 9 8 7 6 5 4 3 2 1

Printed in Canada

For the young who want to*

Talent is what they say
you have after the novel
is published and favorably
reviewed. Beforehand what
you have is a tedious
delusion, a hobby like knitting.

Work is what you have done
after the play is produced
and the audience claps.
Before that friends keep asking
When you are planning to go
out and get a job.

Genius is what they know you
had after the third volume
of remarkable poems. Earlier
they accuse you of withdrawing,
ask why you don't have a baby,
call you a bum.

The reason people want M.F.A.'s,
take workshops with fancy names
when all you can really
learn is a few techniques,
typing instructions and somebody else's mannerisms

is that every artist lacks
a license to hang on the wall
like your optician, your vet
proving you may be a clumsy sadist
whose fillings fall into the stew
but you're certified a dentist.

The real writer is one
who really writes. Talent
is an invention like phlogiston
after the fact of fire.
Work is its own cure. You have to
like it better than being loved.

*From *Circles on the Water: Selected Poems of Marge Piercy*, Published by Alfred A. Knopf, NY
1982. © 1982 by Marge Piercy

So You Want To Write

Contents

An Introduction to the Second Edition

This book is a product of workshops we have given together for many years and the thousands of writers we have worked with over that time. One of the many lessons we've learned is that effective workshops aren't performances but dialogs that expand and evolve, reflecting not only the knowledge of the leaders but also the interests of the writers who participate. We've discovered that no two workshops are ever alike. No matter the material we came prepared to cover, writers in our workshops were of many levels of experience and worked in different genres. They had different needs and questions about their work. Releasing a Second Edition of *So You Want to Write* has enabled us to include a variety of topics that we've developed since the original publication. You'll find new chapters on short story writing, genre writing (historical, science fiction, and mystery), humor writing, selecting a title, and how to avoid writing like a victim; many new writing exercises and examples; a personal essay on the illusions of fame; a section on the career pitfalls that many writers fall into; additions such as the writing of sex scenes and how to characterize emotion; and a lot of new information that comes from our personal give and take with writers, reflected in the updated Frequently Asked Questions and Practical Information sections.

We usually teach personal narrative or fiction together, but each of us has also taught a version of both courses alone. In actual team-taught workshops, we divide up the topics, but we have each worked on every essay in this book. The "I" throughout the manuscript is one or the other of us; we felt it did not really matter which, and was less awkward than the royal "we" when speaking of something one of us wrote or did.

In workshops, we use examples from many writers—but the problem of paying for permissions has led us to use only our own work or those of writers published by our press, Leapfrog. It is not egotism but the desire to keep the price of this book down that has led us to quote so freely from ourselves.

You will find that throughout the book we will refer you to many memoirs and novels. We do this in the earnest hope that you will not only read, for example, the beginning of a piece cited as having a good one, but go on reading. Since we've begun teaching these master classes together, we've noticed an alarming trend. Students ask us what to read to improve their writing and seem disappointed when we do not refer them to the hundreds of books that have appeared on the market in the last decade that are "about" writing, or "the process" of writing, or the "path" or the "journey" taken by writers. Reading itself—the habit of reading, the immersion in books, learning how other writers have solved the same problems—seems to some emerging writers less important than developing the perfect attitude toward writing or fitting writing into a life the way they might schedule time at the gym. Great writing has been done in prisons and cramped hotel rooms and commuter trains, on rickety tables in noisy restaurants, at four in the morning before the twelve-hour workday begins. Such writing has been done by people who experienced the need to write as strongly as they experienced thirst. People seem to take it as a given that great movies have been made by those who have immersed themselves in the cinema, who find true passion on a screen in a room with no windows. Yet these same people bridle when we tell them that to be a good writer you should be as well versed in literature as Martin Scorsese is in the films of John Ford. You would not want to be defended in court by a lawyer who had read a book called *The Attorney's Journey* and neglected to study case law. Likewise it seems absurd that people who want to write memoirs don't think it necessary to read the memoirs others have written before them.

Of course if you are not writing primarily to be published and read, you may not need or wish to be informed of the state of your art. The choice to write in journals for therapeutic reasons and for self-expression is a righteous one. Some journals, after intensive editing, have been published and cherished by readers. Often these have been the works of experienced writers or people who have lived through extraordinary times. Such memoirs have been more carefully shaped than the word "journal" might imply.

Nevertheless, this book is about writing to be published, about learning the elements of craft that modern readers have come to expect, such as the ability to seduce your reader with a good beginning and to create characters who are more than stereotypes. Most writers use notebooks in one way or another, whether in the form of a laptop or a Palm Pilot or a spiral pad or even scraps of paper napkins: some way of capturing random ideas or snippets of dialog overheard or insights from a nightmare. This note-taking is not to be confused with the journal kept by a young man in one of our classes who had more than a thousand single-spaced handwritten pages about his family that he expected us to tell him how to turn into a novel. For years he had been dutifully writing down his thoughts when he woke up every morning. Now he was overwhelmed by the task of recopying and editing these impressions and memories into a manuscript with a shape: a beginning, a plot, and characters who could come to life in a mind other than his own. (For instance, a man who had needs and motivations and a history understandable to a reader, as opposed to the workaholic bully who was all the writer saw when imagining his father.) Eventually, he decided to start from scratch on the novel and use his journal as a reference.

Where we have included exercises, we recommend actually trying them to get full benefit. We ask people to do these in our classes and have found they work. A number of people who have taken our workshops have gone on to publish, some quite successfully; many make the leap to submitting their work to book publishers and zines, while others have joined writers groups or used these essays and exercises to motivate their own students. We don't for a moment imagine that our advice is the last word on writing. It is simply the distillation of many years of professional experience in literature and publishing. What we most hope to communicate, in our classes and in this book, are the skills necessary to read critically. That is, what to look for as you read, what questions to ask. How have other writers solved the problems of drawing in a reader who is faced with thousands of other titles? How have other writers used dialog to advance their plot?

We have a dear friend who hates cookbooks. Whenever she makes a casserole or creates a soup, she insists on inventing from scratch. She thinks it's more creative, or that she's avoiding the reenactment of her mother's tired life. The product leaves much to be desired. Roast lamb really isn't very good well-done in salsa. Cashews are seldom found in tomato soup for a reason. We hope you won't write like this dear woman cooks. You don't have to reinvent the wheel or the novel. There is always room for innovation, but you won't know what's new and what's tired if you don't read widely and critically. This book is a craft workshop on paper, but if you only read it without trying out at least some of what is suggested, you won't get the maximum benefit.

1

Sharpening Your Innate Skills

I believe the barriers to creativity are both inner and outer. The distinction between madness and sanity is one made by those around us: they honor us or they commit us. An act that brings admiration in one society will get you locked up in another. Seeing visions was a prerequisite for adulthood in Plains Indian societies, and quite dangerous today. Societies also differ in how they regard the artist, how integrated into the ordinary work of the community she or he is thought to be, how nearly the society regards artistic production as real production, as a reasonable adult activity—a job, in other words.

Working in any of the arts in this society is a self-elected activity. Although parents may applaud their children's performances in school plays, I have never heard of a parent who did not try to discourage a child who decided to become a professional actor. Even the occasional bit of back-slapping advice you get from peers is usually based on the misapprehension that writing is much easier than it is and that it is infinitely more well paid than is the case. If you tell a friend one week that you are trying to start a novel, likely they will ask you what you are doing the next month, be astonished that you are still writing the same novel, and so on; and when you have finished, they will ask whether you have sold it yet, as if selling a novel were easy.

Basically there is little support in our culture for apprenticeship. Even in a relatively sophisticated movie such as *Amadeus*, the proof of Mozart's genius is that he doesn't correct, doesn't hesitate, but the music gushes out of him almost too fast for him to write it down.

In writing there is always more to read, study, learn, try out, master. The more you as a writer are open to understanding the United States and the world in which we live as richly and variously cultured, the more there is to learn, the more different strands of language and crafts to which you will apprentice yourself. It is not nearly sufficient to know and know thoroughly British and American literature, even if you throw in, as we increasingly must, Canadian and Australian authors. Who would strive to understand contemporary literature without Atwood, Munro, Keneally, White? But lacking a knowledge of Japanese literature, of French, Italian, Spanish, South American and Mexican literature, of Russian, Scandinavian, Greek, or contemporary African writing, all makes us stupider than we can afford to be if we mean to write. Most foreign literatures you will read in translation, although being in command of at least one foreign language helps a writer immensely in understanding her own.

If you want to write a memoir, read memoirs. If you want to write science fiction, read science fiction. Often in workshops, participants will ask us to recommend a "how to write" book—like this one. But the truth is, the best books you can read on how to write are books that are in the genre in which you want to write. What we hope to teach you, in part, is to read like a writer: to read noticing craft. The books you don't think work well may teach you as much as the ones that wring admiration from you. Whatever the author is doing, you want to ask how and look at the choices made.

All of this notion of apprenticeship is at odds with the model of success in the arts so many young people bring to bear, mostly from the careers of rock musicians. You can make it as a rock musician with three or four chords and a gimmick, at least for one record, but you can also be a has-been at twenty-two. There are equivalents among writers, but not many. Basically you may publish an occasional poem or short story in college, usually in the college literary magazine, but few serious writers reach visibility before thirty to thirty-five.

Giant conglomerates control the big media and own the New York publishing houses. They are run the same way as other large conglomerates, and in spite of the wishes of many dedicated editors, they would like to put out generic products like brands of toothpaste or breakfast cereal with an assured cut of a guaranteed market. As one delighted publishing CEO gushed in his company's year-end report, "Fewer titles have translated into more attention for each book, greater publishing success and higher revenues." Books, real books, are risky. Better financial projections can be obtained on the *All Chocolate Eat Yourself Skinny Diet Book* and thrillers that, like the movies *Halloween 16* and *Die Hard 56,* offer exactly the same product in a slightly jazzier package—the romance, the success story. It no longer shocks people to hear that chain and the large on-line booksellers rent space to publishers the same way that supermarkets sell the most ideal shelves for corn chips and pretzels. Publishers can pay to have their titles stacked at the front table, or positioned face-out at the checkout counter and at the ends of aisles. Large publishers, of course, can better afford the thousands of dollars it may cost for a fifty-copy display or a large window sign. But of course they expect a return on their investment and the best chance of getting that return is with a product—or author—that got one before: one with name recognition. It's not some evil plan, just a business plan. But these marketing strategies work against all writers just starting out or those who want to do original work.

The inner and outer barriers interact because we tend to internalize rejection and lack of recognition, and because we are programmed by the media and our peers to believe that writers who are "successful" produce better work.

Work in the arts requires your best energy. That means figuring out how, in the course of a life that usually includes another full-time job whether paid or unpaid, you can organize your time so that you write with your best energy, not your slackest. That may require getting up before everyone else in your house or your close circle; it may mean working after everyone else is in bed. It certainly means having time that is devoted to work, when you pull the phone out of its jack and do not answer the door. If you have children and thus cannot quite cut yourself off from interruption, you can attempt to make it clear that only an emergency is suitable for interrupting you. You may feel guilty setting boundaries, but what kind of adults will grow from never having learned that other people have boundaries that must not be crossed? Should they not rather learn what I hope you have realized, that work is precious and concentration is to be valued, to be sharpened, to be refined? We look more carefully at organizing time in the chapter "Work and Other Habits."

What I will return to again and again is the ability to use your mind mindfully and purposefully. To know when to go with the flow and when to turn on the cold critical eye. To know when to loose your imagination and when to keep it under control. Concentration is learned by practicing it, just as is any other form of exercise or excellence. Even when the focus of the concentration is something in the past of the writer or some nuance of feeling or precise tremor of the emotions, the writer at work is not the emotion. Work has its own exhilaration. You can be happy as a clam—precisely because you are not self-regarding at all, but doing your own tidal work—when you are writing a poem about how somebody was cruel and nasty to you. You can even have fun writing a story imagining your own suicide. You can experience joy writing a story about total nuclear destruction, because in that clear high place where concentration is fully engaged, there is no feeling of self. Learning to reach that state and prolong it is another apprenticeship we all undergo. You have to find the work more interesting than you find yourself, even if the work is created out of your own guts and what you are writing about is your own life.

In the ancient and very modern approach to spiritual energy and experience, the Kabbalah, which is my discipline, we speak of developing the adult mind. For a writer that is particularly important. The adult mind can decide not to fuss like an adolescent because our work and our persons have experienced rejection. The adult mind can put victories or defeats into perspective. The adult mind can choose not to allow interference from the worries of the day, not to give way to irrelevant fantasies when trying to craft a meaningful fantasy. The adult mind has learned to focus and to retain focus for a much longer period of time. We can all have bad days and we can all be distracted; it is a matter of degree and how often we can combat our idiotic and self-regarding tendencies.

Beside my computer is a window and on the ledge of the window are twelve rocks. They have accumulated over the years. Each represents some place I found sacred or meaningful. When I need to focus and center my mind, I pick up the rocks and weigh them in my hands. Eventually I will settle upon a particular rock to contemplate: maybe the rock I picked up after I climbed the Acrocorinth from the ruins of the temple of Aphrodite there. Maybe one from the Oregon coast from a dawn when I experienced a strong vision. It does not really matter which stone I select. What matters is that to me these are meaningful and radiant objects that I can focus on to get rid of clutter and distraction. It is a matter of closing down the noise of the ego, of worry, of casual boredom, of gossip, of concern with what people may think, thoughts of who has not been sufficiently appreciative of my great virtues lately. It does not matter what particular pattern you use to bring yourself into sharp focus on what you are about to write. It is only necessary that you do so. For some people, their screen saver works in the same way—or a piece of meditative music. Whatever works for you, use it.

Now, as a writer, one of the things which you learn to mine at will, to call up and to relinquish, is memory. Again it is a case of being able to focus on the present when that is required and appropriate, but also being able to focus on a particular area of the past when you need that.

One of the resources of the poet, the novelist, and the memoir writer alike is memory. Vladimir Nabokov called his memoir *Speak, Memory*; in Greek mythology, memory is the mother of the muses. You may say you have a good memory or a bad one. An eidetic memory I believe is inborn, but you can improve your memory as you can improve your tennis game or your aim.

By practicing, you can recover pieces of your childhood that you were not aware you remembered at all. There are also false memories that are interesting to explore. We all remember scenes from our childhood that we never witnessed. I have distinct memories from before my birth. These came from hearing stories as a child and imagining them so vividly that they became my own experience. You can learn to have a vivid memory again. There are books and books on improving your memory, but what they are usually dealing with is the problem of remembering the name of the insurance salesman you just met or recalling vocabulary words. We all know simple mnemonics. Before I go on a trip, I always have last-minute chores I must remember to do in the morning. I invent an acronym for them. Let's say COLACU. Feed CATS; OPEN hotbed; take LUNCH; turn on ANSWERING MACHINE; make thermos of COFFEE to go; UNPLUG computer.

But the memory I am talking about is sensual memory; it is memory that comes like Proust's, unbidden from a crumb of cake. It is memory that can be taught to come through patience and concentration. You can use what you do remember to move into what you have forgotten, by concentrating and extending your stroll through old rooms and old gardens and along half forgotten streets. Some of what you will remember you know is not so. I have memories from early childhood of enormous buildings that were not there. They only seemed enormous to me because I was so little standing and looking up at them.

To a fiction writer or a poet, it does not much matter whether a memory is a true one—to the extent that any memory is "true" since five peoples' memories of the same event are five different and quite distinct and often contradictory memories—or a fused memory or invented memory. If it has resonance, emotive content, meaning, then it is a useful memory to possess. Memories also change, of course. If we have grown angry with a friend, the past changes. What may once have seemed a wry sense of humor is now revealed, in light of our changed perspective, to be the mean and sarcastic streak they've always used to cut us down. We have become disillusioned and what appeared before as obvious virtues and good will are shadowed in retrospect. So we rewrite big and little history as we go.

Indeed, if you are writing a memoir of your childhood and you talk with your siblings, you may find that every child grew up in a different family because each experienced that family at a different stage: the parents were older or younger, more or less affluent, getting on with each other well or badly, suffering from problems or having solved them. The world of the family is very different for the first born, the middle child, the youngest.

An Exercise in Sensual Memory

This is a simple exercise I have been using with writing workshops for twenty years. Sometimes, I use it myself. It's almost a meditation, so it is best attempted in a comfortable position, whatever that may be for you, and in a quiet place, where you are not likely to be interrupted.

I will ask you to return to some particular place that was important to you in your childhood. I suggest returning to between four and eight years old, but it's your choice. In your imagination, walk down the block or the road leading to where you lived at that age, remembering you are small. If you pass a privet hedge, you do not look down into it, but you look sideways into its green density. When you come to the door, you may have to reach upward for the knob or buzzer. The door may be heavy for you and require effort to open.

I want you to enter the house or cabin or apartment you lived in at that time. I want you to pass through to a place that held some emotional resonance, some emotional importance for you at that time. Perhaps you were happy there; perhaps you felt safe; perhaps you were frightened there; perhaps you felt conflicted or uneasy. I want you to enter that room or place and experience it fully. Look at everything carefully, remembering your size and the angle from which you see the furniture. The underside of a table may be as important as the bearing surface to a young child. I want you to look at the ceiling; at the walls; at the floor. What covers the floor? I want you to touch everything. How does it feel? Is it rough, smooth, tacky, damp? I want you to use your sense of smell. Do you smell cooking odors, flowers from outside the open window, mustiness, your father's or mother's cigarette smoke, perfume, disinfectant? What do you hear? Are there windows and are they open or shut? Do you hear voices through the walls, the ceiling? Are the voices talking, singing, arguing? I want you to spend a period of time going over every inch of the room or place (I say "place" since it might be a basement, an attic, a root cellar, a garage, a hallway) and recall in full sensual detail as much as you can. Then I suggest you write down what you remember, trying to give not only the details but a sense of their resonance for you. Be extremely concrete and explicit about the details. Style is not what you are after here but emotional resonance.

I learned to do this when I was just starting out as a novelist. When I wrote a full-length memoir, I did a great deal of it in order to recover pieces of my childhood I had forgotten, and to render more vivid the parts I did recall.

Writing a memoir, of course, is the intersection of memory, intent and language. Both fiction and memoir are built out of words. You use words every day to order lunch, to answer the telephone, to greet and discuss, indicating friendliness (or the lack of it if you are shrugging off unwanted attentions), pass-ing time, exchanging information, giving advice or asking for sympathy. But when you write, you are using language in an even more purposeful way. Language is the stuff of your craft as acrylic and canvas might be that of a painter. You make out of words portraits, actions, everything that does and doesn't hap-pen on the page and therefore in the mind of the reader. Yes, we all use language, but casually, often sloppily. Writing fiction or a memoir is not the same as writing a memo, a letter, a journal entry, or an essay question.

You must become aware of the attributes of your medium: language. Language is a shaping of the air, the breath, into sounds and silences, in order to convey meaning and often, to convey emotion. The nature of those sounds and the lengths of those silences can be used to create effects that further the intent of the writing.

Language contains in it attitude. Slender and skinny, svelte and bony are all used to describe a person of the same weight. You meet a dedicated seer. I meet a fanatic. Or the familiar conjuga-tion of the verb: I am firm, you are stubborn, he is a pig-headed mule. I have a strong sense of justice and the courage to speak up; you are an irritable zealot who flares up at nothing. Attitude is built into language. Scientific language attempts to be neutral, but as physics tells us, we change what we observe. The history of science, as Stephen Jay Gould has so frequently described to us, is the history of attitude. What we perceive is colored by our culture, shaped by it. In the chapter on description, we will return to the practical application of those attributes of language.

As Gershom Sholem wrote about the Kabbalah long ago, much in the mystical experience is constant across culture but the forms it takes are culturally determined. Jews are more apt to hear voices uttering prophecy or see words than Christians, who usually see images. A Buddhist will not see the Virgin Mary; a Catholic mystic will not be vouchsafed a vision of Krishna or the Great Grandmother of Us All. We are all imbedded and imbued, dyed through and through with our culture.

Trying to get rid of attitude and culture merely impoverishes you. One human being isolated and alone is not a human being. We are social animals and we are artifacts of our culture. Being aware is not the same as trying to be without. We can become aware of our attitudes and our prejudices and our predispositions and choose which of them to foster and which of them to fight. But in other cultures, we are always a bit like tourists, going to the great cultural flea market and buying a great necklace or a headdress or a musical instrument to play. Until you have lived for a time in a foreign culture, immersed in its daily life, you have no idea at all how American you are.

In writing, much of this becomes important not in first draft, the early stages of creation, but in the critical stage of that process. After we have honed and practiced our concentration to the max and produced something, then we must break that oneness. We must step back mentally or even physically, by putting the work aside for a time, and then exercising the cold critical eye on it that says, of what I intended, what have I actually wrought? Maybe all, in two percent of cases. Maybe twenty percent of what I imagined is on paper. Maybe fifty percent. That is the time for putting in and taking out, for altering and stretching and chopping, for rethinking choices that may have been the wrong ones for that particular work. It is time for making conscious choices about form that may have been made instinctively in first draft, rightly or wrongly. One thing that workshops and books like this one can teach is a set of questions to ask of the work after the first draft, when it is not what we want it to be. What can we do now to make the thing come out right?

In fiction, did we choose the right viewpoint character for our story? Do we need more than one viewpoint? What do we gain and lose if we shift viewpoints? Did I start my short story or novel in the correct place in the chronology of the story? Does my memoir have a compelling beginning or am I doing too much explaining before I get going? Do I need all those flashbacks that interrupt the narrative flow? How's my pacing? Is my dialog working for characterization, local color, flavor and moving the plot along? Are my characters motivated and believable? Have I telegraphed my punches? Am I making full use of my minor characters? Do I have too many? Too few? What are the functions of each of them? Do I understand my protagonist or protagonists from the inside? Can I feel them? Have I brought them alive? Am I putting stuff into my memoir just because it happened, not because it is germane to the flow of the narrative I am crafting? It is good to remember as much as you can, but once you have remembered, you have to decide which of those memories are relevant and which are not relevant to the particular work in which you are engaged. Not everything you remember matters to your story. Most of it doesn't.

We are trying to suggest to you questions to ask of yourself and your work when you are not yet doing what you mean to do in a piece. In short, most of what we teach is how to start and how to revise: how to get from the rough stuff on the page to something that resembles the glorious thing in your mind's eye. The rest is how to work and keep working, and what to do with your product.

2

Beginnings

Fiction is as old a habit of our species as poetry. It goes back to telling a tale, the first perceptions of pattern, and narrative is still about pattern in human life. At its core, it answers the question, what then? And then and then and then. And memoir is equally old: it's telling about your life, perhaps originally to children or a prospective mate or a new acquaintance.

Poetry is an art of time, as music is. Rhythms are measured against time: they are measures of time. A poem goes forward a beat at a time as a dance does, step by step, phrase by phrase. Narrative, whether fiction or memoir, is about time. First this, then that. Or this—then before it was that. Therefore this. From the perception of the seasons, of winter, spring, summer, fall, of the seasons of our lives, of the things that return and the things that do not return, what we seek and what we find or fail to find, and the dangers and temptations we encountered en route: these are the sources of the fictional intelligence. If you make such a choice (being kind to an old woman on the road, running down an old man, marrying Bluebeard against all advice, apprenticing yourself to a witch), what follows?

Why do ordinary people read fiction or memoirs? The most primitive answer is the most real: to get to the next page. To find out what happens next and then what happens after that; to find out how it all comes out.

That desire for finding a pattern in events—for not all happenings will satisfy us, not nearly, only the "right" ending, the proper disaster or the proper suspension or the proper reward—still functions as a major hunger we bring to the novel. We want stories that help us make sense out of our lives. We want to see all this mess mean something, even if what we discover is a shape perhaps beautiful but not necessarily comforting. Similarly, we don't want a life like a diary: I went to the store and on the way back I met my old friend George and we talked about the Red Sox and then I ate a banana. Shapelessness loses readers.

Again, the novel is about time and patterns in time. It is not a simultaneous art but one of transition and sequence. You can do a lot with juxtaposition, cutting, transitions, or the lack of them. The effect of simultaneity can be created but only by illusion. A novel or a memoir takes time to read. Therefore, the art of the novel and the art of the memoir involve much persuasion. You must convince the reader to start reading and continue reading. You must persuade her not to put the book down on page one or page one hundred. Not to skip. Fiction and memoir and indeed any kind of narrative requires constant persuasion. The uses of suspense and one of the uses of identification with characters is to make the reader go on turning pages.

You can spend six hundred pages on one night or pass over a hundred years in a sentence. You can start in the classic epic manner *in medias res*. You can start at the beginning: Josephine was born on a wild wintry night just as the old cow died. You can begin at the end: Josephine was buried on a wild wintry day just as a calf was born to the old brown cow. You can start at the end and go back to the beginning. You can start anywhere on the continuum of days and years and proceed in either direction. You can go in one large or several smaller circles. You can overlap blocks of time from different viewpoints. You can move into parallel or alternate universes. But time is always your servant and master and substance.

Our urge to read memoirs and autobiographies stems from the same source: the desire to understand a life. We believe that by looking at the lives of other people, we can better comprehend our own, both the choices that may or may not be open to us, and the values that have informed someone's life.

The motive to write about one's own life may stem from a desire to understand that life, to make sense out of it—in other words, to find a pattern in those events. Or it may stem from a desire to explain oneself, justify, apologize, demand justice. Or from a desire to teach: do as I did, and here is how I did it. Or, almost as frequently, here is how I went wrong, and don't you do likewise. Or an account of the descent and the ascent, the victory over some obstacle whether inside (addiction) or outside (race prejudice).

The beginning is the most important part of your story or your novel, because whoever does not read the beginning will never read the rest of it. You can't take the leisure to develop slowly in the first few pages. You are competing for the reader's attention with the media and everything else going on, plus all the other stories and pieces in that issue, or books on that shelf. Plus, long before that point, if you hadn't gotten an editor to read your manuscript, you never got published to begin with. Basically you can count on an editor reading your first page in a short story, maybe the first two pages; in a novel, you can count on the first ten pages. If you haven't grabbed them then, you're sunk. I am not saying, get your sex and violence up front. That is what a lot of writers do, but in fact it turns off as many people as it turns on, and too much of either right there may draw your pornographic voyeur but get rid of the rest of your potential audience.

However, here is the beginning of an erotic novel by a young writer, about a young woman who uses her sexuality to control and keep men at bay:

From *Look At Me* by Lauren Porosoff Mitchell:

I brought another one home tonight. This one had a small birthmark behind his left earlobe and cool skin that smelled of coconut milk and lemon leaves. I catalog them this way, by the most minor of their physical details, because otherwise they are not prone to distinction. The drink is always the same; though the color varies from pink to clear to amber, its effects are consistent. It convinces him that he is the one luring me away from the bar to a more private place—my bedroom, with the bare walls and white bed, antiseptic as a hospital and well-trafficked as Union Station. But private, yes. The walls of my apartment are insulated, so when I get on top and ride one of the men my neighbors don't hear. I am screaming, grunting. Sweating as my body rhythmically contracts. I rip pleasure out of them, one at a time, evening by evening. And by day I ignore the oily feel of them that does not wash off.

Sometimes I am drunk, and I awaken with a headache to find one of them asleep in my bed, his hair daubed in sweaty clumps to his face. Then I rise from my bed and sit at my laptop in the next room, typing in the dark until the sky bleeds vermilion. It is this light or the clicking keys that wake him; I do not know which. He sees me like that, writing in the morning light, spread out naked with one foot up on either corner of the desk, and I watch as the shame passes through his body. He goes soft. He feels he has violated me somehow, that he has transgressed some essential privacy. I observe with interest as he considers his own voyeurism, and I think every time it is silly, he probably still has the taste of me in his mouth. And yet he is afraid, inadequate, discovering me like this in the dying dark. He puts on his smoke-stinking jeans and sweat-damp polo shirt. He stumbles putting on his expensive sneakers that were flung in the entryway the night before. All the time I watch him. I don't stop watching until he half-kisses me and leaves and shuts the door softly behind him. Only then do I delete the page of *O*s and *J*s and ampersands and percent symbols, make pancakes, and start my work.

Here the sex is relevant to the theme of the novel and elicits a curiosity about this woman, who seems to have more on her mind than pleasure.

It is the curiosity of your potential editor and all your other readers that you must arouse. You may use your style to draw them in, you may use a skillful and compelling scene. Description works sometimes, but it had better be rather unusual description. I can think of a Tanith Lee novel about werewolves, *Lycanthia,* that begins with the description of a traveler arriving at a deserted train station deep in the wilderness during the winter. Although it is description, it is laden with evocative details that suggest something rather dreadful is about to happen, or perhaps has happened.

From *Storm Tide:*

When the winter was over and my nightmares had passed,

when someone else's mistakes had become the subject of local gossip, I set out for the island. I made my way in increments, although the town was all of eighteen miles square. To the bluff overlooking the tidal flats. Down the broken black road to the water's edge. To the bridge where her car was found, overturned like a turtle and buried in mud.

The color of bleached bones, the shape of a crooked spine, the Squeer Island bridge was a product of willful neglect. Every ten years some town official proposed a new bridge and promptly fell into a hole full of lawyers. The beaches were private, the summer people moneyed, the year-rounders reclusive. No one wanted the sandy ways paved or the hedgerows cut back. Your deed bought more than seclusion on Squeer Island; here life as you knew it ceased to exist.

There had been a family named Squeer, but only Stumpy was left. If you asked how the island got its name, people would say, "'Cause it's queer over there," and they didn't mean homosexual. They meant queer things happened. Peculiar things. Uncommon for a small town.

During high tide there was no access by land. The road to town flooded. Ducks paddled over the bridge. Fish darted through the guardrails. The summer people stocked their shelves with vodka and paperbacks and waited uneasily for the tide to recede. The residents lived for its return.

I left my car on the island side of the bridge. I slogged along the mud banks of the creek, driving fiddler crabs in front of me like herds of frightened crustacean sheep. The grasses were four feet high at the edge of the bank, an inch wide, sharp as razors. They mentioned lacerations across the palms; one in her right eyeball. I closed one eye. I wondered what it was like to sink in this bottomless liquid clay, this mud the fishermen called black mayonnaise. What did it feel like to die this way? They said her hair was encrusted with seaweed and crabs, that an eel had eaten into the armpit. They say she must have struggled to free herself, that as she grabbed at the grass her efforts only increased the suction of the mud. They still call it an accidental death.

What you're trying to do is get something lively or intriguing or mysterious or fascinating or peculiar moving and moving fast. Then you can go back and insert your necessary backgrounding and context. No one needs to know the name of the dead woman in the excerpt above, or why she died, or what kinds of weird things happened on the island. At this point you're competing for the reader's attention. You're hoping those questions will occur to the reader and they'll want to read on. The day has long passed when you could count on the patience required to sit through the first scene of a play (as Ibsen often did) in which the following transpires:

> MAID
> So the Master comes home today, Mr. Ives. And here we are knocking ourselves out to put the house to order.
> BUTLER
> It's been ten years to the day since the Master rode off, Lucy, and all we've heard have been those nasty rumors of duels and wild doings in Paris where he has been studying.
> MAID
> And he hasn't once written to his sweet mother, who took to her bed on the day he rode off and hasn't been downstairs since. What do you think has happened between them, Mr. Ives? Some say they had a quarrel about that young Bates girl he wanted to marry, Sally, who killed herself by jumping over a cliff not three months after he left.
> BUTLER
> Aye, and it's been ten years to the day since any of the Bates spoke to any of our family, the Livingstones, although previously they had been the best of friends ever since the two grandfathers settled here together after coming home from the Napoleonic Wars, etcetera, etcetera.

In medias res is the Latin term for in the middle of things, and that's how Homer opened the *Iliad* and that's where you should usually start, although rules can always be creatively broken. Nonetheless, the more things are happening—that we can follow at least mostly—the more likely we are to get dragged into the story and willing to read on. Your exposition needs to be in there, but you have to learn to do it on the wing, subtly, without stopping the story and laying out everything while the characters shuffle their feet and the suspense dies till the story is stuck out in the middle of nowhere like a becalmed sailboat. You have to pass along the exposition with the story, with the characters, as you go. The trick, of course, is not to confuse the reader; she has to be able to follow it all. (We received a submission in which the novelist begins at an intriguing wedding; a very good place to introduce families and their conflicts. But there were too many people not sufficiently differentiated and ultimately it was confusing. Very much like being at a wedding and not knowing the bride's family from the groom's or whose friends were whose. Focusing more deeply on fewer characters and their conflicts might have been a better strategy.)

For instance, if you are writing science fiction or speculative fiction, you must indicate some unusual things in the beginning, but not by getting lost in the hardware. You want to let the reader know right away that this is perhaps another time, another place, another planet, an alternate reality, but it is more important to introduce your characters and get your plot underway. It is more essential for the reader to be engaged and interested in what is going on and the people to whom it is happening, than that the reader grasp every detail of the situation you have created. That you have to do on the fly, in bits and pieces as the story moves on.

From *He, She & It:*

> Josh, Shira's ex-husband, sat immediately in front of her in the Hall of Domestic Justice as they faced the view screen, awaiting the verdict on the custody of Ari, their son. A bead of sweat slid down the furrow of his spine—he wore a backless business suit, white for the formality of the occasion, very like her own—and it was hard even now to keep from delicately brushing his back with her scarf to dry it. The Yakamura-Stichen dome in the Nebraska desert was conditioned, of course, or they would all be dead, but it was winter now and the temperature was allowed to rise naturally to thirty Celsius in the afternoon as the sun heated the immense dome enclosing the corporate enclave. Her hands were sweating too, but from nervousness. She had grown up in a natural place and retained the ability to endure more heat than most Y-S gruds. She kept telling herself she had nothing to fear, but her stomach was clenched hard and she caught herself licking her lips again and again. Every time she called up time on her internal clock and read it in the corner of her cornea, it was at most a minute later than when last she had evoked it.

There is certainly a lot to be explained in the above excerpt. Backless business suits? A clock on the corner of her cornea? The Yakamura-Stichen dome? But it's the familiar situation in the midst of all this weirdness, the custody battle, that grounds the reader and compels attention, that causes the reader to identify with the people to whom it is happening.

Similarly, if you are writing historical fiction, you want to give a flavor of the time and place you are writing about, but it is the characters and the situation that take precedence, not what kind of clothes they wore or the type of sailing vessels then current.

From *Gone to Soldiers:*

> Louise Kahan, aka Annette Hollander Sinclair, sorted her mail in the foyer of her apartment. An air letter from Paris, "You have something from your aunt Gloria," she called to Kay, who was curled up in her room listening to swing music, pretending to do her homework but being stickily obsessed with boys. Louise knew the symptoms but she had never learned the cure, not in her case, certainly not in her daughter's. Kay did not answer; presumably she could not hear over the thump of the radio.
>
> Personal mail for Mrs. Louise Kahan in one pile. The family stuff, invitations. An occasional faux pas labeled Mr. and Mrs. Oscar Kahan. Where have you been for the past two years? Then the mail for Annette Hollander Sinclair in two stacks; one for business correspondence about rights, radio adaptations, a contract with Doubleday from her agent Charley for the collection of stories *Hidden from His Sight.* Speaking engagements, club visits, an interview Wednesday.
>
> The second pile for Annette was fan mail, ninety-five percent from women. Finally a few items for plain Louise Kahan: her *Daily Worker,* reprints of a *Masses and Mainstream* article she had written on the Baltimore shipyard strike, a book on women factory workers from International Publishers for her to review, William Shirer's *Berlin Diary.*
>
> Also in that pile were the afternoon papers. Normally she would pick them up first, but she could not bring herself to do so. Europe was occupied by the Nazis from sea to sea, an immense prison. Everywhere good people and old friends were shot against walls, tortured in basements, carted off to

camps about which rumors were beginning to appear to be more than rumor.

For instance, if your story is about a doctor, you *could* use the first page to tell us how old she is and whether she went to an ivy league med school or a state school and what she chose to specialize in and whether she's a risk taker or plays it safe; or you could begin in the middle of open heart surgery and allow the reader to discover her background while seeing her in action. You could begin the story of this doctor at her birth and move forward through medical school, to the daring new type of heart implant that won her fame around the world. You could start with the bomb that killed her as she was washing up after the operation and go back to her birth and the difficult struggle to make it to college, no less med school, coming as she did from a dirt-poor Appalachian family. You could start with her first sexual encounter with her childhood sweetheart, Malcolm, in which she insisted on retaining her virginity, having watched her mother give birth to eight children, and thereby losing Malcolm to another girl. There are as many ways to begin as there are stories, but the most important thing is that whatever beginning you choose intrigues the reader and entices them to read on.

This does not mean that you should stare at your computer and freeze up and write nothing until you discover the perfect place to start. Never be afraid to get going on something. You can rework your beginning endless times. All writers do. You don't have to have the perfect beginning to get to the middle—not at all. Several of my novels began at what later became chapter two. In *Small Changes*, I actually began with what is now Chapter Six, which goes back in time and brings Miriam from her childhood up toward where we meet her in chapter three. It was only when I had written Miriam up to where she meets Beth that I went back in first draft and started chapter one with Beth's marriage. Both of Ira's novels, *The Kitchen Man* and *Going Public* have as a second chapter what was originally, in early drafts, the first chapter.

From *The Kitchen Man:*

I am a spy at the elbow of the powerful, a fly on their wall.

Ignored, I mingle, privy to the secrets they drop casually. I deliver pleasure. I loosen their tongues with champagne. And smile. And remember.

By night, I listen. By day, I write.

Naked, I begin the transformation.

The jeans of my day balled in a corner, I shimmy into black wool trousers, shark skin smooth, alive with prickly static. My starched shirt crackles as I break it from its cardboard bondage, my patent leather pumps twinkle sapphires of blue light.

Upstairs, rushing feet drub the ruby carpets, tap cadence on the marble floors. Chairs clack into place. Ice tumbles into silver buckets. Nervous voices shout last minute instructions and bitter complaints seethe, whispers in the cavernous hallways of Danish castles.

I tug cautiously at the wings of my tie. I flick stray fuzz from the pleats of my cummerbund. Snapping my onyx cufflinks into place, I inspect my nails. I catch my waistcoat as it tips, satin cool and shimmering, from its wooden hanger. Combing my thick moustache into perfect symmetry, clicking my heels, I turn to the mirror and bow. I am perfect. I am ready. I am a soldier in the service of the appetites of the rich. A waiter at Les Neiges D'Antan.

The Snows of Yesterday. The finest restaurant north of New York City. Number one choice in the haute cuisine category of every magazine in which we advertise.

Until fifth draft, *Gone to Soldiers* began with what is now chapter four. The decision where to begin is extremely critical and often subject to much experimentation. There are two different versions of F. Scott Fiztgerald's novel *Tender is the Night*, as I recall, one in Rosemary's viewpoint and one in Dick's.

I can give you three rules which, if not golden, are certainly useful: Do not confuse the Beginning of the Story with the beginning of the events in the story. There is infinite regression in all stories, or they would all begin with the Big Bang when the universe started. The particular events you are shaping may start with the birth of your character, but that is not where the Story starts.

Second, never confuse the Beginning of the Story with how you begin to write it. In hindsight, there is usually a correct place to begin in the plot, but in your own work, begin writing where you can. Sometimes if you are having trouble entering a character, you can find a scene you can imagine yourself in, a point of commonalty, of empathy, where you can make a doorway into that character. Perhaps it is a piece of your own life. That might be the first scene you write, even if it turns out to be in the middle or even at the end of the finished product.

Third, no matter how cute or compelling or chic or gripping your beginning may be, if it does not lead to your story, be prepared to scrap it rather than distorting the entire book in the service of a good start. I knew a writer who won two awards on the strength of the first chapter to a novel, from which the novel not only did not but could not follow. But she could never abandon that chapter, because it was the strongest part of the book. It was arresting, all right, but all the fireworks were burned out by the end of it and it could not develop into the material she really had for a novel. Therefore, while the material paid off financially for a while, she never got a novel, never got more than a couple of excerpts published and never got on with her writing.

Even more to the point, if the rest of the book does not follow from the beginning, you will draw readers who will be disappointed. They thought it was blood and guts, but it's a tender psychological study of a boy who loves a pigeon; they thought it was going to be a humorous trip through contemporary adolescence, but it is a psychopath's revenge. The beginning must be powerful or inviting, and it must begin what you are actually going to continue.

If you are working with multiple viewpoints in a novel, it is worth serious consideration which character should open your book. Sometimes it is a matter of chronology, sometimes of opening with the most intriguing or inviting character. There is no reason it should be the most important, unless that's a great idea for other reasons. Since I use multiple viewpoints a great deal, I often shuffle my early chapters until I find the best arrangement. The beginning is that important: it is all important. Without a good beginning, no one with the possible exception of your mother or partner will ever bother to continue reading what you have written.

Don't be afraid to start in the middle of things. If you're telling the story of a life, you do not have to start with childhood. Yes, someone's life starts with her birth, of course; but that doesn't have to be where your story starts. Does your story begin with your birth? With your parents' births or marriage? With your graduation or meeting your life partner? Does it start with a discovery or the desire to understand something puzzling, to solve a mystery or to change your life in some way?

From *Rookie Cop* by Richard Rosenthal:

Sol Hurok immigrated to the United States from the village of Pogar, Russia in 1906 and made a small living for himself by producing concerts for New York City's ever growing number of labor societies. Over the years, the workers' craving for highbrow entertainment grew to such an extent that his concerts were staged in the Hippodrome, an enormous amusement hall built by P.T. Barnum. Hurok became the personal manager of the great Afro-American contralto Marian Anderson and arranged the first U.S. tour for the young violin sensation and son of a poor Israeli barber, Itzak Perlman. Within several generations, Hurok became known as The Impresario, importing cultural institutions such as the Comédie Francaise and the Old Vic to perform for American audiences. A more beneficial, or benign profession would be hard to imagine. Except that the talent he imported also included the Bolshoi Ballet and the Moiseyev Dance Company and there were those who wished to disrupt the ties between the United States and the then-Soviet Union—by any means necessary.

Hurok had been warned many times that he was to stop bringing in Soviet performers. Bottles of ammonia had been uncorked during a number of his events as well as during shows produced by Columbia Artists, a rival company that also imported Russian talent. Live mice and stink bombs had been used to cause upset to the audiences. Some performances had been disrupted by shouting. Annoying as those actions might have been, they hadn't proven effective enough. It was thought that perhaps smoke bombs, delivered right to Hurok's office, as well as those of Columbia Artists, would make the point.

A young man was given some money to buy the chemicals

(hypnole and an oxygenator) in order to produce the devices. Although an effective smoke bomb needed only a few ounces of the two materials when combined, he purchased a hundred pounds of the stuff, the reasoning being, if a little smoke was good, a lot of smoke would be better. Then he and another fellow made up two bombs, each weighing thirteen pounds and placed them inside two cheap attaché cases, a small fuse jutting inconspicuously outside each, ready for the match.

This memoir does not even begin with the author, the protagonist, but with the beginning of a critical situation in his undercover work. We meet him after we have a notion of what kind of situation he had been plunged into. He is using a bombing—which will lead to a death—to bring us into the story of an episode in his life when, as a rookie cop in the New York City Police Department, he was sent undercover, without training, to infiltrate an organization that had just come to the notice of the Bureau of Special Investigations, the Jewish Defense League.

Some characters in fiction or some people writing their memoirs may have had a fascinating childhood that should be covered in depth. For other characters or for yourself, you may want to whip though childhood in a few paragraphs or pages or tell significant bits and pieces of it on the fly. In the memoir *Rookie Cop*, the author mentions his childhood only briefly, well into the narrative, and only to explain why he chose to enter the police department. The same holds true if your novel or story is about a particular incident. You can start in the middle of World War II and go back to its beginning, to when your main character was drafted. You can start in the middle of a safari, as Hemingway did in "The Short Happy Life of Francis Macomber," when the main character has just committed what he believes is an act of cowardice, fill in the beginning of the story through conversation and move to the end, where his wife blows his head off with a 6.5 Mannlicher rifle.

You have to decide your best way to open. Maybe it's an event, a marriage or ceremony where your main characters are all assembled. Dorothy Allison in her novel, *Bastard Out of Carolina*, puts all the important characters, the women in her family, inside a speeding car with the implication that something important is about to happen and with a strong sense of the social class and regional flavor of the characters. Maybe you want to start with a moment of revelation, when everything that came before it comes suddenly into perspective and everything afterwards is seen through an enlightened perspective. Maybe your story starts with a moment of outrageous good fortune, the birth of a child; or a moment of torment, such as the death of one. Maybe it starts with a strange coincidence: seeing an old lover again after ten years or overhearing a phone call that terrifies or enlightens you.

You might start with a general statement about yourself that you hope will generate curiosity or empathy or identification in your reader. This is the opening of my memoir, *Sleeping with Cats*:

> Do I have faith in my memory? Who doesn't? How can I not trust memory? It is as if I were to develop a mistrust for my right hand or my left foot. Yet I am quite aware that my memory is far from perfect. I frequently forget events and people that my husband Ira Wood remembers, and similarly, I remember incidents that have slipped away from him. I rarely remember things incorrectly; mostly I remember clearly or I forget completely.
>
> I have distinct memories of events that happened before I was born or for which I was not present. This comes from having heard the stories told vividly by my mother or my grandmother when I was little and imagining those scenes and the people in them so clearly and intensely that I experience them as my own. I have precise memories of the voice and face of my mother's father, who died ten years before my birth. Stories about him that I heard as a child were so real to me that I created him as a living personage.

In our experience, the best way to learn how to write good beginnings is to read what others have written and discover how they solved the same problems you will face. Don't worry about imitating what they've written because your vision, your plot, your characters will be unique to your story. Nor should you worry about liking every beginning you read. You can learn as much from writing that you consider to be dreadful as you can from the pieces you admire.

There are a number of books on writing that emphasize the necessity of starting with a snappy first sentence. We are more concerned with the *situation* you choose to begin with, and the way various writers have solved the problem of attempting to hook the reader.

Gore Vidal begins his memoir, *Palimpsest,* with the wedding of two members of high society in "the church of the presidents" across the avenue from the White House, where he was one of the ushers, JFK was another, and Jackie Kennedy went off to the bathroom with the bride and showed her how to douche, post-sex. Name-dropping, the hint of scandal, the promise of gossip and the insider's view of the lives of the rich and famous, are Vidal's hooks.

In *The Mambo Kings Play Songs of Love*, Oscar Hijuelos attempts to seduce his readers with nostalgia as he evokes the kind of inner city neighborhood few of us live in anymore. On LaSalle Street, in Brooklyn in the 1950s, kids play in the courtyard as mothers doing housework watch from their windows, everybody's kids, not only their own. Mrs. Shannon, the Irish lady "in her perpetually soup-stained dress" calls out to Cesar to tell him his favorite episode of *I Love Lucy* is on, the one in which his father and uncle appeared as Cuban cousins of Desi Arnaz at the Tropicana nightclub. Most readers have heard of *I Love Lucy*; many would be intrigued by a young kid whose relatives were somehow attached to the show.

Piri Thomas starts his autobiographical collection of short stories set in prison, *Seven Long Times*, during a stick-up in a bar. He recounts the role every member of his gang had played many times before; where each man positioned himself and how they silently signaled each other, how they herded the customers against the wall and approached the bartender. But this time something goes hopelessly wrong. Curious?

Lillian Hellman begins her memoir, *Pentimento,* one foggy summer morning on Martha's Vineyard when, during an ordinary swim, she is sucked under by a sudden riptide and almost drowns. She bashes her head against the pilings of a pier and, thinking she is about to die, imagines herself in a conversation with her former lover Dashiell Hammet, "a man who had been dead five years."

Simone deBeauvoir decides to start *Memoirs of a Dutiful Daughter* on the day she was born. Turning the pages of a picture album, describing photographs of her proper French family, she risks losing many readers who would be fascinated with her courageous and unorthodox life but bored by an ordinary bourgeois childhood until, describing her relationship to her little sister, she proves herself to be anything but an ordinary child. "I felt myself to be much more interesting than an infant bundled up in a cradle. I had a little sister; that doll-like creature didn't have me."

Cesare Casella (with Eileen Daspin) tells the story of his life in a cookbook entitled *Diary of a Tuscan Chef*. Family experiences are intermingled with recipes in this memoir and in the first chapter he posits that he doesn't exactly know where he was conceived but if he had to guess, he'd say the kitchen, and goes on to describe, in delicious sensual detail, the room, the region and the people that so influenced his life. Anyone who hungers for "dusty rounds of pecorino put up for the winter, tins of salted anchovies to eat with bread . . . and liters upon liters of vino delle colline Lucchesi" cannot fail to be seduced.

William Gibson begins his cyber-punk novel *Count Zero* with his hero Turner being chased through the ghettos of India by an intelligent bomb called a Slamhound filled with "a kilogram of recrystallized hexogene and flaked TNT." What's a Slamhound exactly? Why is it chasing him? Is there such a thing as recrystallized hexogene? Who cares? Turner is blown to bits and it takes three months to put him together again, with eyes and genitals bought on the open market. It's the speed, the violence, the absurd details of the author's future world that keep the reader wondering, What the hell is going on?

There are beginnings that seduce simply by creating an identification between the readers and characters. In the short story "Storm," Edna O'Brien begins with a mother, a son and his fiancée on summer holiday together. We are drawn into the mother's thorough observation and growing jealousy of their relationship, and her admission that watching these young lovers makes her feel old. Mary Flanagan begins her story, "Cream Sauce," with Lydia, the world's slowest cook. Lydia likes to drink Bordeaux as she prepares dinner, while her suffering family is enticed by "tantalizing aromas accompanied by interminable waits" likely to be followed by "not infrequent failures which must, out of sheer physical necessity, be consumed." Anybody who cooks, or lives with a cook like Lydia, would read on.

Creating An Irresistible Beginning

The decision about exactly what should be on page one of your novel or memoir is extremely critical, so don't hesitate to experiment. In our workshops, our first assignment is to write a dynamite beginning. The catch is, it doesn't have to be the beginning of anything you plan to finish or even to write. The goal is simply a beginning that is irresistible, that when read aloud (we ask the participants to write one page only) those hearing it will demand to know what happens next.

When we give this assignment on the first night of the workshop, people always groan. "An irresistible beginning? You're cruel! We can't do that!" They start to tense up, at which point Ira always tells the following story:

Some years ago, before he became a well-known essayist, a friend had received what at that time in his career was a prestigious assignment. He had been hired by a national environmental organization to write the cover copy to accompany their annual Beaches of the World calendar and he was to be paid a very large stipend. I was excited for him and asked, every time I saw him, how it was going. The first time, he said he was doing his research, walking local beaches and driving down to Connecticut and up to Maine when time allowed. The next time I asked, he said he was considering a trip to Florida, stopping on the way to visit the beaches of Cape Hatteras. A couple of weeks later, he still hadn't started the piece and when he said he was pondering a trip to the Pacific Northwest coast, I understood that under the weight of succeeding brilliantly, he had tied himself into a knot and was afraid to start.

"You just have to ask yourself one thing," I told him. "Who the hell reads a calendar?"

Later, he told me he began the piece the next day and finished it soon after.

You have to remember not to take yourself too seriously. In this exercise, we're asking you to make up a beginning that doesn't necessarily lead to anything; hence, it may be the beginning of nothing. No beginning (especially something that is the beginning of nothing) is chiseled in stone. You can tear it up, rewrite it, place it in the middle of the piece, save it as something you might use later on. The trick is simply to begin. If you don't begin, you will never finish. Moreover, be real; nothing you are likely to write will become as important as the Bill of Rights or the Magna Carta or even *War and Peace*. And even if it should become important, it wouldn't have if you did not begin. Remember, you can always change what you write, but if you don't write it, there's nothing to improve upon. So now, begin!

Exercise: Beginning in a Different Place

Take a story you have already written. It can be the first chapter of a novel or a memoir; it can be a short story. This is an exercise most easily carried out on a computer. Try starting the story in various different places and print it out each time to see what you have. Did you find a better, more engaging beginning?

Exercise: Changing the Plan of Attack

Again, take a story you have already written. Try starting the story then in a completely different way. If you began with a general scene setting or narration, plunge us immediately into an ongoing situation. If you began in the middle of a situation, try starting with dialog, something striking or startling or intriguing that one of your characters says, and then launch into the scene or into the story. See with each choice what happens to your story. You may find you need things you did not include before or that, more likely, you can cut whole paragraphs and perhaps whole pages.

Where to Start the Story of Your Life

As we suggested earlier, you want to start a memoir with an event that was involving, intriguing, dramatic; something that arouses curiosity or surprise or amusement. But how do you choose one event out of all those that comprised a long life? It seems overwhelming. Remember that the place you start writing need not be what will become page one of the story. You can change it later on. Nor do you have to begin chronologically. You can start anyplace at all in your life. Here are some exercises that might get your engine going.

Exercise: Finding an Emotionally Moving Event

Perhaps you should start with an event that you found emotionally moving in some way. Maybe it was a traumatic event—a time in your life when you felt in danger or when what you cared for most was ripped from you or you were afraid it would be taken from you. Perhaps it was a sickness—your own, your partner's, your mother's, your brother's. Or it was a death—a family member, a friend, a lover, even an enemy? Or a stranger whose death you witnessed?

Perhaps it was something that deeply shamed you—a party thrown for you to which no one came. A time you were caught publicly in a lie. Perhaps you had invented yourself a family that sounded more interesting than your own, and now your parents stand before your friends and you are unmasked. Perhaps you pretended to have attended a better school than you had or to have earned a degree, when in fact you dropped out before commencement. Maybe you lied to get a job. Or lied to impress a possible lover. Maybe you tried to make yourself important in some other social context.

Perhaps it was something that made you so happy you could not believe you had won that prize, that award; that the person you had been daydreaming about suddenly turned and indicated that they were aware of you, too, and interested. Perhaps you suddenly inherited or were given something you had always wanted but never expected to possess. Perhaps you were plucked from an insignificant role to take over the lead in a theater production or a business project.

It's possible you came face to face with an old phobia or a latent fear—of a fierce guard dog suddenly loosed into your path, a feral animal such as a bear encountered on a trail. Or did you waken in the night to smoke and flames and only seconds to figure an escape route and grab a baby, wake your mother, grab your cat or dog? Perhaps your tire went flat late at night on a country road in the years before cell phones and you had to figure out what to do. Perhaps you woke up to sounds of an intruder.

Maybe a strong experience was that time you had a sudden and powerful breakthrough in your personal life, your work, your creativity, your understanding. A strong religious or mystical experience can work in this manner, although this sort of event is extremely hard to describe in a way that others can understand—but some writers have been able to do so successfully. A sudden move to a higher level in some manner of performance can feel magical and strongly empowering. Sometimes the Aha! moment, the click, is one that is political or philosophical. This is not as easy to render dramatically as many of the other types of experiences we have considered, but it can be done. Remember Helen Keller.

All of these "supposes" are dramatic places in which you might be able to enter your life and start writing about it. Any one of them might be page one, or might eventually be turned into a scene or two in the heart of your matter. But sometimes a time and place in our lives with a strong emotional resonance is a scene we can pry ourselves into and begin to write about.

A Fictional Version Of The Same Exercise:

Instead of mining your life for a traumatic or otherwise emotionally compelling scene, you can give entrance to a character who has been giving you difficulty by doing the same thing with him or her. You pick out an outstandingly powerful and emotional scene, a time that shook them for good or ill. You write that scene as a door into that character. Writing them in action and reaction at a pivotal point in their lives may give you a handle on the character and help make that person you are creating more real and far more vivid to you. Any of the events we suggested above are excellent for this exercise, or choose an event of your own that has equally powerful emotional resonance.

3

Characterization

It is easier to talk about some of the factors that make for unsuccessful characters than it is to say simply and straight out what makes characters work. You'll discover that some people will tell you that a given character is excellent and believable and others will find the same character uninteresting or unbelievable. That is standard and you learn to accumulate many opinions before deciding for yourself. In fiction as in real life we find some people charming whom others find boring and are repelled by some people who, we notice with chagrin, others adore. There is a personal chemistry side to the characters in novels which it is folly to ignore and impossible to explain. It would be irrelevant in approaching Rodin's statue *The Thinker* to feel that you would like to have dinner or take in a movie with him, but when we are dealing with characters we read about, that irrational chemistry side does matter. We have to be able to find Vronsky attractive to identify with Anna Karenina; if we take a violent dislike to Little Red Riding Hood, we will be rooting for the wolf, and the story will be quite different. Often, readers can only generalize when they try to tell you why a character worked for them—because the character is funny, they might say—and less than honest when a character displeases them—because the character may very well remind them of someone they don't like or something they don't like about themselves. (Ira got a very honest rejection letter once from an editor at a major New York publishing house, passing on his novel *The Kitchen Man* because, the editor said, she hated the main character, Gabriel Rose. He reminded her too much of herself.)

However, when several readers tell you that the same character is not believable or comprehensible, you are in trouble. Often in the work of apprentice and aspiring writers there are three kinds of characters that don't work.

The first is a character based upon the writer herself, but one in which her self-hatred is in charge. Often young writers set up a piece of themselves to castigate and punish and perhaps kill off as if by that means they could get rid of the parts of themselves they most detest. Indeed, writing about some aspect of your life or yourself that you find traumatic or painful is often a way of dealing with that pain. But self-hatred can be a besetting sin or weakness to a novelist. The desire to punish yourself vicariously distorts the work. The writer is unable to differentiate himself or herself from the character, and therefore unable to create a character that is multi-dimensional and interesting. We wonder why we are supposed to want to read about this person. Often such a character is both boring and unpleasant. We may desire to step on him or her after a chapter or two as we might step on a large ant, but we have no desire to enter their experiences and live them.

At Leapfrog Press, we receive a manuscript about every two weeks in which the non-adventures of a young man are recounted in full—usually his failures to get laid, to find an interesting and glamorous job, to receive the recognition he feels himself entitled to. Usually such narratives are short on characterization as well as action. There is a lot of casual cool conversation, lots of going to bars and parties and not much else. The protagonist is a blank. His friends are hastily drawn caricatures. Females are characterized by how they put out or reject the protagonist and are otherwise simply collections of body parts. The writers always wonder why readers or listeners do not respond with enthusiasm.

Now, you could retort by pointing to the work of Philip Roth, for instance, whose characters may come right out and say, not only as far back as *Portnoy's Complaint*, but in later works such as *Sabbath's Theater*, something like, I am a crazy person, I do detestable things, but the difference is in the tone. The character doesn't hate himself for it. Or, put another way, the character thinks it's his only choice. In fact, acting so crazy is the right thing to do, the only thing he can do; he'll tell you a hundred different reasons for it, reasons that you can even identify with. Roth's Mickey Sabbath is a hostile, self-indulgent man who treats people badly and relishes weird sex . . . but does so in response to his terror of dying. And he does it with a kind of manic energy you're drawn to. This character is handled with a different tone than the twenty-something barfly with major complaints about the way life is treating him. Don't overlook the fact that Roth's character is an older man with many accomplishments and life experiences under his belt. This doesn't give him moral license to be nasty and unpleasant, but since he's lived a full life, and since he's near death, the reader is more prone to accept his reflections. The reader might have less tolerance for the complaints of a twenty-something slacker still living at home.

Look at Kafka's Gregor Samsa, or Bruce Jay Friedman's *Stern*, same *schtick*: they transcend self-hatred because they take it to its ridiculous limits (turning into a large cockroach; a grand metaphor for how one is treated in the world) or find themselves in situations that are pathetic (being terrified of your suburban neighbor), but with which you are able to identify. It is not that you can't write about unsympathetic characters. The problem is to give the reader something about them with which identify, or to be fascinated by, or curious about. It can be their humorous take on the world, or their very strange world view. You're attempting to give the reader a reason to spend time with them.

The second common problem, and this is especially relevant for memoir writing, arises with characters drawn directly from life. Often they do not work, especially if you do not know or cannot bring yourself to imagine the person intimately enough. It is not that you cannot use someone you know as a model for a character—you can, as long as you understand that you may only be dealing with a piece of them. The grandmother you adore and admire is also a person in her own right. Concentrating only on the kindness you have known from her (and neglecting, for instance, her early life, or her ornery side, or her heated feuds with members of the family) will make her less interesting than a more fully imagined eighty year-old woman. And the opposite situation: you can certainly write about a person who has done you wrong, as long as you are not exercising your ambivalent feelings towards them in a way that interferes with the creation of a believable character in a believable plot. Revenge is not the best motive for writing a story. It distorts too often.

Many times you will hear a story in a workshop and criticize the behavior of a character only to be told, but that's the way it happened. Too bad. If you do not understand a character, then you will not be able to write well about that character. If someone provoked you in real life too much for you to empathize with them or to grasp their motivation, then you will not do any better with them in print. The reader will not understand them either, and that's a problem.

Often, in real life, we do not really know what a character means the first time we encounter such a person. It is only the third or fourth time we meet a particular constellation of characteristics, of traits, that we can understand what is true strength and true weakness. How often have you admitted to a friend that in the beginning, you were wary of them; you really didn't like them? As we get older, we find out how a lot of stories turn out in real life, and what motivates a person's behavior, and that enables us to understand our characters better and to build richer ones. After we have come to understand the characters of those around us by watching them in action under stress, in good and bad times, over many years, we can build better and more convincing characters in our stories and novels. One way to do this is to show your character acting differently in various situations, with different people. In college I had a beloved teacher, one I admired for his insight and humor. However, walking across the street from his house one day I saw him in a temper, kicking his dog in the stomach. I never again saw this kindly man in the same light because I had glimpsed a piece of his character I had never imagined. Try to imagine your characters interacting in different situations. To whom are they kind? Impatient? To whom do they prostrate themselves? How do they treat animals? Children? The elderly? Allowing the reader to observe your characters in interactions with others is an excellent way of showing the diversity of their personalities.

The problem may be that you saw only one aspect of a character, and that was an aspect you disliked. Let's say it is a racist school teacher. Or a high school drug dealer who hangs out in the mall. It is not that you cannot use someone you dislike as a model for a character, but if you're going to concentrate *only* on the parts you dislike, and not imagine them more fully, it's best that that character function only as a walk-on in your story. If you have malevolent or ambiguous feelings about someone, you may not be able to allow yourself to fully imagine them as a person with an interior life as well as outward behavior. If you do not intimately understand a character, that is, take the time and make the effort to imagine all their contradictions—the good in them as well as the bad, the people they treat with kindness as well as the people they hurt—then you will not be able to write well about that character. As writers we're fascinated with the ambiguity of human behavior. Life is not simple; motivation is complex. People act out of a variety of motives. We may kill out of intense love; we may compliment someone because we strongly dislike them. A mass murderer may be very kind to his elderly parents. The reason the legend of Robin Hood has lasted for more than five centuries is that he was a mugger with sympathy for the poor.

The third type of character that tends to be less than successful is the character type drawn not from knowledge, not from observation, not from musing about people you have known and your own reactions and motivations, your weird little foibles, your personal superstitions, but from other writers, or commonly, TV and movies. With each imitation, such types are farther from reality, more plastic, and a reader feels that diminution. Such characters are made of words, not from information or observation or insight that informs those words. What are some types? The tough guy detective. The Jewish mother. The proper librarian. The dumb blonde secretary. The Valley girl. The stoned-out surfer dude. The pistol-toting drug dealer from the projects wearing a baseball cap and heavy gold jewelry.

It is not that we cannot work in types. Much comedy involves types and often, so does genre writing. Most writing involves some use of types. But for stock character types to work, they must be entered and made to come alive.

Let's take an example: the tough guy detective. How do we make this tired old type interesting?

1.   You can write a parody by exaggerating the type. He keeps whiskey in his desk and when he wants a drink he bites the neck off the bottle. He speaks in mono-syllables only; wears his shoulder

holster in the shower; keeps a gun behind every door in his house, including the refrigerator and one taped under the toilet seat.

2. You keep the type but humanize it. He is a tough guy detective but all those years of drinking have nearly done him in, and he is a vociferous member of AA. He takes vitamin pills by the handful and is concerned with food additives. How many detectives in mysteries today love to cook?

3. You work against the type. In *Play It Again, Sam* you have Woody Allen trying to be Humphrey Bogart, looking ridiculous in a trench coat and fedora, coughing when he lights up a cigarette. This is a standard device of comedy, also, the comedic character who longs to be a different type than he or she is: the *shlemiel* who wants to be Don Juan. The *klutz* who wants to be an athlete. The bookish librarian with wild sexual fantasies.

A variation would be Columbo, if you remember the show. Instead of a tight-lipped Joe Friday, you couldn't shut the guy up. He was always interested. Drove his suspects crazy with his questions. "Oh, gee, Mr. Moneybags, is that how you use arsenic on your lawn to keep down the sowbugs, that's absolutely fascinating." A slob and a family man and always having a little trouble with his car instead of zooming around the LA streets in your standard car chase, Columbo acted so dumb the perps would sometimes condescend to him by answering his questions, and always find themselves in deeper trouble.

You can work farther against type altogether by having a high school girl as a vampire-slayer; or a sweet little old lady like Miss Marple as your detective. Agatha Christie, by working against type, created a type in itself, the apparently delicate but very bright spinster who seems like somebody's maiden aunt till she traps the killer. A standard in today's mystery novel is the "amateur sleuth," an ordinary person drawn into a crime they must solve. Andrew Greeley's Father Blackie Ryan is a priest detective, a Bishop, no less. Barbara Neely's Blanche White is a street smart African-American domestic.

Exercise:

Think of some stock character or literary stereotype and figure out how to make it new, more engaging or more sinister. Strike, in Richard Price's novel, *Clockers*, is a crack dealer in the projects. Not your typical rock-tough, fast-talking, inscrutable heavy, he has a nervous stomach, and instead of sitting on a park bench sipping malt liquor, he's rarely without a bottle of Maalox. Zel, the dentist in William Goldman's *Marathon Man* adds another dimension to a profession often typed as a self-important milquetoast: he's a Nazi war criminal sadist. Figure out some of your own: the Jewish Mother assassin? The pro boxer whose passion is hybridizing day lilies? The male prostitute street hustler who is a serious student of zen?

Now when you are in your character, they experience emotions. Often that's where writers lose their characters in clichés. "His heart was in his mouth." "She thought she would die of shame." "He was on top of the world." "Her heart sank." "His stomach clenched in terror."

You have to make the fear, the terror, the joy, the shame, the anger, the desire happen, not tell us about it or feed us clichés. Find fresh metaphors. Find more accurate physiological responses. Describe what is producing the anger, the joy, the fear so that we can experience it, too. Build into what you are presenting the aspect of it or her or him or they that is producing the emotion. Make the fear happen, don't tell us about it with abstractions. Maybe this event is calling up something in the past that is reinforcing the emotion. Explore the situation to see what you can pull from it that will help us understand your character.

In Maureen McCoy's novel, *Junebug*, the narrator, seventeen year-old June Angel Host is visiting her mother, Tess, in prison, on Mother's Day. Tess has been incarcerated for murder since June was five. In this excerpt, Tess stops an idyllic conversation with an unbearable confession:

From *Junebug* by Maureen McCoy:

> "Junie," she said, and hearing my name broke the fantasy. It about killed me the way Tess could say it, the charge I got hearing my mother say, "Junie."
> Playtime's over was the message in her eyes.

Shhh, no, Mama. Please, no.

I sat across from her, tables in a row, the room manic with sound, like the brain's surprise when lightning hits. My arms stuck to the table's graffiti scars, and I knew like the absolute end of childhood that Tess was going to mess up our world all over again and for good. I was her daughter and I knew this much. She'd been playing with me, and now . . . she was finally going to answer the question no one asked. My heart was drumming the way hearts do on cue when terrified. I tried for a really mature thought: *I can deal.* But as my blood rushed through swells of sixty-eight percent water, girl life went down with the flood. And on she went, fast and creaturish. I heard my mother's voice as if it came through the hand-held bull-horn used in the exercise yard off the nursery where little kids were allowed to run, where I used to giggle and clap my hands at flies and weeds and the tiny sky above.

Her voice was smoking, telling this story of death, reasoning it out left and right, which she had refused to do in court, or with any other human being all these years. I couldn't look at her, I, her reason and love, as her voice faded into pure heat, like sex talk fanning my ear. I tried to shut it off. I can't hear, I said; I am flooding, I am a current rushing away.

Now of course, the first thing we notice about somebody when we are approaching them from the outside is their physical appearance: size, style, coloration, race, age, what they are wearing, the way their voice sounds, the accent, the vocabulary, the sense of style.

Nonetheless, the most important thing about your characters is seldom how they look. There are characters who are incredibly real to us, and we cannot begin to say really what they look like. What does K. in Kafka's *The Trial* look like? Is he tall or short, blond or dark? Who cares? One of the total clichés of fiction is to have your viewpoint character look in the mirror right off so that they can tell the reader exactly what they look like. Action stops, the story stops and we get a meaningless description. You may well want the reader to know what your character looks like, but often in apprentice writing, that's all we find out. What does their size mean to them? Do they think of themselves as normal size, when you would look at them and think, What a little guy?

Do they think of themselves as oversized? You might judge such a person handsome or merely passable, but how do they feel about themselves? People's self images are often at odds with what other people observe. A woman who appears to you very attractive may think of herself as that fat kid who wore braces and had acne. Think how that might affect her behavior. Would she walk proudly into a party or enter quietly? Would she tend to stay in a bad relationship, despite everyone who observes her wondering why? When the reader observes her buying clothing for herself, is she opting for large sizes that hide her body? Will she never go to the beach when her friends ask? Your characters might be stuck back in high school popularity contests, still trying to make the team or join the ruling clique, while they are in reality astronauts or congressmen.

Similarly, we have all known people who were raised by doting parents and who truly believe themselves to be devastating and act accordingly, no matter how the world may fail to agree. Their self-confidence and their pleasure in the mirror never falters; it is the world that is wrong. If a man fails to accord her the value she places on herself, she thinks him afraid of a strong competent woman. If a woman fails to respond to such a character's advances, she is frigid or scared of sex and can't handle a real man. If you are over forty, you know former athletes now gone to flab who still have that confidence that came from being the best at something that was widely admired, even though those glory days are long gone. So if you describe such a person as a fifty-two year-old flabby man with a big belly, you are missing the essence of that character, who still sees himself as the basketball star, the quarterback, the ace pitcher. Remember Inspector Clouseau of the "Pink Panther" movies. He runs into a wall and blames the wall. "Stee-u-pid Architect! What a ridiculous place for a wall!" Writing prose allows you the freedom to wander around in your character's mind and to exploit and develop their arrogance, their fears and insecurities, their great narcissism—traits that can bring your character alive for the reader.

Each character must be given a name. That name can suggest ethnicity, can define or not define the sex of the character. The name can suggest character. We all can remember names of the characters of Charles Dickens that define a type perfectly. Ebenezer

Scrooge. Uriah Heep. Tiny Tim. Madame Defarge. Harold Skimpole. Mrs. Jellyby. Wackford Squeers. Basically, you must believe you have chosen the true name of your character. Sometimes you will find that after a draft, you may change the names of one of your important characters because, as you have come to know them, the name is no longer appropriate. When you are writing a memoir, you have a decision whether to call a particular character Charlie Browne, or just C. or whether to tell us you have changed the names to protect the privacy of the people with whom you are dealing. In the latter case and in all fiction, when you are inventing a name, you might as well make up one that does a little of the work of characterization. Think even of the most commonly used names in English. Each has its own flow—Michael versus Mike. The prideful, multi-syllabic "Elizabeth" versus the tight, more controlled "Beth." The formal use of the name "John" versus the free-wheeling "Jack." Who uses each form of the name to call the character? What does the character prefer? How do they introduce themselves? Do they have a nickname? Is it flattering or derogatory? Who uses it?

How do they smell? Of sweat? Of lily of the valley? Of that ghastly stuff they spray on you in department stores if you can't run fast enough? Of coal dust or wood smoke? Of sweat and sugar icing after working in the bakery?

And what is the quality of the person's voice? How do they laugh? How do they move? How do they sit and stand and walk? How much space do they occupy? Some people contract to occupy minimal space and some, who are physically no larger, expand to occupy the entire back seat of a luxury car. The difference may depend on how much space they believe they are worth, or, how they react to others touching them. As a writer, that's your raw material. You can mine it.

You might have a character that would go through four hundred pages without your ever describing a single piece of clothing, and you might have another character for whom what he or she wore would be an important element in characterization. Similarly there are certain characters who are evoked in our minds by some items of clothing, such as Sherlock Holmes's deerstalker hat or Robin Hood's green tunic.

When you are entering a character, you have to feel how they move. Do they move in spurts, in long fluid motions, rapidly, mechanically, carefully? Think of a dancer; think of an old lady making her way across an icy street. What is their natural speed of action and reaction?

What senses are most important to them? When they enter a room, do they respond first to sight, sound, smell, to abstract characteristics of the space, or to the social dimension of what is in the room? Some characters will be very observant. Their heads will be full of colors, of sensations; others will interpret the world in terms of sounds, rhythms. What work a person does will affect their perception of the world. A doctor will see cases, diseases; a dentist will look at people's teeth and bite; an accountant will consider someone's financial stability; a model will look at everyone else as being fit to be photographed or not. An aging stage actor may pay attention to who recognizes him and who treats him as a nonentity.

In dealing with the nonphysical characterization devices, one set includes the shallow devices of tics, hobby horses, tags, obvious habits of speech, running jokes. Deep characterization methods include fears, anxiety, desires, passions, attachments to things and to people, friendships and antipathies, real beliefs. It's a good idea to combine both methods of characterization with any of your reasonably prominent characters.

The most important thing of all to know about your protagonist or any other very important character is this: What does that character want? It is what the protagonist wants and does not want that can set the plot in motion and certainly should be one of the chief mainsprings of the action. Wanting is not always positive. A character's chief passion could be to avoid pain, rather than to achieve pleasure. A character may just want to stay alive, to continue to exist. Jack London's famous story, "To Build a Fire," has, as the primary motivation of the only character, not to freeze to death. A character may desire to escape from a prison, a relationship, a danger. When a character wants something that another character wants also, or wants to prevent the first one from having, we have the beginnings of action. *Character A* wants to leave a marriage; *Character B*, the partner, wants the marriage to continue. But as I have tried to suggest, most important characters in fiction cannot be so simply defined. *A's* cannot simply be the desire to divorce. *A* must have a past, an inner life, fears and desires, relationships, fantasies, preferences, tastes, habits.

Minor characters have many uses in a book besides setting the major characters in a social context. But without that social context, we may not believe. Why is this woman totally alone and totally dependent on this guy she has just met? Where are her women friends? Where's her family? If she has no friends, why not? What's wrong with her or her situation? That social context helps us understand the major characters. Why would a young girl of eleven roam the cold city streets at night—because we've given her a mother, a minor character, who is always out drinking and desperately trying to pick up a man. A character's friends and family can say a lot about a character. And something else again if she has no real friends at all.

Minor characters may also help to shade something in, represent alternatives the protagonist did not take, represent different choices or opinions or alternate fates. Sometimes minor characters represent other aspects of the major character, the darker or lighter side, if you will, their youth or their old age. Sometimes minor characters give local color, help to make a place real, alive, vivid. In *The Kitchen Man*, minor characters are extremely important. The protagonist, Gabriel Rose, is an aspiring playwright and a waiter in a pretentious restaurant. His friends, all fellow waiters, represent choices he does not make —Geller marries and has children; Matthew, a gay man, sleeps with his famous customers—and they also comment, freely and sarcastically, about Gabriel's choices. Besides helping to create the back-biting, late-night, gossip-fueled world of the restaurant business, one of their important functions is to help portray Gabriel as a young man who is still very dependent on other people's opinions. A lot of the shading in fiction depends on skillful use of minor characters. There are also the joys of the bizarre minor characters, sometimes named as in Dickens for their grotesquerie. On occasion, the sharply drawn or amusingly caricatured minor folk are what we most fondly remember from a book. Sancho Panza. Dr. Watson. Queequog. Merlin. Tinker Bell.

Another function of characters, whether major or minor, is to give an alternative view of each other. In *Three Women*, Suzanne, a law school professor and an appeals lawyer, sees herself as a bird of prey going after the rats of the system. Her estranged daughter, Elena, sees Suzanne as a fussy, tight-assed control freak compelled to micromanage everything in her life. Her best friend, Marta, sees Suzanne as someone who is too generous with herself. We begin to understand a person when we not only comprehend how that person sees herself, but how others see her, both positively and negatively.

When you can't tell the minor characters apart without going back repeatedly to check their names, the story is in real trouble. In a novel, that might conceivably happen with some very minor character, although it's best to be careful in dealing with the little guys that you do inform the reader each time in some reasonably subtle way just who that character is. You can do it simply in passing, in ways such as: "Susan saw Charles coming up the steps of the porch. Loretta nodded at him and looked away. It seemed to Susan that Loretta was not pleased to see her brother coming to the house."

Sometimes, of course, you just have to bite the bullet and make a chart. In *City of Darkness, City of Light*, a novel about the French revolution, there are six viewpoint characters and a cast of thousands. The publisher asked for a Cast of Characters, a little guide, so that if you don't happen to remember as you are going along who the Bishop of Arras is, or Collot d'Herbois, the handy dandy list will remind you.

Your minor characters can be catalysts that draw out the different and sometimes conflicting emotions of your characters. Through the main character's interplay with minor characters, we get to see the protagonist in action: How she acts in relation to an authority like a boss. How she treats a homeless guy on the street. Does she fight back when a stranger in a bar paws at her? Does she empty her bank account for a boyfriend who's been hitting her up for months? Or for a family down the street who's about to be evicted? Minor characters can serve as devices that spin your main characters into action—by making demands, by drawing them into trouble, by presenting temptations—that force your main characters to make a revealing choice or challenge them or force them to react under pressure.

When you're working with your major characters before you really begin to write your story, you might want to accumulate dossiers on them. You'll want to answer many deep questions about these major characters, beside the obvious questions of age, sex, and physical description. You'll want to imagine them doing some characteristic action such as dancing, playing tennis; some kind of physical or mental work; you'll need to know their family and education and class and ethnic background; and of course their name.

You might ask yourself whether they have close friends and how many. Who are their acquaintances? Their enemies? What do they seek in friends? Yes-men, siblings who mix rivalry and affection, mommas and daddies, challenges, supporters, networkers, someone who is primarily interesting because useful? What do they do when they're lonely? Turn on the TV? Call up Mom? Go down to the corner bar and have a drink? Try to pick someone up? Get stoned? Eat? Meditate? Pray? If so, to whom and for what?

What does your character do for a living and how does that person feel about working? What is their work history? What would be their fantasy job? What do they do for fun?

What happens when they are thwarted or blocked? Do they show anger? Conceal it? Swallow it? Who do they blame for their troubles? Themselves? Their mother? Blacks? Jews? Asians? Native Americans? The rich? Women? A hated rival? Everybody else?

Does your character identify more with their mother or their father? What kind of childhood did the character have? What do they tell themselves about their childhood (as opposed to how it was); how do they present it to others?

What is the person's relationship to objects? You might ask yourself what possessions they have and whether any of their possessions mean something particular—obsessive or simply enjoyable or prideful—to them. Do they hoard? Do they have certain beloved objects we associate with them? How do they relate to technology? What kind of relationship do they have with their vehicle?

What discrepancies are interesting in the character between professed or even deeply held values and behavior? How honest is the person about those failures, to him- or herself? To others? It is in such contradictions and the way a character may handle them that we sometimes grasp their essence.

Some of these questions will be useful and some will not and so you may generate your own lists. However, I will share with you one question I find extremely useful whenever I am having difficulty entering a character. Empathy is part of the necessary equipment of any novelist who aspires to more than rewriting their own early or current history. But sometimes empathy fails. One of my own ways is then to ask of my character what is asked in the next to last position of a Tarot reading: What is most hoped for and/or most feared? Often that is a key to a character.

My last little trick for entry is to give the character some little piece of myself, some moment of my childhood or my adult life, to give it over and thus lose it. But often that little blood sacrifice works, and the character then can be entered and comes alive. Basically, you enter a character wherever and whenever you can so that you can look at the world as that person sees it and sees themselves. Fiction is preeminently the art that requires both empathy and imagination. Autobiography will only carry a writer so far, maybe one good novel of youth and one of middle age, unless she or he has a truly extraordinary life or mind. Once you grant that the novelist works out of other people's lives as well as her own, you grant her a license to write about old age while in her thirties, about the loss of a child while hers are secure, or even unborn or never to be conceived, about passion out of tranquility, about ax murder and poison when she will not set a mouse trap.

Fans of a particular novel may assume the author is the protagonist. Sometimes a reader will become incensed if you explain that a particular character is not literally yourself. Sometimes such a reader will assume you are attempting to fool them; that you are a hypocrite who lacks the courage to stand up and be revealed as an ex-mental patient or a lesbian mother or whatever. The second common reaction is annoyance and disillusionment. I thought it was true and now you tell me you just made it up. We still have a Puritan mistrust of the imagination as a vehicle of truth, an unwillingness to understand that the patterns and forms of art may be true in ways that are not literal, but profound. Successful fiction has been created out of the deeply felt stories of wolves, cats, dogs, horses, Neanderthals, intelligent arthropods, gods, beasts and robots. Sometimes the urge to fiction comes from exploring selves not lived out. I am aware of countless possibilities I did not choose, myriad alternate selves I might have become had I acted otherwise or had chance descended on me with a different leverage. The urge to fiction is, I suspect, partly the urge to explore those alternate universes of possibility. Every character I have created in every novel has some aspects of myself built in and I have lived that character while writing it. Thus even when we are writing about lives extremely different from our own, choices we will never have to make, events we will never in our own flesh experience, we can still learn a great deal about ourselves as we create and explore very different characters in fiction.

One device for giving a sense of character I have not discussed is voice. Often when I am using various viewpoints in a novel, I take care that each one has a different voice. I want it to be the case that if you pick up the novel and turn at random to a page, even if there are ten different viewpoint characters, you will instantly be able to tell from the language and the style exactly which character's mind you are in. I believe that even though I used ten viewpoints in *Gone to Soldiers*, if you read random pages in the novel, you can tell from the voice and diction in whose viewpoint I was writing.

Often if you are writing in the first person in a character, characterization through choices of language and style, diction and word choice, are particularly important. But it is also a good idea to create this clear differentiation in the third person. Take another look at the work of some of the masters of creating voice: Grace Paley, in her short stories. All Kurt Vonnegut's novels. Mark Twain's *Huckleberry Finn*. Barbara Kingsolver's Taylor Greer in *The Bean Trees*. But the first person voice can be especially important if you are writing a memoir.

Writing sex scenes is partly a matter of taste. Unless you're writing pornography, the graphic description of body parts inserted into body parts is not the best way to go. One exception to that statement is when you are aiming for something cold. It is the description of a woman having sex with a man she loathes, going through with it for some reason other than desire. Then the bare physical description would work.

The other extreme is to go all metaphorical. A few well-chosen metaphors are dandy, but too much reliance on metaphor can get ludicrous. You have to watch your language carefully. You want to infuse the scene with the emotions of your protagonist, if she or he has them. Sex can be a great door into character. How someone thinks about sex is a good clue to character. Is he making love, establishing possession, making a conquest, proving his superiority as a male, taking from another man? Is she submitting or making love or establishing her own desirability, taking from another woman, having or letting herself be taken? Is making love a pleasure or an investment? Is your protagonist sharing or spending?

Also, the way someone makes love can demonstrate character. Does he always make love in the same way? Would it make him nervous to change position? Does she always want to be a bottom or a top? Is she orgasmic? Does he make love brutally, slam bang, or is he conscious of the woman's reactions and interested in giving her maximum pleasure? Is she knowledgeable about the male body or ignorant? Does she think about what she is going to wear tomorrow as the act continues? Is she making To Do lists in her head? Is he fantasizing about someone he saw on television or his old girlfriend? Is there role playing involved? Some lovers make animal noises. Some wail or scream. Some are silent. Some speak words they consider dirty. Others say they love the partner, over and over again, whether or not in fact they do.

You have to consider how to reveal character; you have to consider what effect you want your scene to have. Is it romantic? Is it sensuous? Is it boring? Is it distressful in some way to one or the other participants? Is it painful for one of them? Is it disillusioning? Is it startling in some way? Is it some kind of breakthrough for your characters or just the usual? Is it sex for money without involvement? Is the woman faking an orgasm or the man faking emotion?

Don't, unless you are writing romance or pornography, have your characters achieve instant simultaneous ecstasy when they tumble into bed. Sex is as complicated as anything else in our lives, one reason it is useful for characterization. If the sex is too perfect, we won't believe you.

Some writers put in too many sex scenes, as if afraid the action will bog down and the reader will lose interest. Such writers do not trust their own storytelling and think they need to seduce the reader into continuing with one sex event after another. But repetitive sex scenes are as boring as any other kind of scene that is repeated too often.

Other writers are too embarrassed or prudish or proper to write sex scenes at all. If you are writing about two people flirting for forty pages and then getting it on, mostly we do not want to skip that part. We want to find out what really happens between them in that bedroom. It need not go on for pages, but mostly we do need to be present. We've been waiting for them to get together, and we cannot be cheated of that moment.

Now, if you are writing about your own life, whether you give yourself a new name or write in an openly autobiographical memoir, you may think there's no problem creating characters—and certainly not in depicting yourself. Think again. Often people who are writing directly out of their own lives have more trouble trying to characterize themselves or their intimates in a sharp and memorable manner than do writers who are making up the inhabitants of Dodge City or the Orion Nebula. Whether you are writing fiction or a memoir, the means of characterization available to you are the same. Much of what I have written about characterization in fiction applies to writing personal narrative just as strongly. Once again, deep characterization methods include the uses of a character's fears, anxiety, desires, passions, attachments to things and to people, friendships and antipathies, real beliefs. It's a problem when someone writing about themselves fails to imagine themselves as a character; that kind of writing makes the assumption that character development is not important, that the reader knows all about them because, of course, the writer does.

It is a problem, too, when you are writing about your life if you do not understand the other characters you are presenting to us and their motives for acting as they did, but it is not insurmountable. Mary Gordon's memoir about her father, *The Shadow Man*, is a piece of detective work, an account of trying to understand who he was. She attempted to discover his family background, the forces that distorted him, who he really was. It is the quest to understand her father, whom she did not easily understand, that is the moving force of her story.

In many ways it does not matter whether you are writing a novel or short story or memoir: the devices of characterization are pretty much the same. The characters must be vivid and differentiated whether they are invented or your own Aunt Sharon and Uncle Jack. In one case, you must turn your imagination loose; in the other, you must mine memory for the richest scraps of observation and recollection, ways of speaking, ways of being in the room and in the world. When you're writing a memoir, you might want to accumulate a simpler dossier on each of your major characters than you need in fiction, a dossier that consists of everything you can remember about the person, and what other family members and friends may remember, if you ask.

Although we'll address the implications of writing about families and relatives in the chapter "A Scandal in the Family," it is quite true that in some cases, especially if information on them is not available to you, you may have to re-imagine family members (attempting to be true to your recollections as well as your knowledge of their motivations, desires, etc.:) before they become successful characters. Since you don't know all about them (remembering them, for example, from the vantage point of childhood, how could you?), you'll have to re-invent them at different stages in their lives. You'll have to ask some of the same questions about your great grandfather when he was twenty years old that you'd ask about any character.

There are in any life a great many minor characters, major of course in their own lives, but minor in the one you are writing about. Sometimes it is necessary to meld some of these people together into one person for the sake of simplicity and to avoid introducing too many characters and confusing the reader. You could make your two best friends in college into one confidant. I remember reading a memoir about a stroke survivor in which she explained she had turned several of the friends who had helped her while she was recovering into one person, for clarity and in order to better focus her story.

One important way of characterizing your people is by the language a character speaks, the way they use words, their use of jargon or inflated or rough language, what they say and do not say. Often you remember someone as much by the way they spoke as by any other salient point about them. If you can give that flavor to their speech, or mine your memory for particular phrases they used often, you are a good way toward creating a person the reader will believe in.

In writing about ourselves, there is something that we shouldn't forget. It is not uncommon that someone will be a lively talker, full of anecdotes and lively language and comparisons that startle you or make you smile. But sometimes when that very person sits down to write about her life, instead of writing with flavor and energy, she writes in a flat boring manner. She leaves out all the juicy details and the local color and gives us a sort of abstract summing up that has no life to it. It's not clear why this happens. It may be that a certain inner censor comes into play, which says to the writer, "Oh, you can't include that!" Or, "Get on with the story. That detail isn't important. Who are you to take up so many pages, anyhow?" Or perhaps the situation is so real to the writer that she feels her reader will somehow automatically see what she sees, hear what she hears because, of course, it's all there so vividly in her mind. Maybe it's pure embarrassment. "My God! I can't really tell people my father's nickname for lecherous Uncle Richard." Whatever the reason, the writing lacks all flavor and originality. It sounds like the kind of writing you find in a local newspaper. Check out the chapter on Dialog and remember, your character's language is an important tool in making him or her alive for the reader.

CREATING CHARACTERS: THE DOSSIER

We fill out this questionnaire with every major character we create. We suggest you key it in to your computer or make photocopies for later use. Answering these questions in full (and adding any more that are helpful to you or more specific to your project) leads to the creation of a rich and useful record of physical, emotional, and historical information, information that the reader may never see but that will send your imagination digging into surprisingly fertile new places. For minor characters, you might want to answer only some of these questions. For people in your memoirs, people you assume you know well, you'll be impressed how creative speculation can make a familiar person come to life on the page.

NAME:

WHAT DO THEY MOST LIKE TO BE CALLED:

DO THEY HAVE A NAME THAT THEY MOST RESENT BEING CALLED? WHO HAS CALLED THEM BY THIS NAME:

AGE:

PHYSICAL APPEARANCE:

WAY OF DRESSING:

HOW DOES YOUR CHARACTER FEEL ABOUT HIS OR HER FACE AND BODY?

WHEN YOUR CHARACTER THINKS ABOUT HIS OR HER BODY OR FACE, WHAT ARE THEY MOST VAIN ABOUT?

WHAT WOULD THEY MOST LIKE TO CHANGE ABOUT THEIR PHYSICAL APPEARANCE?

VOICE AND/OR ACCENT:

KIND OF LAUGH:

DO THEY SING? WITH OTHERS? ALONE? IN THE SHOWER? WHAT DO THEY SING?

WHERE WERE THEY BORN? WHAT CITY?

WHERE DO THEY LIVE NOW? WHY? DO THEY LIKE IT?

WHAT EVENTS GOING ON IN THE WORLD WHEN THEY WERE LITTLE WERE ADULTS MOST LIKELY TO TALK ABOUT WHEN THEY SAT HAVING COFFEE?

WHERE AND HOW EDUCATED?

ARE THEY PROUD OR ASHAMED OF THEIR EDUCATION? HAVE THEY EVER LIED ABOUT IT?

OCCUPATION?

IS THAT WHAT THE PERSON EXPECTED TO BE DOING AT THIS POINT IN HIS OR HER LIFE? BETTER OR WORSE?

IS THAT WHAT THEIR PARENTS' EXPECTED OF THEM?

WHAT DID THEIR PARENTS URGE THEM / INFLUENCE THEM TO DO?

AT WHAT AGE DID THE PERSON FIRST WORK? WHAT WAS THE JOB?

WHAT WERE THE BEST AND WORST JOBS THE PERSON EVER HELD? WHY?

WHAT WOULD BE THEIR FANTASY JOB?

WHAT KIND OF VEHICLE IF ANY DOES THE PERSON DRIVE?

MARRIED? LIVING WITH SOMEONE? WHO?

CHILDREN? WITH THEM OR NOT?

WERE THEIR PARENTS HAPPY TOGETHER WHEN THEY WERE BORN? LATER?

WHEN THEY WERE GROWING UP, DID THEIR PARENTS ARGUE? ABOUT WHAT?

SIBLINGS?

CURRENT RELATIONSHIP WITH PARENTS AND/OR SIBLINGS?

OTHER IMPORTANT RELATIVES (AUNTS, UNCLES, COUSINS, GRANDPARENTS):

WHICH OF THESE RELATIVES WERE THE MOST IMPORTANT FOR GOOD OR ILL?

WHICH RELATIVE DID THE CHILD HEAR THAT HE OR SHE LOOKED LIKE, AND HOW DID HE OR SHE FEEL ABOUT THAT COMPARISON?

FIRST EXPERIENCE OF DEATH IN OR OUT OF THE FAMILY:

SOMETHING HAPPENED TO YOUR CHARACTER WHEN THEY WERE YOUNG, PERHAPS IN GRADE SCHOOL THAT THEY ARE EMBARRASSED ABOUT TO THIS DAY. WHAT OCCURRED?

WHO IS YOUR CHARACTER'S BEST FRIEND, IF THEY HAVE ONE?

IF THEY WERE TO CONFIDE IN SOMEONE, WHO WOULD IT BE? A FRIEND? BARTENDER? FAMILY MEMBER? RELIGIOUS LEADER? DOCTOR? THERAPIST? STRANGER?

IF YOU SURPRISED YOUR CHARACTER IN THE STREET, WHERE MIGHT THEY BE GOING THAT THEY WOULD LEAST WANT YOU TO KNOW ABOUT?

WHAT DOES HE OR SHE DO WHEN ANGRY?

WHAT DOES HE OR SHE DO WHEN DEPRESSED?

WHAT IS YOUR CHARACTER'S MOST CLOSELY GUARDED SECRET?

IF YOUR CHARACTER COULD UNDO ONE THING THEY HAVE DONE IN THEIR LIFE, WHAT WOULD THAT BE?

IF THEY COULD HAVE ANY WISH, WHAT WOULD THEY GET?

WHAT DO THEY DO FOR FUN OR AMUSEMENT OR TO UNWIND?

FAVORITE FOOD OR TYPE OF MEAL?

SET YOUR CHARACTER IN MOTION ACROSS A ROOM AND DESCRIBE HOW HE OR SHE MOVES:

WHAT IS THE MOST PHYSICAL THING THAT THEY DO REGULARLY (WORK OUT, WALK, DANCE, CLEAN THE HOUSE, HAVE SEX, PLAY TOUCH FOOTBALL)?

DO THEY HAVE ANY PETS? DID THEY AS A CHILD?

IF THEY HAD THE POWER TO HURT ANYONE WITHOUT BEING PUNISHED, WHO WOULD THEY HURT?

WHAT IS THEIR BIGGEST FEAR? THEIR MOST IRRATIONAL FEAR?

WHAT DO THEY RESENT MOST THAT ANOTHER PERSON DID TO THEM OR CAUSED TO HAVE HAPPEN TO THEM?

WHAT IS THEIR RELIGIOUS AFFILIATION, IF ANY?

WHAT DO THEY REALLY BELIEVE IN?

HAVE THEY EVER HAD A NICKNAME? AS A CHILD? AS AN ADULT? HOW DID THEY FEEL ABOUT THAT NICKNAME, AND HOW DID THEY ACQUIRE IT?

HOW OFTEN DO THEY FALL IN LOVE AND WHAT HAPPENS?

DO THEY HAVE A PHYSICAL OR CHARACTER TYPE THEY REPEATEDLY ENGAGE?

FANTASY LIFE? CONTENT AND FREQUENCY OF DAYDREAMING?

Exercise:

Write a brief static description of a minor character in your novel or memoir. Use some of the answers to questions in the dossier above. Then write one scene in which one or more salient characteristics of your person is revealed in action and dialog.

4

How to Avoid Writing Like a Victim

I recently read a manuscript that could have been the saddest book in the world. It was written by a single mother who works two jobs to pay the bills for herself and her young son. Drawing on parts of the writer's life, the book is about a woman who moved to LA when she got out of college and lived in a bug-infested third floor walk-up in a building full of junkies. She loses her job as an assistant to a Hollywood character actress and finds one as an exotic dancer. She's dependent on speed and booze and worse, she falls for the sleaziest, most arrogant, least responsible guys in LA: guitar players in heavy metal bands. After sex they forget her name; they steal her money; they hit the road with groupies. She makes her living from the dollar bills that drunks tuck into her G-string. The guy she truly loves—and marries on a weekend bender—has her committed to a mental hospital, and then some bad things start to happen.

The events in this book can bring you way down, but it was actually a lot of fun to read because the writer told the story with a tough, ironic voice; because she completely accepted herself, her bad choices, and the consequences of those choices. She snorted crystal meth. She screwed around. She lived in a dump. But she didn't feel sorry for herself. She wasn't asking forgiveness. She'd been down and out but she wasn't trying to teach other girls not to go down the primrose path. She'd been badly treated, but she certainly wasn't trying to lay blame on anyone. She was simply setting down the facts of her life, one after another until they snowballed into absurdity.

Readers often bristle when writers present themselves as victims. Having been deeply hurt, offended, wrongfully treated, as we all have been at times, it's difficult to avoid conveying self pity. It's harder still to be even-handed, to see different sides of an event or relationship. Sometimes a person had no hand whatsoever in causing her misfortune. So how is she to write about it? There are probably as many answers as there are writers who take the time to solve the problem, but there are some techniques worth mentioning. One is humor.

Sometimes we can catch readers off-guard if we can make them laugh at situations that, treated in a more conventional way, might seem self serving or self-pitying. In one of our classes a woman presented a piece that, in the hands of a less skilled writer, might have sounded like your typical my-husband-left-me-for-a-younger-woman story. Except that she compared her husband's trophy wife to a white lab rat and kept the metaphor alive (including references to her spare, vegetarian diet; her quick, nervous movements; her overbite) until the class was in stitches.

I'll never forget a story by Primo Levi about three friends who were prisoners in Auschwitz who had not had a drop of water to drink in days. Parched to the point of near madness, they were nonetheless assigned by the Germans to strip the scrap metal from an old basement. Two of them, working together to wrest an old pipe from the rubble, find some rusty water trapped in the elbow of the pipe and selfishly drink it all. Marching back to the camp, the third friend senses their sudden contentment and confronts them. The story is about how people treat each other in desperate situations and how victims can turn into abusers. Writers who experienced the Holocaust have every reason to portray themselves as victims, yet in the hands of a brilliant memoirist like Primo Levi, a story may be as much about the complex social hierarchy in a concentration camp, and thus about the nature of survival and free choice, and become even deeper in its universal implications. It is difficult to remember that in any horrible situation, there are many things going on at the same time as the horror. People like and dislike each other; power struggles develop; petty resentments do not disappear, nor do human longings. Writing about these other aspects will not dissipate the horror but might make it all the more real. Two lovers meeting in the midst of war is not an common device for allowing the reader to more deeply feel war's personal consequences. *The Diary of Anne Frank* is especially moving because each member of the families in hiding is not a helpless lamb, but a person with very real and sometimes quite selfish human needs.

The oldest chestnut of the creative writing class is *Show, don't tell.* Make a scene in which an action unfolds, rather than simply report it. In attempting to avoid writing as a victim, making the decision to allow a situation to unfold in a scene permits your readers to participate in the situation and make up their own minds about its implications. Stating "My father was an irresponsible drunk who always let us down," might be less effective than a scene in which a father comes home to his hungry children on Christmas Eve with an armful of meat pies given to him by a charitable neighborhood baker and then, drunk as a lord, stumbles on the way upstairs and crushes the pies. It's well to remember that as a child we may have been unhappy, but we didn't always think of ourselves as victims while the situation was unfolding. We were sometimes focused on those pies. More often than not there were other people involved and we were thinking of their welfare or privilege. Or strategizing about how to save ourselves. We may not have been thinking at the moment what we now can put into words as adults.

In Frank McCourt's *Angela's Ashes,* it was a given to the children that their father drank. They didn't think of Dad as evil, but as Dad, and that Dad liked his whiskey. They thought a lot about food and being cold and their mother and the neighborhood and strategized how to steal fruit from the corner store. One of the reasons *Angela's Ashes* kept so many people riveted, instead of throwing the book aside in despair, was the author's ability to charm the reader. He used humor. He used language. He created a memorable voice. He drew vivid scenes that allowed the reader to become involved in the action, to hear and breathe the world of Limerick, and to be kept in suspense about what in the world would become of this unlucky family. In telling this story, a less skilled writer might have simply poured on the misery. But young Frank McCourt was not a victim. He was a plucky kid whose father drank too much and whose early life was one of intense desire: for food, for warmth, for safety, for peace between his parents.

The key is control. Victims do not control situations, but writers do. Although the heavy metal musician screwed-around on the L.A. stripper, she continued to dance for a living even though he didn't like it. She retained her attitude, her opinions, her friends, her very bad habits. Primo Levi was refused food and water and badly mistreated, but he retained his critical involvement and his interest in his society. The same is true for Frank McCourt. Poor and hungry, he never lost his curiosity and his wit; his ability to comment on the adult world. He continued to mastermind schemes for getting food; to be an active participant in his neighborhood and his family. Although in each of these examples, the characters have been deprived or ill-treated, the ill-treatment did not totally overcome them or define them. They continued to be active participants in their world.

Exercise:

Choose a situation in your life when you felt you were treated unfairly, or a time that was particularly hard on you, and try to write about it a way in which you do not come off as a victim but as an active participant.

You might write about it with humor, using exaggeration, or unusual description, or intriguing images (think of the metaphor of the rat, for instance). Or let the action snowball into absurdity. (See the chapter on writing humor for more techniques.)

You might use explicit detail, so that the reader is focused not on you but on the situation.

You might focus on the society; that is, the social interaction going on between the characters.

You could center on your specific needs and desires at the time, getting what you want (like those pies) instead of how badly you were treated.

You might simply allow the action to unfold, event by disastrous event.

What you do not want to do is to tell the reader how to feel. The object of this exercise is to allow readers to make their own judgments from the facts. But because you the writer are supplying those facts, you have a great deal of control indeed over the reader's judgment.

5

The Uses of Dialog

One of the most foolish mistakes a prose writer can make is to overlook the uses of dialog. To ignore what dialog can do for you is analogous to using a computer with an 80 gigabyte hard drive as nothing more than a typewriter; why only write letters with a tool that can run your entire house? Because a play or a movie script looks like it's entirely made of dialog, it's easy to assume that dialog is more important for the playwright or screenwriter than the writer of prose. It's also easy to think that dialog is simple; just a couple of people talking.

To the extent that there are rules of dialog in writing fiction or the memoir, they are a loose set of rules. In the same way that writers of stream-of-consciousness do away with conventional sentence structure, some writers disregard conventional methods of punctuation. They don't use quotation marks; they may not use a new paragraph for each speaker; they employ colons or em-dashes to introduce a new speaker. Although this is not wise, it is not illegal. It's all in a writer's style, a personal issue. There is no Great White English Teacher in the sky, with a bolt of lightning in one hand and a red pencil in the other. The only really important rule is this: The dialog has to work in context—meaning, on the most basic level, that the reader always has to know who is speaking and what they are saying. (This is not as obvious as it sounds.) On a more advanced level, it means that once you understand what dialog can do, it will work for you, becoming a vehicle you can employ to carry some of the load of your storytelling.

Many writers of non-fiction, of memoirs and autobiographical novels, write long passages of absolutely boring and sometimes incoherent dialog. Then they justify the mess by saying, "But this is exactly what people sound like." Or worse, "I taped it."

Having a good ear means writing dialog that *sounds* idiomatic. Just because you are writing about things that actually happened, does not mean you want to transcribe the way people actually speak. If you have ever listened to a tape of a normal conversation, you will hear a great many repetitions, interruptions, non-sequiturs and unfinished sentences. Conversation typically meanders, repeats, meanders some more.

People spend an enormous amount of time talking about the weather, about how-are-you, about television and what they had for lunch and nothing at all. There is a time for banal conversation, mostly when you want to reassure someone that you are sympathetic, that you mean them well or want to put them at ease. But your book is rarely the place for an exact transcription of human speech. You're a writer, not a courtroom stenographer. There are very skillful writers who describe people's dreary lives in what would appear to be the most commonplace exchanges, but Ann Beatty and Harold Pinter have labored long and hard to construct dialog that sounds as if it were lifted from an elevator and, in point of fact, is highly compressed and worked over. Lillian Ross, the legendary *New Yorker* magazine interviewer, regularly made her subjects sound like egomaniacal boors by seemingly transcribing what they said. In fact, as the novelist Irving Wallace observed about Ross's book on Hemingway, she was "selectively listening and viewing, capturing the one moment that entirely illumines the scene, fastening on the one quote that tells all."

What you are doing with so-called realistic dialog is creating the illusion of idiomatic speech. What you are really doing is creating highly edited, highly selected representations of human speech.

In the novel *Storm Tide*, the main character, David Green, meets Stumpy Squeer, slow and somewhat retarded, but the kind of fellow that can live his life out in the small town where he grew up because people watch over him. Rather than introduce Stumpy as an inarticulate mumbler, which might have been closer to a real life portrait, we decided to choose dialog that infused him with some pride and purpose:

Stumpy was short and thick, fifty more or less, with barrel-like haunches that made him seem to roll forward as he walked.

Judith stood on the steps, "Let's go, you guys! Gordon. David. Lunch!"

"Will you join us, Stumpy?" Gordon's voice was deep and courtly.

Stumpy shook his head no.

"Going to get back to your book?" Gordon asked him. "Stumpy's been working on one for three years now."

"Four," Stumpy said.

"Really?" I loved the idea. Stumpy Squeer, hermit savant. "What are you writing about?"

"Not writin'. Been readin' it," he said. "Almost finished, too."

In good writing, fiction or non-fiction, dialog always exists to make a point, preferably many points at once. Most important, dialog characterizes the speaker. Because the reader takes note of everything a character says, the reader will develop attitudes about that character. Dialog also gives the reader the illusion of discovery. Remember that old chestnut of Creative Writing 101? *Show, don't tell?* Dialog is the perfect vehicle for showing action unfolding or a character's attitude changing in a scene. Moreover, the information learned through a conversation might register more deeply than the information the author narrates or reports, because the reader feels she has overheard the characters say it and has thus discovered it by herself. If I told you a certain Hollywood producer was untrustworthy, you might believe me but it wouldn't stick long in your mind. If you read the dialog of a telephone conversation in which this fellow, within ten minutes of introducing himself for the first time, guaranteed me an executive producer's credit for a film on a book he had not yet read, and offered to buy me a hundred shares of a hot stock to boot, you wouldn't trust him any more than I did. Because you were witness to his own words, his dialog.

In English, due to the French overlay on the Anglo-Saxon, and the Latin and Greek derived words over those layers, we have levels of formality. So, in order for a geneticist to describe what he does in the lab, he can either say:

"I sequence the genetic patterns of the Drosophila mela-
nogaster."

Or,

"I map fruit fly genes."

The use of formality versus informality in speech, the use of
colorful idioms, the use of slang and obscenities, the misuse of
words, all tell you something about the character who is speaking.
Obviously, the choice of formal speech versus slang may tip off the
reader to that character's level of education, even his pretensions.
Further, when that character chooses to use formal speech, or with
whom he uses it, may give insight into that character.

I knew a man who was college educated, well read and articulate. He worked in a white-collar profession. But when he spoke
with blue collar or service trades people, in the pizza joint, at the
auto repair shop, his language reverted to a tough guy parody
of street talk. It might be that the man was insecure, so that his
personality mirrored those to whom he spoke; or perhaps his
background was more blue collar than he liked to let on and he
felt comfortable revealing more of himself around certain people.
Creating ambiguity such as this can enrich your storytelling.
Without telling your readers what to think, you enable them to
develop theories of their own. In *Storm Tide*, the character Crystal
tells different versions of her past to different people. Characters
in books, exactly like people we know in life, are not one dimen-
sional but complex and sometimes contradictory in their actions
and intentions. We can convey that in our dialog.

Mastering the jargon of particular professions is always important to a writer. Too much jargon can be unintelligible, but
English contains many sub-languages, and mastering them can
make your piece seem more real. Not that your characters will
ever really have to sound exactly like a lawyer or a geneticist or
an arson detective would speak, but you should master enough
of their idiom to create the impression of such a person.

Many of the submissions we get at the press sound artificial.
People think because they've seen TV shows about every conceivable kind of character that they can write those characters. But

without taking the time to learn about them, they are seldom rendered as anything more than caricatures and types. We have read manuscripts in which trial scenes were unconvincing because the writer had never bothered to witness one except in TV dramas; novels in which the police behaved in unconvincing ways which any simple review of procedures with a knowledgeable police officer would have fixed.

When writing about the conversation between yourself and another person, one that actually happened, you'd have to have an eidetic memory or a tape recorder to get that conversation exactly. Happily, that's the last thing you want to do, even in a memoir. You want to imply what a person conveyed and how they said it; shorten the conversation and get to the point. In the memoir *Rookie Cop*, the writer, a one-time police spy, wore a body wire, saved the transcriptions of his tapes, and was in the rare position of being able to provide a word-for-word account of his attempt to draw information from a bombing suspect. The conversation meandered for thirteen pages in first draft and was so full of meaningless exchanges, interjections, hesitations, expletives and in-jokes as to render it unintelligible, however accurate. We had to cut it down to a half-page in which the flavor of the cat and mouse exchange was preserved and the important information was efficiently delivered.

Writers who equate reality with transcriptions of speech have similar problems with dialect: vernacular English, for example, and the various forms of rural English, English that has a Yiddish or a Spanish flavor. How realistically should you portray the dialect you are working with? You want people to read and understand what you have written. You do not want to erect an impenetrable wall of dialect between the reader and your work. I saw the classic reggae outlaw movie, *The Harder They Come,* many times, and if I did not catch every word of the Kingston, Jamaica patois, I was carried along with the action, the setting, the music. So I knew exactly what was going on. When I picked up a novel written (by an American) in the same dead accurate patois, I could not penetrate it and simply gave up trying. No one can give you a formula for dealing with this problem; it's a question of style and may well vary from work to work. Flavor is what you are after, not the exact pronunciation of a dialect so thick no reader will be able to understand it. Many good Black writers demonstrate mastery of the levels of idiom and dialect from street jive to commencement address formal, as the demands of the piece and the situation warrant.

In the novel, *Woman on the Edge of Time*, Connie Ramos, a Chicana, is drawn to the door of her New York apartment:

> "It's me, Dolly!" Her niece was screaming in the hall. "Let me in! Hurry!"
> "Momento." Connie fumbled with the bolt, the police lock, finally swinging the door wide. Dolly fell in past her, her face bloody. Connie clutched at Dolly, trying to see how badly she was hurt. "Qué pasa? Who did this?"

The author is using only a few Spanish words to give us the flavor of the speaker. Another way to use foreign phrases is to quickly and unobtrusively translate them:

> The waiter bowed. "Encore du café, Monsieur?"
> I nodded and he filled my cup with thick black coffee.

It is obvious that if you are writing historical fiction, you want to avoid anachronisms, for instance in a piece set during the early nineteenth century. Remember, the farther back you go, the less accurate will be your rendition of the language and the more you will be simply creating an illusion of eighteenth century language for example. If you get too sucked in to writing the language of the period, you will produce something quaint and curious and mostly devoid of interest to modern readers. That verisimilitude is the reason few readers actually made their way through *Mason-Dixon*, Thomas Pynchon's novel, even when they had devoured his previous work.

I had this problem in my novel *City of Darkness, City of Light* about the French revolution. I had to figure out how to convey the highly idiomatic, somewhat secretive, often obscene and usually colorful language of the *sans culottes*, the most revolutionary working class of the revolution. I realized that the nearest equivalent in modern language would be Black ghetto speech. But I also realized after I had played with this, that it would simply render my attempt to give verisimilitude to 18th century life, ideas, manners, the absolute quietus. Nobody would believe these were people talking in 1792. So I gave up that idea and produced a language, not nearly as slangy as the actual language and not nearly as obscene or colorful.

Realistic dialog, no matter how accurate, is not always what you are aiming for. If you are writing a science fiction piece about characters from another universe, your characters should not sound like your neighbors. You would want to give an alien flavor to their speech. Flavor is the key word. It has to be intelligible. All aliens speak English or you have no story, unless your story is about the difficulty or inability to communicate from one culture to another. Similarly, if you are writing about your aged grandfather from the old country in his youth, he should not use current slang or up to date idioms. But neither should he, say if he arrived on a passenger ship from Italy, speak exactly as he did when he got off the ship. His speech has to be intelligible.

Dialog also reveals character in showing what someone is trying to accomplish by what they choose to say. Is your character using words to flatter? Using words to lie? To provoke guilt? The words that you put in a character's mouth inform our opinions about that character. Those words tell us how characters view the world, the way their minds work, what they want, without the author telling us.

We were having an idle conversation about our car breaking down some years ago when an assistant of ours said, "My girlfriend and I think you should get a BMW." A helpful enough comment at face value. But what did her dialog reveal? That outside of work, she and her lover talked about us (we certainly didn't talk much about them) but more important to us, they viewed us as having a hell of a lot more money than we had.

Although dialog can reveal deep character, silence can be equally revealing.

"You're telling me you were not with her?"
Bob sighed, as if preparing once again to endure her paranoid questioning.
"Because if I ever found out. . . ."
He shook his head. He was tired of this.

"She's my best friend, Bob. The only friend I've made in this town."

"For the last time. I was hunting with Reggie. We got a late start back and spent the night on the road. I can show you the motel receipt." He dug into his wallet. "Do you want to see it?"

"Reggie is in Milwaukee. He called looking for you an hour ago."

Not a word emerged from Bob's lips but if he'd been smoking he would have issued a perfect "o."

She did indeed grab the receipt.

It is not necessary to have pages and pages of dialog, and in fact it is in general not a great idea to do so. You can give the meat of a scene in four exchanges. You can pass hours, days, years of time. In the following example, the passages of time are italicized:

I called my agent *just after mailing off the manuscript*. "I think it's the best thing I've ever written."

"I look forward to reading it *this weekend*," he said.

Exactly *three weeks later*, I gave him a call. "What do you think?"

He brushed me off. "I need some more time with it."

I called again in a month, this time after a stiff drink. "He's in a meeting," his secretary said. "He'll call you back."

He never did. *Two weeks later, I strode into his office.* I was not new to this game. The longer they took with their response, the worse they thought of the book. It was back to teaching, if I could get a job after all this time. Just keep your dignity, I told myself, grasping the side of his desk to keep my hands from shaking. "Tell it to me straight," I said.

"I have to be honest with you," my agent could not meet my eyes. "We've looked everyplace. I must have taken it to the country. I think I've lost the damn thing."

You notice that many lines of dialog have a tag. Tags are vital. Now the most common tags, *he said, she said*, are dull but also transparent. That is, the reader tends to ignore them, to use them simply as markers. Sometimes each speaker is distinct enough, identified either through their speech patterns or the content of their response. The reader always knows who is speaking, even in a long exchange. It is important always to check your dialog and make sure the reader never has to go back and count lines to figure out who is saying what. That breaks the flow and takes the reader out of the story. A participant in one of our writing classes told us that her grade school teacher used to hang a chart listing all the verbs you should substitute for *said*. (My own grade school teacher told us that sitting under our desks with our heads between our knees would protect us from the atom bomb.) Likely, she wanted to inject a little action into the children's writing. But don't get too fancy, as in:

"Well, hello, Little Girl!" vociferated the wolf. "You must be off to Grandma's house," he hypothesized.

Action or description tags (in italics below) are great, because they attach the words to bodies, moving or still, and allow us to see as well as hear the characters.

From *Three Women:*

She wakened curled in the backseat to find that Chad was checking them into a motel. They all fell into the bed and more or less slept until it got noisy in the morning. Then they all took turns in the shower and Chad shaved.

"How come you aren't shaving?" she asked Evan.

"I'm going to grow a beard. Great disguise. I look older with five o'clock shadow."

She made a disgusted grimace. "Just don't expect me to kiss you!"

He grabbed her and rubbed his cheek against hers. "Kiss, kiss, kiss."

They were both giggling as they fell on the bed. *Chad came in whistling.* "Leave you guys alone for five minutes and you're at it. In permanent heat, that's what you are."

Elena said, "I think we should all do something to change our appearance."

Chad shrugged. "Who's looking for three kids. Runaways are a dime a dozen."

"Your father's going to want his car back."

Chad waved that away with an airy gesture. "We'll have to ditch it at some point and get another."

"Oh, sure. We can trade," Evan said. "Hi, want to trade your old Ford Escort for a nice BMW, no questions asked?"

"For the time being, let's get as far as we can in it."

"I've never been to California," *Elena said, curled up again in the backseat with a bag of potato chips that would do for breakfast.*

They walked around the mall until the traffic thinned out. Finally, Chad saw what he was waiting for. A guy pulled up in a dark blue Ford Taurus. His girlfriend was waiting in the passenger's seat while he ran into the liquor store. He left the engine running.

Chad yanked open the door on the passenger's side. "Out." *He shoved the gun into her neck.*

"Don't hurt me!'

"Don't scream, or I'll shoot. I don't want you, just the car." *He pulled her out.* "Evan, drive." Evan flung the backpack behind him and fumbled for the parking brake.

Chad motioned Elena into the backseat, and they lurched off. "Okay, Elena. Where do we go?"

"Turn right at the light." *She turned on the overhead and looked at the map Evan had bought.* "Okay, just keep going. We're heading for the interstate."

You should also be aware of the uses of direct versus indirect dialog. Direct dialog shows us your characters speaking. Indirect dialog (italicized below) sums up what they said.

When I last saw Rebecca, it was in the lobby of the J.W. Marriot on 54th Street. She was charging toward the elevators, followed by a bellman pushing a cartload of matching Gucci luggage. "This is the most amazing coincidence," she said. "How long has it been? We must have dinner. Come up to my room for a drink first. I'll be here until Monday and then I'm flying down to Miami. To see Mom," she added, as if, five years after our divorce I still referred to her mother that way. *I said that I was only here for a sales conference and would be leaving that evening.* "Oh come now. You can't stay a few hours more?"

I replied that I was sorry, no. Rebecca fixed me that reproachful glare. "Oh, yes. I imagine, Doreen, is it? . . . would be absolutely incapable of spending another night without you."

When I said I had to get back because someone was house sitting my cats, Rebecca glowed with a rosy smile, "You're no longer married, are you?"

Indirect dialog has a flattening effect that can be used for irony, humor, distancing; to diminish the importance of one speaker in order to emphasize the other. It can also be used to summarize action or information the reader already knows and that you don't want slowing down the action by repeating.

"Good morning, Mr. Chalmers," I said to the principal of my fourth school in as many years. *I began my story, but he simply glanced at the fat file folder on his desk and told me not to bother.*

In the following example, Bud Hiller, a very minor character is depicted solely by indirect dialog. What matters here is not what Hiller says but the fact that Suzanne is under economic pressure and forced to take on certain types of cases:

From *Three Women:*

It was not a case she wanted. She contained herself, listening, questioning him, taking careful notes with Jaime backing her up. Bud Hiller had inquired coldly who Jaime was upon entering her office, but now it was as if Jaime were a cat on a chair.

Hiller orated on, his injuries, the stinginess of his dead father, the perfidy of his siblings and their spouses, how his previous lawyers had failed him and his just cause. She listened, she took notes, and she thought how she would love to show him the door, but this case leaked money through all its flimsy seams. She had come to a financial crossroads where she must take cases that would pay her bills instead of cases that excited her legally or ethically. She was still the litigator she had always been. She could find a new angle to use. She began to plot her strategy in getting Bud his money and doing his siblings out of theirs.

Unless someone is telling a story, a very involving story, watch out for long speeches. Even if someone is giving a speech in a story, you can give the flavor of the speech in a paragraph or give us some important highlights, interspersed with reaction. Dull dialog is a much more common problem than too much clever repartee, but that also can carry a book astray if it gets out of hand.

Some writers choose to use no direct dialog at all, while others rely heavily on dialog. Again, there are no hard and fast rules. Dialog can hasten the unfolding of your story by revealing elements of the plot that the reader and/or the other characters do not know. In the following example, a woman discovers that she and her friend Michael did not just spontaneously fall into bed.

From *Waiting for Elvis:*

When Jane wakes up, she sees Mike propped on one elbow, looking at her. They have slept barely two hours, between sunrise and now. He kisses her immediately, against her protestations of morning breath.

"How can you look so appealing, first thing in the morning," he says.

She tells him she is probably a mess, that he must just like her with rumpled hair and without her glasses. Only then does she realize that Mike did not wear glasses last night, nor has she seen any contact lens accoutrements in the bathroom. "Can you sleep in your contacts?" she says.

"Don't get mad."

"What do you mean?"

"You'll be angry," he says.

"What are you talking about, Mike?"

"I wanted to see you," he says, "All of you."

"And?" She feels herself blushing, but still does not know what he's getting at.

"I picked up some of these contacts you can wear overnight."

She gets it, now—this is the same as stopping at the pharmacy on a condom run—he was laying-in seduction supplies. She is touched that he wanted to look at her in bed, but a question remains.

"Did you get some of those for last weekend, when you were here as my houseguest?" She wonders if he will answer truthfully.

"Well, yes, but. . . ."

Again, dialog allows the reader to make up her own mind about a character, because she is judging the character in action, on the character's own merits, from the character's own words, rather than being told by the author what to think. The use of dialog makes it easy to create dramatic scenes that alternate with straight narration, and thereby show the action of a story enfolding.

Exercise:

In no more than one page, create an interaction between two characters, written all in dialog, attempting to incorporate the following techniques:

1. Using dialog to pass time
2. Using action or descriptive tags
3. Using indirect dialog.

You can create a situation of your own choosing, or use one of the following situations. (Remember that when there is conflict, when one speaker wants something the other does not, there may be an interesting element of dramatic tension in the dialog).

A very worried parent tries to convince his/her child that her (or his) boyfriend or girlfriend is a bad choice.

A person who can no longer stand living with his/her roommate is trying to suggest that the roommate move out of the apartment they share.

A diner in a high-priced restaurant finds a worm in his salad and wants his dinner free. The management finds this request excessive.

Two people who dated twenty years ago meet by chance at a conference. One would like the relationship to resume. The other is not convinced.

A taxicab pulls over for a fare at rush hour. Two people reach it at the same moment, each attempting to convince the other they need it more.

A woman in your building just got a new dog, an adorable little Pug that begs to be picked up. As you do, the hyperactive little thing squirms out of your arms and falls on the hardwood floor, breaking a bone. She suggests you pay the vet bills. You don't think it's your fault.

A very persistent person at a bar sits next to you and suggests you get to know each other. That's the last thing on your mind.

You're home for Thanksgiving. You really want to please your mom, who you haven't seen in a long time. She is anxious for you to meet and like her new boyfriend, who not only has politics that are opposite yours but aggressively baits you.

The guy in the upstairs apartment has come home at 2 A.M. again and pumps his stereo up full blast. This has got to stop and you go upstairs to tell him so.

Exercise:

It is late at night in the suburbs or in the city or at a resort—your choice. A couple has returned to their room from a party, where one of them is upset with the other for what they see as excessive flirtation. Create dialog using physical tags and silences as well as what is said out loud in order to suggest the dynamics of the couple—who is the stronger? Who loves the other most? Who is the most possessive? What kind of shape is this relationship in—stable, rocky, dying?

Exercise:

Take this same kind of argument—Who has been flirting too much?—and move it into a public place such as a restaurant or on the subway or at the party in a corner. See what happens when there are other people around who may overhear. Do each of them care equally who hears them arguing? Is one more embarrassed by a public argument than the other one?

Exercise in Indirection:

As we have said, not all characters tell the truth. A person may be withholding information or actually lying. You want to create a situation in which the reader can guess or suspect that the character is not being truthful or not being open—their conversation is not transparent. They are intentionally misleading or throwing another character off track. Such a scene is interesting to write. What you want is to arouse the reader's suspicions. Perhaps one character does not feel comfortable lying outright, and manages not to answer the question or provide the information requested. Instead they change the subject, pretend to misunderstand the question, provide a great deal of verbiage or information but not to the point of answering the actual question asked. This is a subtle exercise, but one that can be fun to write.

Perhaps you want to use the context of a murder mystery. Perhaps you like the context of a jealous partner trying to find out whether their significant other is having an affair. Perhaps it is a mother or father questioning their teenager about where they have been so late or who they have been with. Perhaps it is a manager in an office who is trying to find out what happened to some document or office supplies. Perhaps it is a professor trying to find out whether a student plagiarized a suddenly insightful and well-researched paper. Perhaps it is an ex trying to find out whether their previous spouse is seeing someone new.

6

Plot In The Novel

True story: I know a writer who told me he needed a motel room to start his novel. What he would do was push all the furniture to the middle of the room, then cover all four walls floor-to-ceiling with a blank roll of newsprint. He would then proceed to outline his book, chapter by chapter, to the end, listing every incident in a flow chart. He thought visually, he told me. He needed to see it all written out on paper. Ideally he would sequester himself in the room with pots of coffee and finger food for however long it took. When finished, he would have the book entirely worked out. All he would now have to do was to transcribe the incidents to his laptop, fill in description and dialog. I was skeptical but kept my mouth shut. Every writer I know has a different way of going about it. A friend who writes novels as well as for Hollywood writes at night, sometimes all night, beginning after dinner and typing until dawn with the TV blasting for company. A Pulitzer Prize winner we know wrote his first three novels on the Long Island Railroad, commuting to his job in New York City. He liked to roughly sketch every scene on a different index card and then fully compose it on a legal pad. Now he's the chairman of a writing department and has an oak paneled office overlooking a lake. Still starts with the index cards.

It wasn't the motel room that worried me about the outline man or the days of powdered doughnuts and coffee. It was the idea that he could completely control the story without involving himself in the inner lives of his characters. He wanted to control every speech, all the action and reaction like a puppeteer, ignoring the process of entering his characters' states of consciousness and experiencing the world through them. He wanted to by-pass the mystery of the writing process, the frightening walk down unknown roads.

The danger of over-plotting, of imagining that you can entirely avoid the unknown and list the elements of a novel like the ingredients of a recipe is perhaps as dangerous as jumping into a project without a clue. Of course there are writers who do just that. Some fine writers start with a piece of blank paper and nothing more.

As we have mentioned, a large number of the submissions that we receive at the press every year are by young men who believe their adolescent experiences are the stuff of great fiction. There are a lot of scenes in bars; a lot in bedrooms—not sex scenes, but in bed, trying to decide why they should stub out their cigarettes and get up. The problem is that besides bitching about their jobs, school, women, their parents, they have very little to say; nothing happens. After ten pages maybe a friend will come over, and start bitching about jobs, school, women, their parents. Thinking about plot beforehand can help a writer avoid the problem of getting to page fifty and feeling written out without a thing left to say.

All writers face the problem of how to shape their ideas and experiences into a form that maximizes meaning and dramatic tension, that seduces a reader into wanting to turn the page. This is obvious for writers of fiction. However, people who have their own stories to tell of a life full of incident, sometimes imagine that all they have to do is remember their stories and type them up. Then they wonder where they've gone wrong, why editors reject their work and their very exciting lives, why even friends find reading their output makes for tough going. Because these issues are somewhat different for writers of memoir and autobiography, we've devoted an entire chapter to Personal Narrative Strategies. But for those who choose to fictionalize their life's adventures, however close to the truth, they, too, need to know something about plotting.

Some writers plot out the book from start to finish and know their ending before they begin. Some writers have only a vague idea of the ending, plot a few chapters ahead of themselves, write a draft of those chapters, and plot out a few more until they find the ending. There is no right or wrong way to go about it.

Plot is the element of fiction most often in disrepute. It is considered by certain critics that truly serious fiction should somehow be free of this basic element of every story. But you dispense with it at your own risk. It is so basic to the narrative impulse that even a simple tale that has no characterization beyond labeling (the prince, the princess, the wicked witch) is nonetheless identifiable as fiction because it tells a story.

One basic plot is The Quest. Simply put, the main character wants something and sets out to get it. The "something" can be physical, emotional, conceptual; anything from a lost treasure to lost confidence to the answer to a secret. They can lose something and need to get it back. They can feel they are lacking something and set out to achieve it. They can be hired to take it away from somebody else. They can be commissioned to discover it. This concept—the protagonist wants something and sets out to get it—seems almost too basic to include in an essay for people who have undertaken serious fiction writing, but we are continually amazed, as we plow through stacks of submissions, how many writers fail to begin by asking the most basic question: What does your main character yearn for? What do they want? What sets them in motion? What gets in their way?

Take Little Red Riding Hood. (Fairy tales and myths are often as sophisticated structurally as they are symbolically and deserve serious study.) She's given a mission: Take this basket to Grandma. Think about it. Would there be a story at all if she never left the house? What if she set out to go to Grandma's and made it there without incident? No trickery, no wolf, not much of a story.

Now of course you could write the story of a little girl who never leaves the kitchen. You could write the story of a little girl getting to Grandma's and having lunch. Who's going to stop you? Such a story would not rely on plot; you'd have to employ other elements to keep the reader turning pages. Description: the careful poetic description of the rare forest flora. Character insight: Riding Hood hates her mother and longs to be reunited with her absent father and Grandma is her only confidante. Lively dialog: "Grandma," Riding Hood takes the old woman's hand, "you're so frail. The doctor says you may not make it through the night. Tell me, Grandma. How can we best honor you, with burial or cremation? What is your wish?" Grandma musters the last of her strength and shrugs, "Surprise me."

You will want to employ *all* these elements in your writing: description, character insight, dialog. But you do not want to ignore the element of plot.

Think about *The Odyssey*. In its most basic form, Ulysses wants to get home. Obstacles get in his way: some really bad weather; Polyphemus, the Cyclops; Calypso, who saves and seduces him; Circe, the enchantress who turns Odysseus's men into swine; the Sirens, those sea nymphs who sing Odysseus's men into a trance; the lotus eaters. This is a plot as good today as it was 2800 years ago. In his novel *The Wanderers*, Sol Yurick created a modern version of *The Anabasis* (a Greek classic about the return of an army in hostile territory), recasting an army of Greek mercenaries making their way from Babylon to the Black Sea into an urban street gang encountering cops and rival gangs as they cross New York neighborhoods on their way back to their home turf in Brooklyn. The reason for obstacles, of course, is to enable your readers to see your characters in action, under stress, making choices either right or wrong, that will determine the outcome of the story and their lives.

The simplest way to begin thinking about the plot is this: First, figure out who your main character, or protagonist, is. Develop her dramatic need. Then, figure out obstacles to get in her way. This yearning, this dramatic need, need not be obvious to the reader, or even to the protagonist herself, but you should know what it is. Nor is a character in a novel so simple as to want only one thing. But there is often one desire, however difficult it may be to articulate, that is more central than all the rest. In Dorothy Allison's novel, *Bastard Out of Carolina*, the main desire of the protagonist, a teenager named Bone, is to be loved by her mother. She isn't aware enough of herself to articulate this. She's a richly drawn character, a complex young woman. The obstacle to that love is the abusive man whom her mother is sexually obsessed with as well as the grinding poverty in which the family lives (and of course because of that poverty, the lack of choices the family has).

In a detective story, the dramatic need may be to find the murderer or the evidence; the witness or even something meaningless. The Maltese Falcon is the object of every character's desire in Dashiell Hammet's famous noir mystery novel of the same name.

But what is it exactly? Why is it so desirable? The author tells us that it is a fabulously valuable gold statuette of a falcon, created as tribute for the Holy Roman Emperor, Charles IV, but not many readers really give a damn. It's the action that rivets their attention, not the statue. If you say the Maltese Falcon is hot stuff, then the reader believes it's hot stuff. The movie director Alfred Hitchcock called such objects "the macguffin," a made-up name for a made-up thing, the sole object of which is to create a yearning that will propel characters into motion, make them want to overcome all obstacles to get it. In fantasy or science fiction, you are free to invent anything you can render believable; nonsensical elements in plot work just fine. You want space travel? Invent the warp engine with a sentence. You want time travel? Invent the time machine. You want totally equal sex roles as in *Woman on the Edge of Time*? Invent the brooder. But even in realistic fiction, you can invent the world's biggest emerald or a new element or a formula for curing AIDS. The reader will not believe it if your protagonist survives in the last ten pages because of a sudden new cure for AIDS, but if that cure is carefully posited into the plot with convincing medical details and you are dealing with the effects on a country suddenly liberated from sexual fear, then posit away. The reader will accept your premises if the story is a good one and the characters are convincing.

There are many in-depth studies of plot, from those that analyze the elements of story structure in fairy tales and myths to the writing of screenplays. Many of them talk about the nature of The Quest, the search to satisfy a yearning or a need. They present the protagonist in the beginning of the story as existing in a kind of limbo; that is, knowingly or unknowingly, spiritually or materially, in an incomplete or unsatisfactory state in their lives. Perhaps, as with Oliver Single, in Le Carre's *Single & Single*, they are in hiding; or as with David Greene in *Storm Tide*, the protagonist finds himself with neither a career nor confidence in himself. In Richard Price's *Clockers*, being a drug dealer literally makes Strike, the protagonist, sick to his stomach. Suzanne, in *Three Women*, has yet to reconcile with her mother and her oldest daughter.

Sometimes it is called an Inciting Incident, or The Call to Action, but invariably some event shakes the protagonist out of his/her present state and sets him or her in motion to change.

Oliver Single suddenly receives notice that five million pounds sterling have been deposited into his bank account; David Green meets a seductive older woman who recruits him to run for political office; Suzanne Blume's adult daughter loses her job and moves back home and Suzanne is presented a note in court: her mother has had a stroke.

The traditional three-act structure (set-up, confrontation, resolution) common to many plays and almost all commercial movies is the standard model used when talking about plot. Some books that discuss the finite number of recurring plots in literature even list films as examples. But here you have to use common sense. Novels are not screenplays. Novels do not have to conform to a rigid structure. Many novels are adapted for screenplays and rewritten to fit the classic three-act structure and in the process sometimes bear only a token resemblance to the book from which they were adapted. Indeed, the most truly faithful novel-to-film adaptation I've ever seen is the British Granada Television version of Waugh's *Brideshead Revisited*. But of course, this was a TV mini-series that ran about twelve hours rather than the standard Hollywood ninety-minute theatrical release.

Novels are about change over time, about memory and reflection, about characters and their most intimate thoughts. No less an important medium in our time, films are about characters changing through action. Novels depend on language to tell a story; films, visual imagery. Others have compared fiction and film far more knowledgably and in depth. We bring up the issue here only to make a point about not confusing the two. Many writers who want to write fiction are more knowledgeable about film than they are about literature. They have seen hundreds of movies in their lives and have read only a fraction of that many novels. They are astonished that what works in film does not come across on the page.

As a case in point, in a manuscript we recently read an American diplomat meets and begins a relationship with a third world terrorist. The author was relying on a number of clichés to pull it off: that they were both good looking, tall and thin; that they had good sex, the first time, every time; that the terrorist had been tortured and was therefore sensitive and sympathetic; that the American diplomat was a lonely foreigner.

Every serious screenwriter will tell you that when they bring two characters together with the intention of showing them falling in love, it takes a lot more than two movie stars, some repartee, a series of facial close-ups, reaction shots and a love scene. But it is sometimes the case in writing fiction that we are imagining movies, and thinking in movie language, rather than trying to figure out how to show people making a real connection over time. We made a lot of suggestions to the writer. We asked her to think about imagining her couple more fully: the small physical details that lovers notice, or the fascinating and sometimes even off-putting differences that a person of one culture might notice in a person from another; the conversations but also the failures of language that would draw and repel two such lovers. Whereas it is true that a fine writer can say a lot with an image or a few perfectly chosen words of dialog, fiction allows you the space to spread out and create an entire world, the world that in a film includes all those visual clues provided by the actors and the designers, the costumers and location people. As a fiction writer you're not only writing the script, you're the entire company.

A woman approached me once in a workshop and said, somewhat confrontationally, "I'm a journalist. I don't write fiction because everything I need to say about a story I can say in a paragraph. Then I have nothing more to say." It turned out she did very much want to write fiction, but didn't understand that her five or six sentences were a mere outline of facts; that she was stopping short of the creation of her main character's yearnings, her history, family, friends, neighbors; where she lived, what went on in that town; the situations she looked forward to and those that she dreaded; all the details that would provide her protagonist with the interactions that constitute a believable and interesting life.

In the Afterword to the 20th Anniversary edition of her first novel, *Adult Education*, Annette Williams Jaffee writes about the genesis of a book from an outline:

> In the spring of 1979, two women named Becca and Ulli came to live with me. I had recently started working with the poet and novelist Maxine Kumin, who was teaching in the Creative Writing Department at Princeton University for the semester. I had sent her two very short stories—I couldn't

write more than five or six pages at that time—and a letter saying: "I am a housewife trying to crawl out of her kitchen." Although I had wanted to be a writer most of my life, it was only six months before that I had begun writing with a certain seriousness I had never brought to my work before, meaning I was actually writing, instead of just talking about it.

We were living on the lake then, in a split level contemporary house and the bedroom which had previously housed a series of students who baby-sat in exchange for the room and an occasional meal—other people's difficult adolescent children was how I thought of them—was empty because my children, now 11 and 10, could finally stay home alone. I resigned from all my volunteer activities and gave myself five years to produce one publishable work —a short story, perhaps, in an obscure literary magazine

I had known Becca a long time, although I didn't know her name. For several years I wanted to write about this woman and the times she lived in; sometimes I called her Susan, sometimes I called her Sandra, but I could never get beyond a few flat first-person narrated pages. One of the stories I had sent Maxine was about a dancer named Becca. All of a sudden I knew the name of this woman! I knew she had been a dancer; I knew she had red hair. I knew everything about her. More importantly, I heard her voice—she talked to me all the time. The kitchen, my car, my bedroom became cluttered with scraps of paper with what Becca had to say to me. In fact, suddenly, everything anyone told me seemed to be about Becca. Her friend Ulli arrived differently. I had spent the academic year 1973-4 in Sweden, and Ulli became the culmination of that strange, mysterious, beautiful place for me.

I would meet with Maxine in her office every Monday for an hour. She would read what I brought her and I would watch her elegant face for signs of amusement, confusion, pleasure. She taught me that my stories were really outlines and needed to be filled out with details and dialog. Sometimes she said they were finished as they were, sometimes she didn't have a clue of what to do to save them. After that hour, I would run indoors in the enormous skeletal university gymnasium—like Jonah in the belly of the whale, I thought—on a wonderful spongy track and pieces of fiction would float through my head. With my flushed face and all my pulses beating, it was like being in love.

By May, I had written about forty pages about Becca and Ulli and their husbands Gerry and John and the children, Christopher and Alexandra and Victoria. "Well," said Max at our last session together, "if you can write eighty more pages about these four characters, you will have a novella and maybe we can fix up some of these short stories and you will have a book." (A book!) More importantly, Max handed me on to Joyce Carol Oates for a tutorial the next fall.

"No," said Joyce, when I brought her my 75 pages in the fall. It's not a novella, it's a short novel—about 180 pages—and here is how you begin."

Each Monday at three o'clock, I climbed the stairs at 185 Nassau Street to Joyce's office, usually stopping to chat with Richard Ford across the hall. He had published only one critically acclaimed novel at that point, so I wasn't too intimidated by him, and anyway, he had those lovely Southern manners. I assume he still has. Every week, I brought Joyce the next chapter I had written on the basis of her wise and gentle guidance. One week, I remember I was very distracted and didn't get much done and when Joyce questioned me, I said I was thinking about Thanksgiving and making a turkey. "Well, think about Becca making a turkey," she said.

By April, I had written 180 pages. I remember how Joyce put the manuscript down on her desk and said very seriously, "You are now at a blessed point for any writer. You have a fine first draft of your novel. Treat it as if you will die and this is the only thing that you will leave behind."

In a spy story, the dramatic need of the main character may be to find the mole in the organization, or to bring an agent in from the cold, or to discover the secret formula. In a thriller, it might be to stop some catastrophe before it happens, such as stopping a madman before he sets off a bomb. Novelists sometimes use the device of the ticking clock to maximize suspense; that is, the problem must be solved in a certain amount of time or the catastrophe will occur. This is a common device on television and in films.

Thrillers and detective fiction, books about spies and cops, mysteries are sometimes called plot-driven fiction, although, in the hands of a really good writer, all categories blur. In plot-driven fiction, the incidents that occur in the story mostly derive not from the personalities of the characters, but from external forces out of the character's control, and from incidents of chance.

In James Lee Burke's novel, *Burning Angel*, a detective's house is trashed and two men are brutally murdered. These incidents are obstacles to the main character's dramatic need to solve a crime, but they do not derive from his personality. Contrast this with a novel that is character driven. In James Leo Herlihy's *Midnight Cowboy*, the main character, Joe Buck, a street hustler, encounters many obstacles to his yearning to be truly needed by someone in the world. He's duped by a religious fanatic, fleeced by a con man and continually taken by the johns he's supposed to be taking, but all of this results from his personality. He's a country boy, totally out of his element in New York City; more, he's kind and dense and gullible.

In the chapter on creating character, we talk about the fact that the more you know about your characters, their histories, fears, their likes and their phobias, their habits, their weaknesses, the more there is to write about, the more trouble they'll get into, the more places they are likely to retreat to, the more problems they'll create for themselves. I've often heard people complain about thrillers they'd bought because the plot sounded fascinating, only to find that the book ultimately felt artificial. The characters seemed to be continuously facing obstacles that were created for them, like rides at an amusement park, rather than problems that they were likely to face in real life had the characters been given deeper personalities. The best plot-driven fiction, such as the novels of a writer like John Le Carre´, use all the elements of character-driven fiction. A character's strengths and weaknesses, his or her history and longings, will determine not only the obstacles that he or she will face, but how he or she handles them as well. *Single & Single* is a globetrotting thriller about rogue London investment bankers entangled with the Russian mafia. There are as many explosions, shoot-outs and reversals as any *Mission Impossible* movie, but its protagonist, Oliver Single, is primarily driven by his complex and realistically drawn relationship with his con man father.

We can think of stories as being driven by character when the desires and flaws of the protagonist create much of the action, or driven by events when the structure of the story is provided by a central sequence of external occurrences or crises: World War II, a flood or fire, an invention like the time machine. The characters in such a story have no less necessity to be well drawn, well motivated, convincing, but we are primarily interested in how they contribute to the main event and how they are affected by it.

Similarly, if you are writing what is sometimes termed character driven fiction, stories based on the lives of people who are not in "high concept" professions—bookstore owners, housewives and academics rather than four-star generals, homicide detectives and astronauts—you still want your reader to continue turning pages, and you would do well to pay attention to some of the basic elements of storytelling.

This is not to say that the protagonist is ever *only* about satisfying a need. Your main characters will meet many people and many things will happen to them. Time will pass and they'll make discoveries about life and maybe they'll have more than one great desire or maybe they won't even know what their primary need is, but you, the writer should have an idea about where they are headed and what they yearn for.

For instance, in Myla Goldberg's fine novel, *Bee Season*, Eliza wants to enjoy her father Saul's love and attention, which has always been fixed on her brother; Saul wants a disciple, a progeny who will be brilliant in some way and share his passion for Kabbalah, Jewish mysticism. This is one of the novels in which it is characters getting what they want that gives them trouble.

However, the dramatic need is not always obvious, especially in character-driven fiction. The character thinks she wants one thing, such money, when what she really wants is what she thinks money can buy: respect or freedom. Sometimes a character might think she wants sex, when what she really wants is human connection, an end to loneliness. If this is the case with your character, your story is even more interesting because you're operating on more than one level: on the material level, the quest for money or sex, as well as on the deeper spiritual or psychological level, the quest for love. Your character might even fail to get one thing she thinks she wants and get what she really needs. Or she may get what she thinks she wants and find it does not satisfy her real or deeper needs.

People don't generally read novels or memoirs to observe

characters breezing through life. Nobody gets a free ride. Life is about meeting challenges, solving problems. Characters change when they encounter conflict successfully or unsuccessfully. Just as there are some people who undergo a tragedy and continue forward in their lives with a deeper perspective, others become bitter and wallow in self-pity.

Some readers like to follow people like themselves, meeting or knuckling under to similar problems. Others like to read about people who couldn't be less like themselves: professional athletes, gorilla researchers, double agents; the disabled, the dyslexic, the disinherited. It is true that a terrific writer, in command of her talent, can write an interesting novel about a woman who does little besides think and react to a day's occurrences, but you will often note that the day is very well chosen indeed and manages to bring up important issues and conflicts in that woman's life, as happens in Virginia Woolf's *Mrs. Dalloway.* It's well, however, to remember that a lot of people want to read about other people's juicy problems in order to forget their own.

So what kinds of problems can your characters find themselves faced with? *Interior* conflicts are those problems or issues that arise from the traits inside a character's personality: guilt, greed, jealousy, envy, laziness, self-hatred, lack of confidence, the inability to make decisions, the habit of believing everything people tell you, the need to please authority. Your protagonist could harbor a terrible temper that always makes her blow up at the wrong people; your protagonist can suffer from the fear of being emotionally hurt which might make him run away from people who love him. On the other hand, a character can create serious complications if she has an obsessive need to be loved which makes her attempt to seduce people and thus invite trouble. Interior conflicts in characters as well as the people we know tend to repeat and snowball. In *Midnight Cowboy*, Joe Buck's need to please people gets him suckered time after time until all the money he's saved is gone and he finds himself homeless.

Interpersonal conflicts are problems that arise between people and may or may not result from a character's own personality: a character's interaction with a sadistic boss, a really nasty neighbor, an abusive husband; a father-in-law who always tries to put her down. Rivals for a job or the love of the same person or divorced parents competing for a child's love: these are all examples of interpersonal conflict.

Interpersonal conflicts can happen as a result of pure chance: a band of Hell's Angels who appear in your character's rearview mirror; a lover with whom she had the most exciting sex of her life twenty years ago moves into her building; a lonely widow meets a charming con man in the supermarket line. But it is the convergence of personality and chance that sets up the conflict. In the first example above, an aggressive personality might decide to race the Hell's Angels at a stoplight, while a meeker (more sensible?) person might pull over to the slow lane and let them pass. So many choices: every personality responds to chance in a different way.

External conflicts: The natural world can create some impressive conflicts: A snowstorm made tough going for the Donner party. A stock market or plane crash may dampen a vacation. A large white whale plays havoc with the outcome of a whaling venture. All are disasters the characters had no part in creating, although usually the situation is set up to involve the personality of a leader or decision-maker: someone foolhardy or stubborn or driven who insists on going forward in spite of danger or obstacles.

Things get even more interesting when external conflicts create inter-personal conflicts: An aging but very independent woman has a stroke and must then move into the home of the daughter whose life she never approved of; a bad snow storm causes a writer to drive off the road and be rescued by a sadistic, obsessed admirer. External conflicts can cause a person to act in a way that puts his/her personality to the test: A self-involved Jewish teenager must grow up quickly when the Germans enter Paris and send her family to a concentration camp. Perhaps you're struggling with the issue of how to write about the lives of everyday working people. A prolonged labor strike can throw the citizens of any community into situations in which they meet conflicts on every level. This can happen in a mountain mining town, or rust belt Detroit, or downtown Los Angeles.

Most novels have their characters go through all kinds of combinations of conflicts while short stories tend to deal with more limited conflict, if any. Many short stories are slice-of-life narratives that may, like James Joyce's, offer an epiphany, a moment of insight. Or, like many *New Yorker* stories, they may simply give a quick view into someone's life.

Another way to look at plot is from the standpoint of what happens to the protagonist. The most elementary kind of plot consists of a *change of fortune* on the part of the protagonist, either a rise or fall. The personality, or deep inner character of the protagonist, does not undergo any particular change either for good or ill and no interesting issues, or moral or political or philosophical dimensions, are riding on what happens, although the story may be told to point out a simple moral: money is the root of all evil, Thou shalt not kill, whatever. The story depends on suspense and perhaps surprise or on a simple irony of fate for its effect on us.

When such a work rises above the ordinary, it is generally either because the milieu is tremendously well realized, or because one or more of the characters is strong enough so that we simply want to watch him or her in action. We do not want the character to change, but only to please us by doing what we expect of it, with variations. Arthur Conan Doyle's Sherlock Holmes's stories are of this kind. However, I would point out that in the detective fiction of Dorothy Sayers, her protagonist, Lord Peter Whimsy, changes considerably.

There are other kinds of plots in which the protagonist does not change: those in which the main action is the suffering of the main character, often the heroine. Sometimes the emphasis as in Zola or Dickens is on the societal forces that have produced the misery; for instance, war in Hemingway's *A Farewell to Arms*. Another case in which the protagonist remains constant is the plot in which some particular strong character wreaks havoc and is punished. For all its richness of language and complexity of presentation and milieu, *Moby Dick* does not have a protagonist who changes. Ahab is as obsessed when we meet him as he is when he goes down lashed to the whale.

We have expressed the strong opinion that plot must issue from character. The better you know and the more completely you can enter your major characters, the surer you will be about their longings, what they want to do and what they will then try to do. Certainly the interactions and intersections and collisions of characters partially determine plot. However, the better you know your societal setting and the pressures of the time and place, social class and economic situation, the more you will know how these desires can or cannot be translated into successful action.

Simply put, a doctor wants a fur coat. Her conflict would be largely internal. Is it right to own such a coat? Animals died for her to wear it. Is it appropriate to her life style, her social setting? But a coal miner in Wyoming wants a fur coat. That's a different story.

Successful action in this case is determined by scarcity, competition and consequence. What to eat for supper is not the stuff of high drama to a woman who sells commercial real estate in Manhattan, but to the displaced homemaker living as a bag lady on the street, what she can buy in the supermarket to eat in her doorway—say the doorway of an office building in midtown Manhattan—is a fraught choice. She may not have another meal for two days. And for a mother in the Sudan trying to keep her child alive another day, eating or not eating is the stuff of life and death.

I can show you what I mean by what I know and don't know about the plot when I am writing a first draft with an example from *Gone to Soldiers*. I know that about a third of the way into the book, Jacqueline, a French Jewish teenager, and her mother have a serious fight, so that Jacqueline leaves home, not meaning to run away permanently, but keeping her away from home at a critical time—the night of the Grand Raffle when roughly twenty thousand Jews were picked up by the French police under instructions from the Gestapo. They were taken to a rink used for bicycle races in the winter, where they were held for eight days without food or water, including five thousand children, who died like flies. Then they were shipped to camps.

Now I have to remove Jacqueline from her mother's flat in Paris that weekend, so that while her mother and younger sister are taken, she is not. I would like it, naturally, to be an absence not accidental or contrived—By the way, Mama, this Friday night I will sleep at my girlfriend's. So I figure with Jacqueline being nineteen in the hot summer of 1942 and out of college because she has been forced out for being Jewish, I will give her a boyfriend and she will at this time begin sleeping with him. That, either discovered by her mother or in fact an honest answer on

Jacqueline's part to such a question, would get her into a fight where she would likely storm out of the flat. Such a fight could also make her feel quite guilty, which is useful to my plot. So Jacqueline has a boyfriend, who to keep her out of danger that night, should not be Jewish. Who would be most indifferent at that time to the laws forbidding such association? One of the zealous, the zoot suiters of Paris who defied the Nazis by wearing their hair long and greasy and listening to jazz and acting cool. Okay, now we have Jacqueline's boyfriend, Henri, emerging, and the plot begins to fill in.

When you must have characters quarrel, it is far better if the reasons for their quarrels do pertain (1) to the ongoing needs of the story; (2) to some revelation of character about one or both of the quarrelers; (3) to our understanding of the dynamics of the relationship; or (4) to some point about the politics or economics or general situation of the characters of the society we ought to understand. In science fiction or in historical fiction, this latter reason may be particularly important.

Another common type of plot is that in which it is not so much the change in fortune or circumstance of the protagonist we are concerned with as it is maturing (as in the classic Bildungsroman; *i.e., Portrait of the Artist as a Young Man* or the first three books of Doris Lessing's Martha Quest novels). Or in a variation, the plot is about a learning or changing experience, as in Conrad's *Lord Jim* or *Pinocchio*. But not all change is for the better. There are also tales of the degradation of character: for instance Conrad's, *Heart of Darkness* or Faulkner's *Sanctuary*.

In some novels, the primary learning experience occurs not in the mind of any of the characters, but in what the reader is supposed to understand. These novels do not generally have a simple plot in the same sense that a novel fixed on a single or small group of protagonists may have. Dos Passos' *USA* trilogy, Doctorow's *Ragtime, Gone to Soldiers* are all examples of the genre. Only in the reader's mind will the final story assume its shape, for none of the characters can see what the reader sees or know more than their own stories. It is the pattern of the whole that is the plot and indeed, such novels are usually roughly about some historical event: a war, a depression, a revolution, a particular moment in history.

Another type of plot is the revelation story. This is not the same as a mystery. It is not *who done it*, but *what the hell is going on?* A classic example is Shirley Jackson's much anthologized story, "The Lottery." The suspense lies in the protagonist and the reader figuring out the situation.

Coincidence is part of every plot. Little Red Riding Hood happens to meet the wolf. He could have been off chasing a rabbit or snoozing. Most sizable predators sleep a fair amount. Ask your cat about that, a small predator but one who can explain much mammalian behavior to you, as can your dog. Your hero happens to win the lottery and get rich overnight. Two of your characters meet on a plane after they have sworn never to speak again ten years earlier. A woman behind a fast food counter recognizes a face from the post office wall. Our lives are full of coincidences, and so is fiction. But a light hand is required. And it is far, far better to use coincidence to set up your plot than to use coincidence to resolve it. That is, few readers will challenge you if your protagonist wins the lottery in an early chapter and the plot moves on from there, about the impact of sudden riches. But in the plot mentioned above where the coal miner wants a fur coat, if, in the end, she wins the lottery and gets it that way, we will feel cheated, manipulated. That is the difference between using coincidence to launch versus using coincidence to resolve. It is probable in general that we are able to accept complication from coincidence better than resolution from coincidence.

One problem with apprentice writing can be an over-elaboration of plot. It is something the writer keeps tripping over and that keeps tripping up the reader. Instead of going deeper into character, the writer keeps inventing new events, new schemes, new travels and twists of fate. Often the best plots are the simplest. Sometimes plots are borrowed and reinterpreted. A good story is always there for the retelling. World War II was a whopping good story and a lot of us have had a go at it over the years and many more writers will come to it. King Arthur, Tristan and Ysolde, Robin Hood, Bluebeard, Billy the Kid, Adam and Eve, King David, Helen of Troy, Faust: these names evoke basic stories that can be told again freshly in every generation. They can be made new again and again because they are rich in resonance and each writer finds something different in Merlin, in Guinevere, in

Lancelot. The descent of the hero or heroine into the underworld to confront death in pursuit of knowledge or some item, some person, some task, goes back to the story of Inanna's descent into the land of death as first told by the Sumerians, and we have been telling versions of it ever since. Such stories survive and are retold because they are capable of bearing great meaning, but that meaning changes over time. Arthur is one writer's fatuous fool, another's naïve dreamer, another's failed schemer; for someone he represents what was left of Roman values, for another Celtic strength; for one he is Christianity's hero combating the ancient mother goddess religion, for another he is the last Druid king.

Plot is in many ways inseparable from questions of viewpoint. By looking seriously at Morgan le Fay in the cultural context of her times, by adopting her point of view, Marion Zimmer Bradley got a completely new angle on the Arthur stories. Many basic stories of our culture appear in the long run inexhaustible. Only some truly fresh approach and an apprehension of new and interesting values in the tale is needed.

There are certain plots always capable of reuse even though they lack that mythic dimension; for instance, "The Pardoner's Tale" in Chaucer's *Canterbury Tales* is also the plot of B. Traven's *The Treasure of the Sierra Madre*, just as *Romeo and Juliet* serves as a model for *West Side Story*.

Occasionally a basic new plot emerges. Joanna Russ has identified a plot in the writings of a number of contemporary or relatively so (nineteenth century) women writers that could be called Rescue of the Daughter. Frequently the younger woman is not actually a daughter but is a daughter figure, one in whom a continuity of values or life can be expressed. She is stolen, lost or embedded in a hostile or dangerous situation. This is of course an old plot, too, being your original Demeter and Persephone myth, but it has proved particularly prevalent in women's writing in the West in the last hundred or hundred-fifty years.

No plot contains within its outline any information on how serious it is, how meaningful, how lightweight. Take the basic mystery plot: a crime has been committed from which certain consequences are visible. Who done it? That's your basic formula mystery but also the plot of Sophocles' *Oedipus Rex*.

In the chapter in which we discuss viewpoint, we write about ironies that arise from flawed viewpoint or from multiple viewpoints. There are also ironies that are built into plots. The irony may be in the protagonist's sacrificing everything or working for years to attain something that when she or he gets it, destroys him or proves worthless. The irony may be in the character's trying to get rid of something that turns out to be necessary, precious, vital. These are ironies of plot, built into the basic story and developed through character but not issuing from it.

The most satisfying resolutions of plot tend to be those in which the ending feels "right" to us. However difficult that may be to describe, there is usually a correct reward or disaster or suspension awaiting the characters at the end of every story. This outcome should be one which issues either from the character of the protagonist or from the nature of the important relationships set up between the protagonist and important others, friends or enemies. In plot- driven fiction, the ending may be a stunning or exciting outcome to a course of action which should not be too easily foreseen but which doesn't come out of nowhere, either.

Sometimes you may have to choose between more than one "right" ending (and indeed there are novels, such as John Fowles' *The French Lieutenant's Woman* that include more than one). We've all been disappointed at one time or another by the endings to some books we've otherwise liked. We may have felt that the author let us down, they did not fully think through all the possible choices available to their characters, or they wrote in a happy ending where we expected disaster, let someone off the hook. Unlike today's commercial movies, in complex novels, villains don't always get punished. The ending is your choice. In one submission we received at the press, an ending kept us from publishing the book. The writer began with an eerily created, quietly explosive rural town, a place in which people live in fear and keep their mouths, and curtains, shut. The main character, an army vet pushed to his limits, finally confronts the corrupt and omnipotent county sheriff. But by the end of the book the crooked cop has disappeared, as has the woman with whom the protagonist had begun a relationship, and her jealous, gun-toting half-brother. They simply dropped out of the last quarter of the book and were written off in a sentence at the end. If characters have become real to us and integral to the story, they cannot simply drop from sight or be quickly dismissed.

While all books are unique and it is difficult to theorize about the "right" or "satisfying" ending, you never want to create situations you can't fully imagine. If you can't bring yourself to write a fight scene, don't create a potential showdown between two violent characters that gets arbitrated off-stage by a kindly judge. All our experience would tell us that this is not what would happen. Therefore it doesn't strike us as "right" or "satisfying." When considering the ending to a plot, you don't by any means need to know it before you begin, but be prepared to finish what you start. The plot has to issue from what comes before it. The *deus ex machina* refers to the resolution of a drama in Greek theater by a god being lowered onto the stage to solve or resolve the situation. This would not work nowadays (unless, of course, as in *The Three Penny Opera* you are calling attention to it and attempting satire). Your ending must issue from your story, rather than being tacked on or produced by an outside force.

The theory of story structure can be explored further. There are books that advertise themselves as analyzing the plots of every story ever written and contend that there are only a finite number of plots. There are books that go deeply into the structure of myths, list the common character types and map out sequences of action. There is never a danger in studying what others have learned, only in believing there is a formula for creating. In searching for a formula, rather than mastering the fundamentals in your own way, you're basically renting a motel room, tacking paper to the wall and following a mechanical flow chart. Rather, allow yourself to engage in the mystery of the creative process.

Make 'Em Suffer - An Exercise for Creating a Plot

Some plots in their most basic form are quests. The protagonist wants something and spends the length of the story attempting to get it. When he or she does get it, we the readers feel a sense of satisfaction, because we watched someone work hard to achieve their goal. (Or maybe the protagonist fails to reach the goal—that's okay. You're the creator, you can do anything you want.)

Too many writers know the setting of their story, or the characters they want to write about, but fail to give their characters a material goal or an emotional yearning (or both!). The pursuit of this yearning sets your character into action.

Even fiction that is not about "action heroes" needs complication to set the characters in action.

In this exercise you are going to:

• Create a protagonist (tell us his/her name and something about him or her).
• Give that character a dramatic need, or an emotional yearning.
• Create obstacles to achieving that need or satisfying that yearning.

Remember, we talked about • Inner Conflicts.
                                           • Interpersonal Conflicts.
                                           • External Conflicts.

• And, if you can, figure out how (and if not why not) he/she achieves the goal.

Remember, too, sometimes we set out trying to find something we think we want and end up with something different altogether—and maybe not something tangible, but an emotional or intellectual understanding.

This exercise can be done in outline form. No complete sentences or graphic detail are necessary.

7

Personal Narrative Strategies

Some years ago I had the following conversation with my mother: I was thinking about getting her some novels for her birthday and she said, No, she didn't think so. She didn't like fiction any more. Because I write fiction, there was an awkward moment, but when I pressed her as to why, she said, "Well, because, you know with novels it's . . . like somebody just made it all up."

Right. So I went out and got her a book of memoirs and she was thrilled. She loved it. So I asked, "What did you like about it?" She said, "Some true stories are like . . . I met this one and then I met that one, but this book, well, it's just like a novel."

What she meant was that the memoir presented her with a life that had a shape rather than a mere listing of events. It had a unifying idea and took the trouble to describe places and go deeply into characters, all the fundamentals necessary to lift a life story above the level of mere reporting. In short, it had all the things you find in a novel.

It seems to me we're culture obsessed with personalities; from Walter Scott's "Personality Parade" to *People Magazine* to *Vanity Fair* movie star profiles to celebrity tell-alls, we're nuts to know what goes on beneath the veneer of social discourse and that persona which we portray to others. Some of this curiosity is probably as low-minded as the tabloids themselves: we all like to see the high-and-mighty take a fall. Some of it is based on our own insecurity. We want to see how we're doing compared to the next person. If others suffer some of our same pain and frustration, then we're not such losers after all. But I think, too, that we're all seeking the answer to a fundamental question, What does it mean to be alive? In a world where we're running around sixteen hours a day, who has the time to put things in perspective? So we read about other people's lives in hopes of seeing a shape, a meaning, a direction in our own.

Depending on your tastes, you will select different lives to read about and obviously receive different kinds of insights. We'd like to think that the examined life of a saintly person would give us more moral or spiritual guidance than the memoirs of a movie star, but on a practical level, seeing the long term arc of someone who was admired by millions and then drank himself into ruin just might be all the wisdom we need to turn our lives around.

The two questions we're most frequently asked in memoir workshops are these: How exactly do I organize the telling of a story as large as my entire life? On a more personal level, the question that seems to plague every writer contemplating a memoir: Is my story interesting enough to tell?

Let's take a look at three lives:

One was a World War II combat photographer. The second, a New York City homicide detective. The third, an elderly woman who lived with her cats in Maine. All three were writers. But, although the combat photographer arrived at Hitler's bunker the day after Hitler blew his brains out, then went on to witness the liberation of the concentration camps, his memoirs were returned by every publisher who saw his manuscript.

Although the homicide detective had worked deep undercover, infiltrating a fanatic terrorist group and rising through its ranks until he reached the leadership of the organization, he had been unable to place his memoir in any venue he tried.

The old woman died at eighty-two years-old. Her personal writings, largely about illness and solitude and things as mundane as her garden, her cats, and her friends—few of whom were famous—have been international best sellers, translated into many languages and still in print long after her death.

As you may have guessed, her name was May Sarton. She was the author of some forty-eight books and took the trouble to learn what the two men who lived lives full of suspense and excitement did not: how to write about a situation and make it interesting to a reader.

So what makes interesting writing? I can tell you that in the case of the homicide detective, none of the characters in his original manuscript were well drawn. They were described as tall or short, brash or submissive, but he had failed to infuse his characters with life, to make them real by illustrating the nuances of their behavior, or describing what they longed for, or contradictions that made them capable of bombing a building near a school at the same time as they were caring fathers to their children.

The life may be yours, but there are other people in it. If the story is going to hold a reader's attention, the most important of those people must be created with more depth than mere walk-ons.

I can tell you that in the writings of the combat photographer, he listed one fact after another. Montgomery crossed the Rhine on the night of March 23. The U.S. 17th Airborne landed in the enemy rear areas. The air column was two hours and thirty-two minutes long. Every fact was correct—and devastatingly dull. The writer was crushed; he didn't believe it. He was writing about World War II: the most fascinating conflict of the century. But there were no descriptions of the personal toll of battle on people's lives. The narrator's voice was a constant drone of facts, less compelling than a good newspaper article.

May Sarton's personal narratives, however, take mundane experiences and squeeze from them insights into the writer's own inner life and truths about the world. A subject does not have to be glamorous to be interesting, not if it is treated interestingly; that is, investigated by a curious mind for the human truths that the facts imply.

Let's take an example, in this case a kind of personal writing we all do, writing about a trip. Your diary might list mundane facts:

> Stayed in a small hotel in the Marais. Paris is expensive. Ate in three restaurants then started buying take-out to bring it back to my room. Parisians basically tolerate you when you buy things but otherwise pretend you don't exist.

Your journal might choose certain facts more selectively:

> I was shy about bringing food back up to my room and carried a large back pack at all times, enabling me to preserve

my pride when undergoing the scrutiny of the concierge who never lifted his eyes from his newspaper but surely followed the smell of double creme goat cheese all the way up the elevator shaft. I did my shopping on the Rue Rambuteau, a winding grubby market street where the chefs of many small restaurants split their lists—one shopped for vegetables, the others poultry or fruit—before meeting at morning's end for coffee. I practiced my French outside every establishment, carefully constructing my sentences for the discriminating third assistant apprentice to the pastry chef who clucked at my stupidity while handing me change for a hundred franc note.

In a memoir, however, we might squeeze the situation in order to reach that place where the personal touches upon universal experience:

The large clock at the Gar du l'Est read five-forty; exactly ten minutes until departure.

"S'il vous plaît, monsieur," I said again, as I had after every fractured sentence cobbled from my phrase book. More slowly this time: "Deux billet en seconde pour Limoges, non fumant?"

How hard could it be to book two tickets for a non-smoking car? But through the tarnished brass bars of the cage, the ticket seller appraised my worth. Foreign. Male. Middle class. No one who knew his name or his superior or whose complaint would mean a thing. Nothing I was or had ever been, no accomplishment in my life, no feigned kindness on my part, not even my evident need moved him. I watched the large hands of the station clock move. Five minutes to departure.

Clumsily, I repeated myself.

He sighed. "Je ne peu pas vous comprends, Monsieur."

What did he not understand? What was I saying incorrectly? We had reservations for a rental car in Limoges. A hotel was booked and paid. It was too late to find a room in Paris for the night and we hadn't an extra franc to spend. We had to make this train.

The woman in line behind me cursed. The man behind her shouted something I did not need to have translated.

All our belongings, our suitcases, lay at our feet. The official looked through me, the smudge of sweat on my forehead, the reek of my nervous breath. "Suivant!" he signaled for the woman behind me.

I blocked her path and pressed my face to the cage. "Can you understand English?" I tried one last time. "Can't you please speak English with me."

I saw the first hint of smile. "Naturellement," he said. Of course he could speak English. "Mais pas à Paris." But not in Paris.

In the smug set of his mouth I recognized the disdain I myself had shown the gypsies who surrounded me in the train station in Prague and the old ragged panhandler in Earl's Court. I understood at that moment that the nasty Parisian bureaucrat had forever altered the way I would treat a stranger in need.

In at least one way, autobiography is the opposite of biography. Autobiographers know everything; biographers never know enough. Biographers have to research a life for many years to figure out what to put in; *you* have to concentrate on what to leave out. You can't possibly tell us everything about yourself, so you need a narrative strategy.

The plot of a novel might involve a character with a longing, a need—say, to find someone who ran away with his lover, or an emotional need—to come to terms with her lack of education, to accept herself. The problem of satisfying this longing might be the arc of the action of the book, commonly called the plot. The need can't be satisfied too easily, of course. The reader wants to observe the character over the course of time, wants to watch her interact with others and make decisions in difficult situations. So the writer creates obstacles that force the character into action.

Braided Lives is a novel about a young woman from a working class family in Detroit who desperately wants to be a writer in spite of the fact that she has no financial or emotional support from her family and faces the dead end life of many poor young women in the Midwest of the 1950s. An autobiographical novel was Marge Piercy's strategy for telling her story.

If you are shy about the effect of your story on other people, fiction may afford you the distance you need in order to discuss your life. Obviously, if you label your piece fiction, the reader is never sure what is true and what is not. But just as important, you the writer are encouraged not to stick to the absolute facts as they happened, but to create variations on the theme that was your experience.

The most apparent strategy is to change the names and the places. Once you do even this much, you find that strange characters tend to join the party. For example, if you shift your family drama from Ocean Parkway in Brooklyn to an ocean liner in the mid-Atlantic, you need a captain and a crew and other passengers to make the voyage real. Suddenly there are people around who had nothing to do with your family. Now each character may be true to the role they played in the family—that is, the bitter and demanding old-world family matriarch or the youngest son who steals—but the scenes in which they interact might be quite different. A storm at sea could replace the fire that gutted your third floor apartment. People are true to character no matter what the disaster; indeed, no matter what the time period or setting.

Some writers go back in time to tell their stories, place their characters in historical situations, while remaining true to their own experience. Other writers choose science fiction. Their characters live on distant solar systems, three hundred years in the future. But what concerns those characters three centuries from now may very well be a father and son who cannot communicate, or a daughter troubled by her mother's addiction, or a woman who is in love with her sister's husband. It is naïve to imagine that people in the past were free of the complications we suffer through today, and overly optimistic to think that people in the future will face no interpersonal problems.

Piri Thomas, the author of *Seven Long Times,* chose to write about his life through a series of short stories set in prison. Toni Morrison says that her literary heritage is her autobiography and that through her novels she is imagining the interior lives of her ancestors, slaves in the southern United States. She says, "These people are my access to me. They are my entrance into my own interior life."

No matter which of the narrative strategies you try out or decide to pursue, you still have the problem of looking over your life and deciding what to put in and what to leave out, which will amount to the bulk of your life. Consider that many writers such as Lillian Hellman and May Sarton have produced a number of books about their lives, each focusing on a particular theme, a particular era, a particular significant other or crisis. There are probably as many narrative strategies as there are writers, but a number of them emerge time after time. An obvious one is to start from childhood and work toward the present in chronological order. Some people's childhoods make fascinating reading; they had famous and powerful relatives (Gore Vidal), or they lived through extraordinary times (J.G. Ballard in *Empire of the Sun's* World War II Shanghai) or they themselves (Simone De Beauvoir) had precocious insights.

Another strategy is to start with a particularly interesting time in the near present, as Mark Matousek did in his memoir *Sex, Death, Enlightenment,* and go back to childhood to dramatize the various forces that shaped his personality. Then he resumes going forward to the present. *Sex, Death, Enlightenment* is a spiritual journey, another narrative strategy. The arc of action in the book is the author's search for meaning and spiritual connection.

Kingsley Amis tells the story of his life through remembrances of people he has met; Lillian Hellman does the same. In both cases the authors' friends and enemies are the jumping off points of the piece, allowing the author to riff about the politics and the mores of the times they lived in, their ideas and opinions, places they've lived, meals they've abhorred or remembered, but the actual subject is the author because we're in their viewpoint, seeing and experiencing every encounter through their unique sensibilities.

Memoirs, as opposed to full-fledged autobiographies, often shed light on certain aspects of the writer's life rather than reconstructing their days on earth from start to finish. Writing about subjects that have touched your life, such as people you have known, or cats, or your years in school, or music, or each of your lovers, or every car you ever owned or one particular house you lived in, can be the scaffolding upon which you can build your narrative strategy. Remember, you are writing about yourself and your thoughts and feelings and emotions as they relate to these touchstones. You can go back and forth in time and memory, dip into childhood or the present for a few paragraphs or pages as your story dictates.

Now you may think you know everything there is know about your life, but it's not always clear exactly what your story is, where you fit into it and what you are trying to tell the reader.

The New York Times columnist and host of the PBS series *Mystery!*, Russell Baker, told great stories about his huge family and was encouraged by his editor to write something they both referred to vaguely as "the growing up book." In a speech at the New York Public Library (reprinted in *Inventing the Truth: The Art and Craft of Memoir*, edited by William Zinsser) Baker said that he put it off for years until he decided, in the 1960s, that he needed to communicate to his children some sense of the pride and dignity of their family. At about that time, his mother was stricken ill and he decided out of due respect to her to write about the times he and his mother went through together. Being a reporter, he packed his tape recorder and interviewed his vast array of relatives, transcribed the interviews and came up with a four-hundred-fifty-page manuscript about all the hard but wonderful times of family generations gone by. He sent the manuscript to his editor and waited for a response. And waited. And waited. All experienced writers know that an agent's (or editor's) enthusiasm is inversely proportional to the amount of time they take to read your manuscript and get back to you. Overnight: they love it big time. Weeks: you're in for trouble. When no response came, he knew something was wrong. When he re-read the book, he realized that although this was to be a story about a boy and his mother, known as a remarkable but tough-minded lady, he had dutifully recorded all his relatives' interviews but had left himself and his mother out of the book. It was nothing but journalism, an accurate but not very compelling sketch of the Great Depression.

Baker decided he had to delve deeper. He had access to his mother's keepsakes, specifically her trunk. Inside it he discovered several interesting things. One was a cache of love letters between his mother and a man she had never mentioned; the other was her marriage certificate, which proved that Russell Baker was a love child, conceived out of wedlock. This discovery cleared up a lot of things for him, mysteries about his mother that he never understood, such as the animosity between her and his father's mother. Beforehand, this relationship had been incomprehensible. Now on the one hand, he feared that to mention these very personal discoveries in his book would be airing dirty linen and exploiting his mother's past for commercial purposes. On the other, he felt if he wanted to honor his mother's life, he had to be truthful. He had to show her as a person who acted as she did for good reason. So he decided to rewrite the book concentrating on just a piece of his life, a story line he referred to as the tension between a mother and son. His strategy in this book was to cast light on one corner of his life, albeit a significant one. He left out a great deal of material that failed to contribute to that story—which amounted to most of that original four-hundred-fifty-page manuscript.

Any memoir or autobiography is a way of investigating the substance of your own life or a segment of it, a theme running through it. Others will sometimes come to your writing asking the same questions as you yourself must ask when you are writing: What are the full implications, the essence of my experiences? Perhaps you are writing for the next generation. Perhaps you are writing lest you or others forget something important. Perhaps you are just trying to make sense of what you have done and what has been done to you. No matter what your intention, you can't simply record what happened. You have to shape and examine it.

You can think of the facts as containers—empty until you fill them with meaning and imagination. One day at a family gathering, a boy falls into the river. That's a fact. But what does it mean until I tell you that his father, a jealous and secretive man, bitter about his own difficult childhood, famously afraid of water, terrified of embarrassing himself in public, dives in to save the boy? Or until I recount the shame the boy feels at causing his father to flail awkwardly in front of the relatives to stay afloat; and the boy's guilt, at the same moment he is struggling for air, that he had made his father ruin his one good suit? What is a mere fact in light of the boy's sudden realization that his demanding and inscrutable father deeply loves him? In retelling the facts, in exploring what the facts imply, they may resemble a new situation. The experience won't be exactly like the one you lived through, but more intense. The incident may have been over in sixty seconds while it may take you years to figure out its implications, days or months to write it. As we have remarked earlier, sometimes when you write of your own experience, whether in personal narrative or in fiction, you lose the memory as it happened. The artistic reconstruction of the event replaces what actually occurred on that day or in that year, because it is shaped, more vivid, investigated for its implications. You create a small world of your own with meaning that reaches out to others. If you want people to make the effort to read about that world, you have a responsibility to your reader. You must make your characters real and convincing and multi-dimensional. Your descriptions should make your physical details vivid. Mere reportage and statistics, however faithful to the truth, do not make interesting reading.

When you search out your narrative strategies, you might choose a subject, rather than your entire life, that you can infuse with your unique language and intelligence. M. F. K. Fisher used food. Willie Morris, his dog Skip.

Don't worry if you don't think you have an interesting life. Senators and generals, trial lawyers and movie stars, for all the action in their lives, are constantly writing less than interesting books about them. V. S. Pritchett was right on the money when he said, "It's all in the writing. You get no credit for living."

The Exercise: The Parallel Universe

Think of an incident in your own life. It can be an argument, or an erotic experience, or your first music recital—some memorable incident. The best incidents for this exercise carry some emotional weight: happiness or misery, fear, nervousness, embarrassment. (If it's been an incident you've been reluctant to tackle in your writing, so much the better.)

You are going to write about that incident. You are the main character in that story. But . . . you are going to disguise things in a big way.

Here are some suggestions (choose one or more):

Write in the *third* person.
Pick a main character *that is not you*.
Change the *place* the incident occurred.

126

Change the *time* period (make it happen in the past or the future).
Change the *sex* of the character.

Naturally, you'll have to make adjustments. If your incident concerns a crush you had on the captain of the ice hockey team and you decide to set your piece in Barcelona instead of Minnesota, the object of your affections will also have to change to accommodate the new surroundings (maybe captain of the soccer team? maybe a matador?).

Your aim is to be *true to your emotions* and *your version of the incident* but to distance yourself from it, disguise it so that:

1. The average reader of the piece would not see you in it but feel what you felt and,
2. Perhaps more important, you can write your story without worrying about whether someone will see you in it or whether you are betraying other people.

8

Choosing And
Manipulating Viewpoint

In discussing characterization, we looked at the chemistry involved in characters in fiction—our attraction to them, repulsion from them. Often we respond to them as we would real people or sometimes as we would "selves" we put on. We may even imitate a particular character with whom we identify. There are three basic strategies for dealing with that chemistry.

In the first case, you want the reader to keep an emotional distance from the characters, as in Brecht's *Threepenny Novel,* as in the work of Sol Yurick and in Doctorow's *Ragtime* and *Loon Lake.* You intentionally and repeatedly distance the reader from the characters by the tone, by the placement of the vision, by a maintained coldness, by certain comic effects, by interposing a very strong voice between character and reader, or by adapting an omniscient point of view well above all the characters, in order to make them seem more like robots or ants and less like people we might know.

The second strategy for viewpoint occurs when you want the reader to identify with one character strongly. (Doris Lessing's *Martha Quest* series, Charlotte Brontë's *Jane Eyre*, Margaret Atwood's *Surfacing*, Barbara Kingsolver's *The Bean Tree.*) They will go through your narrative looking out through the eyes of that particular person and only that person.

In the third case, you give the reader a choice of characters with whom to identify, at least two and perhaps several to choose among. In Myla Goldberg's *Bee Season,* viewpoints alternate between the father, the mother, the younger sister and the older brother. Or in the three-generational novel, *Living To Tell*, by Antonia Nelson, the viewpoint moves from family member to family member.

I have usually tried to get readers to identify with my characters. Why encourage it? When we identify with fictional characters, they offer us the opportunity to slip into someone else's skin: a woman, a man, a black, a white, a Chicano, a Native American, a Norwegian dock worker, a Japanese physicist, a politician in Kenya, a midwife in Texas, a Neanderthal woman, a sled dog, a purple arthropod from Deneb 4. When we can empathize with others, we can less easily reject the alien, or what we perceive as the alien, because it truly becomes less alien to us. We enter another consciousness and experience life in somebody else's shoes or boots or moccasins or ballet slippers. Like the life in dreams, it is not real but it can alter our perceptions, change what we think and do.

We imitate fictional characters. How many men still play Hemingway who played his own characters? Byron's heroes in his narrative poems inflamed a generation of young men, and sometimes young women who wanted to play those parts, too. Characters in the novels of The Beats have reemerged to inspire another generation of young people in khakis, black leather and t-shirts just as the popularity of Charles Bukowski's books hatched thousands of new barflies. An acquaintance of mine in college had an affair with an instructor based on the fact that both of them passionately wanted to live in a Henry James novel, in the late style.

Another important tactical choice has to do with how much you want the reader to trust your viewpoint character's observations and reactions. This is quite distinct from whether or not we identify with a character. The power of the sense of dramatic irony often rests in identifying with a character who does not perceive what is bearing down on her or him, while you see and feel the approaching shock wave. Some of the best comic effects can come from our perceiving how a character is "doing it again"—once again digging a grave with his tongue, lying, exaggerating, boasting, whatever is his prevailing vice.

Now there are varying ways of using a viewpoint character, depending on how much of what the characters tells us we are to accept as the truth.

You may choose a viewpoint character who is pretty much

transparent in that respect *i.e.,* you want us to see what they see and believe what they believe, to know neither more or less. Conrad's narratives are like this. So is Nick Carraway in F. Scott Fitzgerald's *The Great Gatsby*. Nick is everybody's friend, and as he comes to understand the characters, so do we.

You may choose a viewpoint character who knows less than we do, a child's viewpoint, perhaps, or, because we are in fact switching viewpoints or getting some commentary in omniscient. We accept that they are honest and perceptive, but we know things they don't yet know. A certain amount of energy can be generated by our sense of how a character's naïveté or ignorance or mistaken beliefs may be about to wound or destroy her or him, or wreak havoc on others. The hopefulness of the narrator's voice in *The Diary of Anne Frank* and her continuing discovery of life are especially moving given what we readers knew to be her fate.

You may choose a viewpoint character who is a flawed, a distorting lens. We learn as the story proceeds to disregard much of what that character believes, as in John Fowles's *The French Lieutenant's Woman* or his *Collector* or Mark Twain's *A Connecticut Yankee in King Arthur's Court*. The character may even be lying to us and, as in real life, we have to try to separate the reality from the obfuscation.

In the first type—the transparent narrator—you are expected to accept pretty much the judgment, changing or constant, of the viewpoint character, whether first or third person; in the second, where each viewpoint character knows only part of the picture, you supplement what each knows with knowledge you the reader have learned elsewhere; in the third—the mistaken or duplicitous narrator—you the reader are required to exercise caution and your own judgment. The character may be lying or may be merely fooled or wrongheaded, but you are on your own to figure out the truth. Humbert Humbert in Nabokov's *Lolita* warns us straight away to beware of a murderer with a fancy prose style.

Another tactical choice is whether to tell a story from a single viewpoint, a multiple viewpoint, or an omniscient viewpoint—or from the viewpoint of a character who in essence sounds as if he or she is omniscient, because that narrator knows how the story comes out and what led up to that denouement. For instance, the novel *The Family Orchard* by Nomi Eve begins with a section called

"I Tell," in which a narrator addresses her husband and talks about how the story begins and suggests she knows things she has not told him, some inside or hidden knowledge. The true omniscient narrator who is above the story was most common in nineteenth century fiction and is common in potboilers today, but far rarer in literary fiction. This narrator knows what everybody is thinking and feeling, what everybody is doing—the narrator knows everything the author knows. With this kind of omniscience, withholding information from the reader, such as who done it or an important character's shady past, is not an option.

Every time you switch viewpoints, you gain information and dramatic irony and new perspectives, but you lose momentum. You may lose the reader. It is a very important choice you make.

What you need to do before you begin any piece of fiction, whether short story or novel, is to figure out exactly where—from whose viewpoint—the story must be told. What must the reader see and know? In whose head are we going to be situated? Or is it a tale without a visible teller? If it is a tale told by someone, then to whom? to what end? And then the question returns, is that someone an idiot, a wise woman, a liar? Once again, is that viewpoint transparent or cracked?

A related tactical question is how close in to what you perceive as the center of the story do you want locate your viewpoint? Let us say we are writing the story of a divorce. The husband's story is one point of view, the wife's another, and alternating them creates an extremely different texture. The viewpoint of a friend who can comment is quite different again. So is the viewpoint of the other woman or the other man, or someone who wishes to be one or the other. In every case, a very different story or novel will be the result of whose story you choose to tell, and whether you wish to present that story—let us say the wife's story is our center—according to how she herself sees it or according to how someone may see it who wishes her ill or well, or who is truly neutral in the divorce. All of those are a priori choices, wisely made before you begin to write.

However, one thing you learn is that when a story or a novel is going poorly, sometimes it is time to stop and ask these questions again. It may be that the story is being told from the wrong viewpoint, and that another is needed to supplement the one being used, or a different standpoint may be required altogether. You may want to add a viewpoint or viewpoints, or simply change the head you are living in to tell the story. The voice of Mary, the homeless woman in *The Longings of Women*, was originally written in the first person viewpoint and in second draft changed, to much better effect, to third person.

If you are telling a complex social or political story, or perhaps the story of a very large family over the generations, you may well need multiple viewpoints. But each time you go into a new person's head, remember what you are losing. You take the chance of confusing the reader. You lose the suspense of the story going forward. You lose momentum. You lose any identification and rapport so far built up. You have to make this judgment freshly for each additional character you conceive of entering. But if you need to have the reader see your fictional world from multiple angles, you may choose to use multiple viewpoints. I often do that—certainly not always, but better than half the time—because while I encourage identification, I want the reader to arrive at his or her own truth, rather than buying the opinion of any one of the characters.

Remember that it is equally important to decide when you are using multiple viewpoint whose life you want to enter, because you want the reader to know what that person knows, and whose life you do not want the reader to see from within, because of destroying suspense. For instance, when the chief suspense element in your plot is who did something—whether it was stabbing the old man in the library with a sharpened back scratcher, or writing a poison pen letter that destroys a friendship—if you enter the life of the person who did the act in question, you owe it to the reader to let her or him know what you know and what that character knows. But not all suspense resides in who did what. A great deal comes from such diverse questions as, Will they realize they're in love, will they learn what X knows, will they succeed or fail, will she finally leave her husband, will he realize she's using him, will he get the money in time, will she agree to the operation? Not only mysteries or adventure stories make use of suspense. Suspense is one of your basic seductions in getting the reader to read and keep on reading.

Similarly, if you use omniscient viewpoint, you may gain a kind of strong narrative voice otherwise available only in first person or with a narrator who lends a definite flavor to the story with their voice. You can go anyplace you feel like and witness anything convenient to your story. But you can't withhold information from the reader, for you are in fact omniscient. That is why omniscience is seldom a good device in a mystery. Omniscience means you the writer are situated well above all the characters and can tell us what every one of them is thinking as well as doing. This may happen in telling or it may happen from simply shifting viewpoints constantly, as you find convenient.

Third person is the style of narration most commonly used: *He strolled down the causeway with his shoes in his hand.* Or: *Dorothy stood at the head of the stairs listening to the conversation below, straining for her own name.*

Second person is a trifle cutesy, used at best for something short. *You walk down the street, you turn and look behind you. You stop at the corner for a light and you remember that guy at the party last night, the one with the throaty voice and the great grin.*

First person is often used in autobiographical fiction but third person is commonly employed to create a distance from the actual teller of the story, a fictional self. There are times it has even been used in personal narrative. In *The Armies of the Night,* Norman Mailer created a third person character named Norman Mailer. Writing about himself in the third person gave him some distance and a sort of dry perspective, enabling him to watch himself from above and comment on his own thoughts and behavior.

In Pam Houston's short story collection, *Cowboys Are My Weakness,* she occasionally uses the second person. In the story "How to talk to a Hunter," it has the effect of inclusion, as if to say, "You all know what it's like to be with a guy like this." There are fewer novels that use second person. In Jay McInerney's *Story of My Life,* it is used by the narrator, Allison Poole, a big city party girl, and creates the illusion of the dialect of a lost young woman.

Second person can work, but it can also feel like someone buttonholing you and insisting you agree with whatever line they are putting out. It's like sitting next to a stranger in a bar who keeps asking, "You know what I mean? You know what I'm saying?" until you wonder whether you really do.

First person is used frequently in fiction and is the most common form used in the personal narrative. First person brings with it the identification available from the colloquial speaking voice.

From *Look At Me*, by Lauren Porosoff Mitchell:

> I stood at the buffet where I could meet just about anybody at the party, except the anorexic of course. My half glass of wine from the cash bar clutched in my hand, I was hoping to get lucky or even semi-lucky, someone to talk to, to avoid resembling a potted plant.

That direct first person invites you in and whispers in your ear and can be used for direct address, exhortation, special pleading and everything in between. It has ultimate freedom because it has the spontaneity of the speaking voice, and it can have that intimacy. You can freely move around in space and time, editorialize and give or withhold information and insight as someone does in conversation. However, its vices are as flagrant as its virtues. It has a tendency toward talkativeness if not kept on a tight hold and can lead to an easy filling up of the page with nothing in particular, the long-windedness that destroys concentration and reader interest. Certain scenes are more difficult in first person. Sex scenes take careful handling.

A strong first person can seduce the reader, or it can put her or him off, for if the reader takes a dislike to your character's voice, the book may go unread. I recently began reading a manuscript in which the narrator was a nineteenth century country woman, a domestic, whose voice was so whiny and irritating I could not finish the story. The question of matching voice to character is another tactical decision. A bad first person can feel like someone shouting in your eat, and that can be tiresome indeed.

Some writers write the whole book in one voice. Others switch voices when they switch viewpoints. It is a matter of preference. Again, there are advantages to staying with one voice, in the unifying flavor it gives to a novel. There are advantages to switching voices if you switch viewpoints, for you have then one more device for characterization, and the reader will pick up quickly which head you are in if the voice is markedly different.

Finding a voice can be a challenge. Oftentimes I find that if I know my character well, I have my voice. It comes from within the character and sounds like her, as Connie's voice goes throughout *Woman on the Edge of Time* in the third person narration that never leaves her viewpoint until the documents at the end from the hospital staff.

However, with ten viewpoint characters in *Gone to Soldiers*, I paid attention to differentiating their voices. I hoped that if you read even a page of any particular chapter, you would know from the voice who was speaking. There were certain rhythms, certain types of idioms, vocabulary, ways of thinking and perceiving that belonged to each character.

When I had finished second draft, I took the book completely apart and wrote the third draft as ten separate novels, so that each character's story would be consistent in language, style, the minor characters, the time line, the feel of that character's world, and ambiance. Then in fourth draft I put it all back together. Many novels only take four drafts. *Gone to Soldiers* took six, and parts of it went above twenty.

Often when a writer of fiction is starting out, all the fuss about viewpoint seems overly technical and he or she may think, I'll just tell the story. But it doesn't work that way. Whose story are you telling? One of the standard exercises to understand viewpoint is to write the same scene from the point of view of two antagonistic characters: say a mother or father trying to discourage a son or daughter from continuing in a romantic relationship; and then from the standpoint of the son or daughter; then from the viewpoint of the lover being argued about. You may find your story is very, very different depending in whose head you situate yourself and therefore your reader. But the exercise works no matter what situation involving a clash of wills that you use.

When you are writing personal narrative, viewpoint may not be as pressing a consideration, but there are still aspects to consider. Most personal narratives are told in the first person, but there are many autobiographical novels and short pieces in which the author decides to put some distance between herself or himself and the story. Sometimes you may begin in the first person and find that it somehow inhibits you when you are telling your own story. You may decide to take another pass at the material by changing the voice to third person. This is a common way to solve the problem of narratives that feel too private for the author to tell us or that might put the reader off by seeming too intimate. The writer may worry that the story told by "I" will seem too full of special pleading or self-pity or self-congratulation. The writer may feel safer, more comfortable with third person.

Sometimes a writer creates an alter ego and writes books in that alternate voice which sees the world through a perspective similar to their own. The short story writer, Grace Paley, sometimes employs the witty and wise voice of a working class New York mother named Faith. Philip Roth has written a number of books through the voice of Nathan Zuckerman, a writer who has become rich and infamous through a scandalous, semi-autobiographical best seller. Creating an alter ego for yourself is a way to blend reality and imagination and have fun doing it. You can always point to your character and insist, "I didn't say that. He did."

There is no right or wrong way to choose and establish viewpoint in personal narrative any more than there is in fiction. If one approach doesn't feel comfortable and it clenches you up to work that way, try another approach. Do what works for you.

Some writers choose to tell their own story in the form of fiction, as we have remarked before, in order to create a greater measure of distance between the story and themselves, and perhaps in order to gain freedom to explore potentially volatile, painful and shameful material. Obviously if you label your piece "fiction," the reader can never be sure what's true and what's not. Perhaps more important, you, the writer, are not forced to stay with the facts but are free to invent scenarios that are emotionally true, what should have happened, what almost happened, what you dreamed happened. It surprises some people that the Chinese restaurant scene in Ira Wood's *The Kitchen Man*, never actually happened. For years after reading the book his mother asked him, "We *never* went out for Chinese food with you and Marge?" Not once, to a Chinese or any other kind of restaurant. But even to the participants, it feels as if it happened because all the emotions and characterizations ring true. That greater freedom may empower you or dismay you. Experiment. Becoming conscious of the various options that are open to you in your writing is one of the biggest gifts you take away from any workshop, course, or how-to book.

Some Exercises

Take a simple story such as *Little Red Riding Hood* and reverse the usual point of view, that of the little girl. Write the story from the point of view of the wolf. YOU are the wolf. Get inside the wolf. How does the world look to him? Remember, he is the hero of his own story. Make at least a start on seeing the world through wolf eyes.

Other suggestions: *The Three Bears* from the point of view of the littlest bear; *Snow White* from the point of view of the Queen; *Rapunzel* from the view point of the witch; *Rumpelstiltskin* from the point of view of the dwarf. Remember that "villains" are heroes to themselves, and the center of the story and the center of sympathy.

Exercise:

Take any scene from your own life and write it, not from your point of view, but from that of another person involved in the situation—perhaps someone antagonistic to you or in disagreement with you. It should prove interesting. Try doing it in the other's first person viewpoint.

Exercise:

Choose the viewpoint of another life form involved in a scene from a story you want to work with from your life or a fiction piece you have been trying to write. Tell the story as the dog or the cat sees it. What does a parrot observe? Get into the body of the animal you are inhabiting and see the world not as you would as a little feathery or furry person, but as a being with a cat or dog's senses and instincts and desires. See what happens. The results may be interesting, but only if you can actually penetrate the distinct world of the animal. It could be a pet of yours or a wild animal observing you or someone else in the forest.

Exercise:

Your viewpoint character is interacting with someone else. He or she makes an assumption about the other character's motives or intentions that we, the reader, realize as we watch the scene unfold is an erroneous assumption. Thus we understand the situation better than the protagonist does. This is a situation that the reader often enjoys, and that also creates suspense—when will the protagonist learn that their take on the character or situation is wrong?

9

Descriptions

Descriptions are places where writers feeling their oats often let themselves go and readers nod off, put down the book or at their kindest, skip. No description should be skippable; every one should be functional. If you describe something, make it work. In a work of fiction, a description might have a function in the plot. Perhaps you plan to use that jaunty red dingy in chapter four.

In both fiction and memoir, a description may suggest character, as in describing someone's bedroom or their apartment or their clothing. It may set a mood. It may place your characters in the socioeconomic spectrum.

From *Small Changes:*

> Beth was looking in the mirror of her mother's vanity. The mirror had wings that opened and shut. When she was little she used to like to pull them together around her into a cave of mirrors with only a slit of light. It isn't me, isn't me. Well, who else would it be, stupid? Isn't anyone except Bride; a dress wearing a girl.
>
> Beth could not help seeing herself in the mirror; could never call up a glamorous image as her younger sister Nancy could. Nancy was sulking in the bathroom because her best friend Trudy had called her a dishwater blond. Like Beth, Nancy had naturally curly, almost kinky light brown hair. They were the little ones in the family. Just yesterday she had picked off the floor a piece of paper with gum stuck in it written in Nancy's fancy new backhand: *Nancy Phail is a petite vivacious blond*

with loads of personality. Nancy could look in the same mirror and see faces from those teen-age magazines she brooded over. But Beth saw Beth lost in a vast dress. She felt like a wedding cake: they would come and slice her and take her home in white boxes to sleep on under their pillows.

With their married sister Marie's help, Nancy had written a description for the paper and mailed it in, though they never printed that except for people like, oh, executives' daughters from the G.E. plant where her father worked at the gate. "Schiffli embroidery and ribbons dip softly over an organza skirt and bodice, with sheer daintily puffed sleeves," Nancy had written. "The train comes away." That meant the thing that dragged could be taken off, with a little timely help.

Description may give us information about the society, if it is exotic to us.

From *City of Darkness, City of Light:*

He went to Versailles with Turgot reluctantly. None of his talents counted. No one cared about mathematics, social theory or philosophy. They treated him the way people behaved when served the new and nutritious vegetable, potatoes, earth apples. They stared at the objects on their plate and toyed with them. So the bored and haughty courtiers stared at him, an earth apple if they had ever seen one, and attempted to toy with him. Ladies of middle rank flirted. He could not flirt back. He hardly found them of the same species. A woman who took six hours to dress, whose hair loomed a foot over her head, who was painted bright gold with red splashes and artificial moles, who reeked of violets and attar of roses and was packed into a dress that stood out three feet on either side of her, inspired him with nothing but a kind of contemptuous fear. All the courtiers were ranked by absurd roles (the countess who handed the Queen's first lady of the bedchamber the royal petticoat; the comte who stood on the King's left as his shirt was buttoned) and their privileges, both formal (who could sit on a stool in the royal presence and who must stand) and informal (the marquis the Queen danced with last night; the lady she smiled at; who had made the King giggle).

Versailles was an unnecessary city, built on ostentation as if on sand. It was larger in land than all of Paris and enclosed by walls. The streets were lined with the houses of officials whose functions were frivolous, and storehouses that held too much of everything. One building housed two hundred seventeen royal coaches. In Turgot's coach as they made their way through the crowded street, they passed the residences of men who cleaned the palace fountains, men who helped the king to hunt birds, who tended his packs of dogs, ten men in charge of crows, six of blackbirds. Scores of almoners, chaplains, confessors, clerics, choristers, the hundreds employed in the royal chapel or in providing sacred or profane music, clustered around the churches. Hairdressers alighted from carriages with the air of great generals, as heavily floured as bakers. The amount of flour consumed in a day in Versailles to powder the court's hair could feed Paris.

Description may make a satiric point.

From *The Kitchen Man:*

Wellfleet.

The summer town where a piece is not a nubile teenager or a triangle of boardwalk pizza but an essay in the *New Yorker*. The town where 1.4 members of every family has an agent, where psychiatrists block the narrow aisles of the local supermarket and sit cross legged on the sawdust floor counseling their sullen children, "Do you *really* want to be sticking your fingers through the cellophane wrap on the ground chuck?"

Lawyers from New Jersey and their wives in unisex resort wear line the sidewalks rubbernecking network newsmen who jog into town for the *Times*. Ex-cabinet members and Presidential advisers have cocktails on the redwood decks of the colleagues they've left behind at Harvard and no one cares more for dressing than to throw a sports coat over what they've worn to pick blackberries. You'll see an occasional Mercedes on Main Street. On a cloudy day a Cadillac full of time-sharing condo owners from Harwichport might pull through on their way to Provincetown to show their houseguests the gays. But the rule is a Ford station wagon, stored on blocks over the winter at a pond-front plot bought in 1954 at twelve hundred dollars—with the house—that is now worth two-and-a-quarter million.

Wellfleet.

On any given summer morning Main Street turns into a drive-in movie parking lot, a frozen field of packed cars facing the post office from six directions. The lot has spaces for ten, and in winter, observing local tradition, people get their mail, peruse it quickly, say howdy to their neighbors, and leave. In summer, entire families park, run through the post office front door and disappear through the back to go shopping. German tourists unload their bikes and coast to the beach. Retirees back in their Winnebago vans. The spry second wives of New York analysts, their children leaning on the horns of vehicles double parked in the middle of the street, cuss out grizzly local oystermen bottlenecked behind them proving that nothing hones rudeness and guile like shopping at Zabar's.

But all of the time whatever you place in the work must do double or triple labor; it must have a reason for being there. Descriptions may fill us in on attitudes of the characters, their background, their relationships, according to what is chosen to put in and what is left out:

From *Storm Tide:*

Yirina had baked both cakes and decorated them. She had sent Judith into Prospect Park where the daffodils were in bloom, to cut some and hide them in a bag pinned into her old coat that no longer properly buttoned. They looked lovely in the vases Yirina had brought with her from Mexico. Yirina had taken out the good tablecloth she always washed by hand, with fine embroidery of birds and flowers. Yirina had had it since her years in Turkey, during The War. Judith's mother could always make a feast. She could make a celebration out of a chicken, a couple of candles and a bottle of cheap Chianti. She could make a celebration out of a sunny afternoon and tuna fish sandwiches in Prospect Park. For Judith's father, Dr. Silver, she was wearing her best red dress of real silk and the diamond necklace that went in and out of the pawnshop several times a year. It was very important that they please Dr.

Silver. Judith wondered if she ever really pleased him. Was he happy she existed? Did he wish she had never been born? She was always covertly staring at his square face, impeccably shaven, and trying to read his feelings for her.

Once again Judith unwrapped the flowered skirt that her mother had wrapped in the same paper, carefully opened the night before. Dr. Silver was a stout man of medium height, a bit stooped. His hair was all white, even the hair that bristled from his nose and ears. His eyes were a pale luminous blue, but Judith had dark eyes like her mother. Sometimes she tried to find herself in her father. She had her mother's dark hair, her mother's pale skin with an olive tint. Dr. Silver was ruddy. She was small like her mother, small for her age. Her mother could pretend she was ten for several years longer, when they occasionally went to the movies. But she had her father's hands, what Yirina proudly called "a surgeon's hands." Long-fingered but quite strong. She had his long narrow feet. Her mother's feet were small but wide. Her mother wore size 5C, a size they looked for in sale bins or rummage sales at the nearby churches of Brooklyn.

My apprentice writing was full of scenes described only because I found describing them interesting, and I suspect that is surely true of a number of you. You may write such descriptions as an exercise, but do not include them in your finished work unless they really belong there.

Similarly, if you are writing a memoir, the specifics you include will tell us a great deal about your family and your friends. They are precious to you because they are part of what formed you, but only your language and your choice of detail can make them precious to us. It is a case of persuading us that we care whether the kitchen of your childhood home had tan and gold squares of linoleum or terra cotta tile on the floor; whether your bedroom curtains were filmy white or blue velvet; whether you slept with a teddy bear or a Barbie doll or a live tabby cat. You must make us care. You have to involve us in your life and involve us in the meaning, the resonance of these memories through vivid sensory language that carries an emotional message, and through an ongoing story that carries us forward.

Avoid words like *beautiful, pretty, ugly, handsome,* unless you do the work to make the scene or the painting or the man or the horse beautiful or ugly or whatever. Learn to describe briefly or in snatches, so as not to stop the story in an obvious way.

Make your descriptions work overtime to give us local color, reveal character, move the plot along, set us in time and place, fill in the socioeconomic picture, hint at the habits of the characters as they react to their surroundings.

From *City of Darkness, City of Light*:

(Here is Georges Danton arriving in 18th century Paris for the first time, without money but with great ambition and greater energy):

> The coach dumped him on the edge of Paris, in a slum festering under a black cloud of pestilent smoke. As he hiked through the narrow streets carrying his two portmanteaux, he choked from the stench of shit and rotten garbage. He was suffocated and deafened at once. In the perpetual twilight of the open sewers between dark houses sealing out the sky, every half block some poor soul was singing at the top of his lungs, bawdy songs, ballads of adventure and crime, topical songs, religious songs: all seeking sous from passersby and selling song sheets, scraping away on violins or banging on drums. Women carrying racks of old clothes pushed through the crowds. Swarms of beggars, crippled, blind, maimed, clutched at him. A man slammed into him. He watched his purse. Two men glared; he glared back. He elbowed his way along. Toughs looking into his scarred face saw someone who would readily fight. They let him pass.

I remember the opening of a memoir written in one of our workshops in which the Greek old world character of the family was given to us through a description of smells of cooking and the food served at a meal characterized by high tension and drama. The emphasis was on the drama, but the food gave us necessary background that made the conflict more understandable.

Sometimes description does even more than that, because the landscape is a character in the drama. The landscape itself may be an actor, a presence as vivid and as experienced as any other character. In Stanislau Lem's *Solaris*, the ocean on the planet is alive and a strong actor in the novel. In Isaak Dinesen's autobiography, *Out of Africa,* Kenya is a character, a strong part of the story of her marriage and her life at that time.

Sometimes "the city" or "the scene" is at the center of a novel, whether it is Hollywood or New York or Paris or Alexandria; and the city must be made new and bright and vivid in those stories. The city may be the destroyer or the seducer or the prize. But it cannot be merely alluded to; it must be recreated. This is equally true in fiction and in memoir. You must make Cleveland or Seattle vivid to us. The story of the writer who goes to Hollywood and is destroyed or falls into temptation and then recovers his or her integrity is an American cliché, but like all such stories, able to be told and retold as long as it is made new and the seduction of the place is created for us so we experience it with the protagonist. We returned a recent submission from a retired professor of English whose description of Chicago was as flat as the city itself. We explained that many major cities have horrific traffic and large parks and rivers running through them and that her Chicago, a place of immense local character, could have been any one of them. She wrote back that we must have mistaken her book for another submission; that in chapter one she specifically mentioned Grant Park and the Wrigley Building. Sorry, not enough.

Descriptions of people may function to tip us off to the attitude of the character doing the looking, the describing. It may contain enough attitude to suggest something of what is going to happen.

From *Three Women:*

> The next year there was a new student who transferred in from Kansas. They both had history with him. He wasn't a jock, a club kid, one of the super students who ran the school, or a burnout who would be tossed, but like them, one of the weird kids. He was between them in height and had pale sleek blond hair he wore to his shoulders. His eyes were a dark haunting blue. He had a scar through one light brown eyebrow. His cheekbones were high and sharp, and his profile looked to her as if it should be carved on the prow of a sailing vessel. He always had shadows of stubble on his cheeks that made him seem older, more experienced. Half the guys had

just started shaving. Evan had a darkish beard but not much of it. He only had to shave every other day, and it took him about a minute, although she did like to watch, cause it was such a male thing to do. She was almost hairless on her body and never even shaved her legs. To each other, they called the new kid the Decadent Viking. "I want him," Evan said.

"So do I," she said. "We'll share him."

They made up stories of capturing him, tying him up and doing things to him. His name was Chad. It seemed a silly name for such a fascinating-looking guy. He was broody. He sat at the back, and even when he knew the answers, he sounded as if he resented being right. She sat down next to him in assembly one day. His wrists stuck out below his shirt. There was a scar on each of them. He caught her looking at his wrists. They stared at each other. He did not hide his wrists. Then he smiled.

If you grew up in Toledo, Ohio, you have to work hard to make it interesting to us; but not if you grew up in Toledo, Spain. Then we want many sensory details of your growing up. If you introduce an exotic locale in your memoirs, we expect that locale to play a part in the story. We expect somehow that the story of growing up as the son of a missionary in the jungle of Paraguay will be different from the story of growing up as a minister's son in Dubuque, Iowa. If it is not different, that, too, is important to the narrative. If your family recreated a little Dubuque in the jungle, that's part of your story, and you want to make that real to us with vivid and emotionally engaging description.

Here is the beginning of a novel about a fourteen year-old girl who has been shipped off to live with her grandmother in the Philippines and who spends all her free time playing fantasy games in cyberspace:

From *leo@fergusrules.com:*

I insist on durian. I love the sweet taste of the meat, and the rotten cheese stench of the skin keeps the curious from my room. I have the maid bring it up twice a day and leave it outside my door. When you're chasing Genghis Khan across the Tekla Makhan or gouging the eye from a Cyclops, the last thing you need is to be called down for supper—especially when it's a plate of hard rice and chicken overcooked in vinegar and soy sauce.

I wrote that in my journal ten months ago when I arrived in Manila. At the time, I was battling my grandmother, Lola Flor, who wanted to impose her medieval notions of order on me. In her house, every day was regulated according to the canonical hours of a monastery: breakfast was served at lauds, just as the sun rose; I left for school at prime; we recited the rosary right after I came home from school at none; we sat down to supper at vespers; and at complin Lola marched around the house turning out the lights. At school, she wanted me to listen for the bells of St. Andrew's and take my lunch when terce sounded, but that meant eating during math class. I tried it once just to see what would happen. I'd no sooner unwrapped my chicken wings than Mrs. Siew sent me to the principal's office.

In descriptions, it is the language that tips us off as to what is happening, the connotations of the words that tell us what to expect, subliminally, the way a score in music will set a mood in a film of suspense, impending doom, romance, serenity. The connotative language is the movie score working on you as you read. The shorter the description, the more power you must build into each word, the harder each phrase must work. Chapter one of *Lycanthia* by Tanith Lee begins with the description of a fast moving train passing through a comforting world of villages and small farms, cottages and sheds and busy peasants, then suddenly plunging into a land of winter, of ice and emptiness and sinister black forests. As the protagonist steps from the train at his station stop, the air is so sharp and cold he can hardly breathe and the train's whistle seems to cry as it leaves him absolutely alone. Such a description connotes imminent harm, a land where nothing familiar, and probably nothing good, will happen.

Some Exercises:

Write a one paragraph description which is powerfully connotative, which is leading to a murder, a frightful revelation, a disaster.

Do not tell the reader what you are trying to convey but do it by language and the objects you choose to describe. Watch your verbs and make them do a lot of the work. Do not rely only on adjectives.

Exercise:

Write a one paragraph description in which you convey the emotional attributes of a place; the way it makes you feel or the way you remember it, the way you want the reader to feel about it. Fearful, angry, cozy, lost. It can be a room, a neighborhood, a school, a town, a large city. Don't name the emotion but attempt to choose words and images, objects and sensual details that may trigger the reader's own feelings about the place.

Exercise:

Write a short scene in which your viewpoint character is encountering a person. Give us a strong sense of that person through what you choose to include about them, what your viewpoint character observes or senses about them—perhaps their clothing, their walk, their attitude; the way they hold your character's stare or avoid their eyes. What do they smell like? What are they clutching? How do they act in the presence of other people: a bag lady? a cop? Here you are using description to characterize.

Exercise:

Create a room or a place that invokes the character who created or inhabits it. Do the work of making us feel the character first through the objects you include. Not a chair but a leather club chair with cracked upholstery smelling of dog. Or a particular type of designer chair, expensive and trendy. Or a horsehair couch in purple evoking the Victorian era in a period house or—more strangely—in a high rise apartment building in a room painted stark white. Not a bed but a narrow metal cot or a sumptuous king bed with a velvet patchwork quilt and swag draperies on the wall behind it or a fake Colonial canopy bed with an off white chenille spread.

What's on the walls? Are they bare? Is there a girly calendar, Elvis on velvet, a reproduction of Van Gogh's sunflowers, a landscape in oils in shades that match the couch, a portrait of the hostess? What's on the floor? What does the room smell like? What sounds do you hear when you enter it? Does the person play the piano or is a piano there for show? Are there music components visible and CDs? If so, what kind? You need not go about and catalog every object in the room, and in fact there is no reason to do so. But choose your furniture and your decorations carefully so that we know what's important to the character who lives in that room. Or keeps it for show.

Exercise: The Spirit of Place

Try writing a dynamic and engaging description of a city, a landscape, a resort in or out of season, a mountain cabin (be specific about the mountain range), a village you visited on vacation. You can introduce yourself as a character experiencing this place or you can provide us with another narrator or protagonist. Or you can make the place itself the primary actor in the scene you are creating by having your narrator react to elements beyond her control: speeding taxis, aggressive panhandlers, freezing rain, and onrushing commuters streaming out of a busy London tube station.

In any event, let your language do a great deal of the work. Select your images carefully. Be as specific as you can—not trees, but sugar maples or Joshua trees or bristlecone pines or royal palms. If you have birds or animals, make sure they are native to the place and name and describe them accurately and vividly. Is there a particular kind of music you hear in those streets or cafés? Are there shutters? What times of day do they open and when are they shut? Make the right kind of architecture inhabit your place—brush huts or high rises with lavish balconies or clapboard three-deckers or pastel stucco buildings of two and three stories with courtyards whose fountains you can hear dribbling on their pebbles.

10

When You Have Research To Do

Frequently you may have a fair amount of research to do on a novel or a memoir. Although there are a few sources particularly useful for personal narrative, there is a great deal of overlap and similar technique no matter what you are writing. For *Woman on the Edge of Time*, I had a lot of studying to do about the brain and psychosurgery, about how it feels to be in a mental institution, and a lot of research preliminary to thinking about the technology in a good future society. For *The Longings of Women,* I needed to study homelessness and murder trial procedure in Massachusetts; I had to make on-site visits to several neighborhoods that are featured in the novel, the Barnstable House of Corrections, the courtroom where Becky's trial takes place, Lesley College where Leila teaches.

But some novels take an enormous amount of research. While I was writing *The Longings of Women*, I was already doing research on the French revolution for *City of Darkness, City of Light*. It has a huge computer database, as did *Gone to Soldiers*, my World War II novel. The database for *Gone to Soldiers* was seven times as long as the novel itself. The database for the French Revolution novel covered thirty-two high density discs.

Searching a database on a computer is fast, but it still takes time. However, it sure beats writing things in a notebook, where you have to go through everything to find anything. It beats ordinary file cards, because from each piece of information in a filing system that depends on spatial location, either in a filing drawer or in a card box, you can only get at that particular goody by one path, one label. It is under WOMEN or it is under HISTORY or it is under NINETEENTH CENTURY or it is under FRENCH COMMUNE or it is under LOUISE MICHEL. Some of those descriptors will prove useful at different times, but you might want a cross referencing system that will get you that little goody by any of those routes.

Whatever system you end up using, I recommend some system to you. It is simply not useful to have the stuff you want and need on random pieces of paper, the backs of grocery lists or lost in the middle of a notebook. The disadvantage of that method, or lack of it, is that you wade through pages of extraneous stuff—stuff that was interesting enough to you when you wrote it down to make it likely you'll get suckered into reading it again now. There goes the afternoon.

I clip periodicals heavily and keep files on subjects possibly useful. Novelists are hungry for information. I am always way behind clipping things, let alone reading them. My house is always full of glaciers of yellowing newsprint creeping through the rooms. Perhaps half the subjects I clip will never become novels, but some of them will, and what I save (I tell my very skeptical husband whenever we move stacks of old magazines to pinpoint the odor of a long petrified mouse) will eventually be useful for me.

Most of my fiction is research intensive and even my memoir required a great deal of digging. But as we've mentioned many times, all writers approach the subject differently. Some are absolutely fascinated by their own lives and do no research at all. Some work directly from memory, some from snippets of inspiration. In the preface to *The Spoils of Poynton* Henry James talks about the problem of hearing too much about an incident, what he calls the "futility of fact." He was at a lavish Christmas dinner one night in London when another guest mentioned in passing that an acquaintance of hers was "at daggers drawn" with her only son over the ownership of the furniture in an old house the son had inherited upon his father's death. James was immediately stung with an idea for a story, "as if the novelist's imagination winces at the prick of some sharp point." As the guest went on with specifics, however, his imagination began to fizzle. James compares that initial story idea to a newborn baby, with all the potential that the metaphor implies, but as she proceeds to supply him with helpful details all she manages to do is "strangle it in the cradle even while she pretends, all so cheeringly, to rock it." Others mine jobs for story ideas. Ira became a waiter, designed computer games and ran for public office in preparation for his three novels. He got a bus driver's license and drove a school bus ferrying Black children into hostile white neighborhoods in preparation for *The Last White Class*, the play we wrote about the violent battle for school desegregation in Boston. The great critic Edmund Wilson used to research long articles about a subject before he tackled a book, a common practice today for non-fiction writers for the *New Yorker*, for example.

Interviewing is an undervalued art. As someone who has a lot of experience with being interviewed, I can tell you it is something usually done poorly. It requires empathy and direction, tact and a sense of tactics, patience and flattery. The best interviewer I have ever experienced is Studs Terkel; the best I've ever watched in action is Barbara Walters on TV. Both are extremely skilled and both massage and stroke the object/victim/target. Neither means harm but both are relentless and yet open, curious, for the moment a little in love. Love is a form of attention and so is interviewing.

I often ask people who have a specific expertise in an area I have written about to look over an entire novel or sections of the novel, to see whether I have committed obvious gaffes, whether I have handled the language or the jargon essential to one or more characters idiomatically. You want to master some of the jargon of a profession, but only use it as flavoring. You do not want to create something so dense that your reader has to take a course to read what you have written.

I asked a historian who had been a bombardier during World War II (and before that had worked in a shipyard) and his wife, who had been a Rosie the Riveter, to go over *Gone to Soldiers* before the final draft and give me feedback on anachronisms. I also had a friend who was in New York during the war check out my milieu details. I had both a Holocaust survivor and a Holocaust scholar check relevant chapters. One of my old French professors checked my French and saved me some real gaffes. I had two other friends who had experienced different aspects of the war check the manuscript, also. In spite of that, a couple of errors got through; some of them I have heard about from readers and was able to correct in the paperback—about five boners, as I recall. A copy editor should have caught at least the most important of those, but they usually spend their time fighting with you about points of grammar they imagine they know more about than you do—and missing grievous errors you would be pitifully grateful if they caught. Copy editors are mad for commas but not so interested in fact checking.

Most of your research you'll have to do at the library, through interlibrary loans, through on-site inspections and visits. You can get bibliography and some sorts of research on the Internet, but books are the most convenient and efficient way to find out what you want to know. The Internet is great for medical information, I've found, but not so great on history. However, there are listservs and forums for almost every conceivable subject, and you can put queries on ones you join.

If you need to interview people, do them the courtesy of finding out as much as you can about them before you meet. Do not lie and do not get caught in oily flattery, but act even more interested than you are. You are taking up someone's time and you owe it to them to be prepared. Never try to make a person replace reference work. It is not right to ask someone to answer questions you could do yourself with an hour in the local library. Remember also that what people remember is highly selective and highly subjective.

Understand that we create the past and recreate it as we examine it. Even small facts are often unknowable. Again, using *Gone to Soldiers* as an example, there is a convoy in the third Duvey chapter, "The Black Pit." I researched the list of ships in that convoy in Washington and in London and in every available historical record; every single list was different. This is a well attested to convoy that should be a piece of cake to track. History fades under our hands. History changes. You must get used to entering the realm of the Maybe So. The finally unknowable.

Although this seems almost too obvious to mention, one of the worst things you can do is borrow a piece of equipment and use it for the first time while conducting an interview. I can't tell you how many interviews have failed because the interviewer was unfamiliar with the tape recorder or microphone and wasted at least fifteen minutes of the hour available fiddling with the equipment. If you must borrow equipment, use it first and try it out until you are familiar with it. Be sure you have enough cassettes with you. Be sure you are carrying spare batteries. You would be surprised how many interviews are lost because of mechanical failure on the part of the interviewer. You want your recorder to be unobtrusive, just sitting there quietly recording. Be alert for the time you must turn the tape or change the cassette. You cannot reasonably expect any person to repeat what they have already said. If they told a great story full of charming detail the first time, they will give you a dry synopsis the second. If you are using a new digital recorder, you don't want to be monkeying with it, calling attention to it, stopping a natural flow to make sure you are recording properly.

In writing a memoir, you may imagine you do not need to do research, but memory is fallible and you want the flavor of the times as well as the facts. To jog your own memory or perhaps even that of someone you know, try songs from the period in question. Often songs are associated with an era of our lives. Movies work less well, but they may work for you. Smells—the smell of a particular flower or perfume or soup—jumpstart your memory. That usually happens without conscious preparation, but you can use a scent to recapture a period.

Old magazines (often available in libraries and sometimes on microfilm) can prove extremely useful in recalling or creating details; so can newspapers. By looking at ads or illustrations, you might recall your mother's dress or your father's hat, or some particular outfit you were dressed in. Ads are useful. So are news stories of the time. Such research can provide you with vivid details, the bits of image, of sound and phrase that make the past real to your readers—because they make it real to you.

Doing research with your family when you are writing a memoir or a piece about your family requires persistence and tact. You need to keep focused on what you are trying to find out (unless you are simply interested in recording everything). Mostly you won't have trouble getting people in your family to talk, once you have persuaded them that you are genuinely interested; but there are stories they do not want to tell, and often those are the ones you want to hear. It takes persistence and it takes tact and it takes a kind of flattering attention, but you will probably succeed in the end. Transcribing interviews, by the way, is one of the most tedious and annoying activities you will engage in and by far the least fun element of your research. But unless and until you transcribe interviews and notes, they are useless to you. I have known people who did many interviews but never wrote a book or even an essay, because they could not bring themselves to deal with the cassettes they had accumulated.

Sometimes reading a children's book that was important to you may bring back pieces of your childhood. Was there a radio program you listened to regularly or a television program you always watched? Did your family regularly watch some program together? Often you can find DVDs for old TV programs that have some significance to you and may be useful. I found cassettes of news broadcasts from World War II that were invaluable.

If you cook a particular dish that your mother or grandmother made, that, too, may bring back memories you have forgotten or render sharper and with far more significant sensual details some memory you do possess, but has faded. Old photographs are an obvious source of information and emotion. You may use them to refresh your memories and use them as a device to get someone else in your family to talk about a particular family member or a particular era or event in which you are interested. You never know what may help. I have a tin box of buttons I took from my mother's sewing drawer after she died. I have found that certain of those buttons inadvertently brought back entire experiences because they recalled to me what my mother had worn on some special day or trip we had taken and which gave me an entire scene. I have a poem called "Unbuttoning" that came from that tin of buttons. For you, perhaps sports memorabilia, old comic books, a book of period toys, rock or movie posters might help. If you jitterbugged or waltzed or watusied, doing it to the right music could bring out bygone times and faces.

Experiment and see what may work for you. These are all only suggestions, but try out whatever you think might do the job.

Exercise:

Pretend you are writing about the life of any particular minor historical figure—you want a minor figure so that you are not swamped in information. See what you can find out on the Internet; then compile a short bibliography and see how you can get the books you need.

Exercise:

Pick an incident in the history of your family. One that you have heard about but did not yourself take part in or witness. Interview family members one at a time, not together, about this incident and then compare your notes. See what is important to each person and what they have forgotten. Notice the different emphases and preconceptions each person brings to their account of the event.

11

A Few Genres:
Historical Fiction, Mystery,
Science Fiction, And Fantasy

Newspapers and other review media, as well as "serious" critics, often overlook genres, but the best writers of any of the genres we are briefly discussing are as good as any so-called mainstream writers. All of these genres can tackle important issues and create compelling characters. Often writers will use one of these genres to examine societal issues not often taken up in what is considered serious fiction, or to ponder human nature or the nature of good and evil, the nature of justice and the existence of free will. While there are specific concerns and problems you might encounter in each of these genres, what makes a detective story or a science fiction tale good is exactly what makes a so-called mainstream novel good—plus the special requirements of the genre. It is not easier to write in genre than it is to write a mainstream novel. Further, you had better like and be well acquainted with the genre. If you have only read five or six mysteries in your life, don't consider writing one. You have no idea what the contemporary landscape of the mystery is. Study your field.

HISTORICAL FICTION

Historical fiction presents its own pitfalls. You don't want your characters to sound like 21st century teenagers or housewives, but neither do you want to create authentic period language. Some writers become so entranced with their material, their research, that they have forgotten their readers. You want a *flavor* of the time—as we emphasized in the chapter on dialog—and you certainly want to avoid anachronisms. Slang dictionaries and the *Oxford English Dictionary* are your intimate friends in avoiding phrasing that is out of its time. Some slang goes back hundreds of years; some expressions and words will be dated next year.

Equally important, that someone wore hoop skirts or silk doublets does not mean that they were any less interested than people in your circle are in their family, their friends, the politics and gossip of their time, getting ahead, getting laid, finding Mr. Right, raising their children, surviving. Make your historical characters real by entering into their heads. Understand that some of their obsessions will be different but many will be yours in a different key. Do not make blanket assumptions that all Victorians were straitlaced or that all Puritans were scared of having a good time.

Research your period thoroughly. Especially pay attention to the minor and colorful details of daily life. John Adams was considered a very abstemious man because he drank no more than six glasses of hard cider a day. We'd judge that to be alcoholism. But what could people drink then? The water from their shallow wells was contaminated by human and animal waste. They had no refrigeration to keep milk. They couldn't hold on to juices. Canning had not been invented. They drank coffee and tea, yes, but they also drank alcohol in quantities we would find alarming—but they were used to it and thought alcohol healthy. After all, it didn't give them cholera or dysentery like their water did. Put things in their context and make a real effort to understand them.

Besides dressing your people in period clothes, feed them what they would eat, give them to drink what was likely and available. Give them the furniture appropriate to their class level and lifestyle and the fashion of the times, if they paid any attention to that. A peasant family in Normandy in 1780 would not furnish with Louis XVI furniture, while a leather merchant in Paris certainly would want to do so. Discover what jobs people really had in the social class you're working with. Read about the period but also read as much as you can that actually dates from the period. If you can see the originals, that can be a big help. I knew of the gutter and rabidly political journalism of the French revolution when I was researching *City of Darkness, City of Light*—but somehow I never imagined that the most obscene and violent street paper would look like an academic journal: small type in grayish columns, no graphics, no big screaming headlines.

Look at the dishes, the crockery, jewelry, wigs: anything at all you can find from the time. Read about the favored scents and who used them. How did people recognize each other's station in life? How would you identify a doctor, a bricklayer, a prostitute, a midwife? How did your characters get their water and food and what happened to their waste products? What were the walls, the ceilings, the floor coverings like? Did people keep pets? What kind? Fashions in pets come and go. How many servants would your character have; if they were a servant themselves, what was their life like? Where did they sleep? How did they wash?

But all of the time you are making your setting as real and vivid as possible, keep getting deeply into your major characters. If they do not capture the reader and provoke her interest, if they do not convince us they are real and lively, we won't care how realistic your details of life in 17th century Amsterdam are.

Occasionally, of course, you reach a dead end. I was researching 1600 Prague and trying to find out what clothing Jews of various social classes wore. But there are no portraits. Unlike occasional examples of clothing from the aristocracy, none of their clothes survive. There were no fashion magazines for Renaissance Jewry. No one at the Jewish Museum in Prague had any idea. I had to pretty much fake it, guessing what they wore and avoiding much detail about dress. Sometimes you just have to guess. But mostly if you pursue your query, you can find out.

Historical fiction works pretty much like any other fiction in its structure, characterization, use of dialog, and so forth. What's different is that certain things happened historically so you have a specific framework into which you fit your story. All of my historical novels use actual events of the time. In many cases, I am using real historical people, so I am at the mercy of what really happened. I find that an advantage, often. There is a great deal of room for empathy and for imagination even when you are working with historical individuals like Robespierre and Elizabeth Cady Stanton, about whom a great deal is known. What you are bringing to the historical personage is your insight into the deeds that are recorded. The dialog, the inner thoughts, the emotions.

You are restrained by the facts. If you want to have Napoleon win at Waterloo, you are writing fantasy, not historical fiction. The "What If" stories —'What If' the Confederacy, or Hitler won?—are in that category. But with historical fiction, the British did burn Washington and Amelia Earhart's plane was lost in the Pacific. Now since no one knows exactly what happened to her, in historical fiction you are free, as many writers have done, to invent her end. You can fill in the interstices of historical events, making them far more vivid to us than history texts can. But you must do it by creating characters we believe in and care about.

Be careful how you work in your details. Laid on too thick, excessive details can keep the pace sluggish and make us lose sight of our characters and their obsessions, their concerns, their problems and conflicts. A lot depends on what you are dealing with and how skillfully you can handle them. Details of a toilette are inherently less fascinating than details of judicial torture. But a good writer can make a hairdresser's work on a lady of fashion absorbing to us.

Letters and journals of the time are especially valuable for giving a flavor of everyday life, as well as a sense of what people of a particular place and class worried about, depended upon, really did and said. Overviews are a good place to start, but you want period details, and overviews and histories cannot give you that kind of richness.

Exercise:

In the chapter on research, we asked you to gather information on some historical personage, preferably a minor one so that you would not be overwhelmed with data. Now take that same person and put them in a scene from their lives, recorded or imagined. Make the period real and make the person vivid. Find a good action scene to sketch out.

SCIENCE FICTION

In the chapter on Beginnings, we talked about the need to seduce the reader, to get something lively or intriguing or mysterious or fascinating or peculiar moving and moving fast. Then you can go back and insert your necessary backgrounding and context. No, there's no law against starting with description, of a place, a time, a character, but at the risk of losing the reader, it had better be an intriguing description. Since science fiction often involves the creation of an alternate world or reality, one that is completely new and confusing to the reader, it can be especially challenging to take a lot of time in the beginning to set up a convincing description of this strange new world. You may want characters, you may want conflict and things galloping forward, so that the reader has something dramatic to draw her into the confusing new world. It takes skill to do exposition subtly without stopping the forward pace of the story, but it's absolutely essential. You have to create a convincing world or a future with enough connection to the present to persuade us it is a possible outcome of where we are.

The following excerpt is from *He, She and It*, and takes place in the year 2059. It describes the clothing styles of the time, in particular those favored by Yakimura-Steichen, the multi-national corporation that employs Shira, the novel's protagonist:

Y-S had fierce injunctions concerning what parts of the human body should be displayed in what circumstances. It went with rigid sex roles—not at work, of course, for no one could afford such nonsense, but in every other sector of living. Women dressing for dinner often bared their breasts at Y-S functions, but the legs were always modestly covered to midcalf. The back was usually bare; the standard business suit, with its deeply cut back, was designed to show both men's and women's musculature and fitness. However, it was the custom to keep ears and nape covered for women, who were required to wear their hair at least shoulder length, often artificially straightened. Malkah, Shira's grandmother, had cut Shira's to a sleek cap just last week. At Uni-Par, her friend Gadi's multi, nudity was a sign of status. The higher you were on the pyramid, the less you wore, the better to show off the results of the newest cosmetic surgery performed on your body. At Aramco-Ford, women wore yards of material and short transparent symbolic veils.

You have to immerse yourself in the world you are creating. If your protagonists lay eggs instead of bearing live children, how does that change their social structure and their gender roles? What kind of social world would intelligent creatures with wings inhabit? If you have three sexes or, if like some aphids, you alternate many generations of asexual reproduction with an occasional generation of sexual reproduction, what kind of changes does that create for courtship, families—if there are any? They would certainly be quite different from ours. But the members of those clans would probably have just as many problems with members of their group as we do. They would be close to some and distant or hostile with others. They would experience conflict over direction and over resources. You have to put on that costume and find out through your imagination what the life of your protagonist is like.

The worst science fiction is usually that in which gadgets and pseudo-scientific babble are predominant. The characters are stock figures—heroic captain, mad scientist, macho weapons wielder, wise old explainer.

Again, in this context, you must find a language that convinces us that these are not people from our time or our world without obfuscating meaning or annoying the reader with impenetrable fudge. You might drop in an occasional made up word for some object strange to us or some alien ritual. You make the meaning clear by context. You don't go:

"Xpldnik waved his tentacle at the merkplod, the viewing window of his floating house." Much better to say, "Xpldnik slithered over to the merkplod to stare out at the fast approaching object, which looked at first glance like an asteroid but was pursuing an erratic path, now up, now down, now to this side and then to that."

In spite of Gene Roddenberry's optimism about the future, it is unlikely that all our societal and personal problems will have been solved. In human history, every solution breeds new problems. The invention of agriculture meant far more people could be fed, but also that people used up land, often ate a less varied diet that gave them deficiency diseases and came into conflict over arable land with other groups wanting the same croplands. Often in interesting science fiction, one variable is changed, and we see how everything changes—but we see it through characters that we can identify with, no matter how different their bodies, experiences or social structure may be. Remember that the fiction part is what makes the speculative part function: believable characters, hard working and interesting dialog, good pacing, incidents that move things along, a vivid setting, actions that reveal character and draw us into the story.

Loosening the Imagination

The line between science fiction and fantasy is blurry. Some novels, such as sword and sorcery tales, are more clearly fantasy, while tales that depend upon changes in technology for their variable are obviously science fiction. But lots of works fall somewhere in between. The borders overlap and labeling doesn't teach us that much. Isaac Asimov, father of science fiction, said that all such works fall into three categories: *What if? If only . . .* and *If this continues!* The first is more speculative, the second more utopian and the third, dystopian.

Many writers are afraid of fantasy. However, it can be liberating to your imagination to move beyond the mundane and the realistic. As a child, you probably entertained yourself or consoled yourself with stories in which you had all the powers of a superhero. Of course the best comic book superheroes, such as Spiderman, have problems as well as powers. Recently DC Comics decided to introduce real character-changing tragedy into the sagas of its trademark heroes, like Superman, Batman and the Elongated Man. They wanted their heroes to grow in a grim time. Nowadays even Superman gets depressed.

We have all felt like aliens at times—dreamed we were adopted by our birth family while our true parents—much superior and more sympathetic and loving in every way—were elsewhere. We had been switched at birth or stolen away from our proper family. Our true family has far more of everything we desire and will simply adore us instead of being disappointed by our gender, our looks, our ability to excel in school or at athletics. Similarly, we have all at times felt out of place—that we did not or could not fit in with a group whether at a job, in school, socially. Introducing an alien into the contemporary world is a frequently used way to indulge in social criticism. Why do we behave as if we were the slaves of mechanical beings who consume petroleum products and excrete toxic gasses? Why do we walk around wearing advertising logos on our clothing? Are we paid for this? We pay them to advertise their products? How peculiar. Why do we pay those who care for our children so little if we truly value our children and pay a thousand times as much to men who toss a ball through a small hoop mounted on a backboard? There are many observations an alien can make about the habits, mores and values of a culture. There is an inherent pathos in being out of place or out of time that can make such a character sympathetic. But such a character must feel vivid and well defined and not merely be a mouthpiece for the author's opinions and observations. She or he should have foibles of their own.

At times we have all experienced suspicion of those normally our nearest and dearest, our family, our friends. We have all at times suspected that somehow people were ganging up on us or talking behind our back or not what they have always seemed. Here is a source of horror fantasy that you might want to develop. Sometimes these feelings of suspicion and mistrust are best explored in such a genre.

Sometimes we can more easily write about very intimate things by transferring the situation and transposing it to another time, another place, another type of being. It might be too painful to deal with incest or abuse, but not if the character is a slave in South Carolina or a child prostitute in Victorian London or a captured sentient feline on another planet. Perhaps it is easier to deal with some traumas in fantasy, where the father-perpetrator is an ogre or a warlock, a monster to the child supposedly under his protection. Many writers have commented on *Buffy, The Vampire Slayer* in which Josh Whedon used vampires, werewolves and demons as metaphors for the emotional violence that so many of us experienced in high school. Indeed, we felt lucky to survive it somewhat intact. Some people never do get out of high school but spend their lives trying to get in with the right clique or win the popularity contests that are high school elections. I can imagine a short story in which young people literally cannot escape or graduate from high school but are trapped in it not for three or four years, but for an eternity of boredom, shame, ostracism, meaningless competition.

Fantasy and science fiction both offer alternate ways of exploring experiences that you may not wish to tackle baldly or head on. You might as a writer come at science fiction or fantasy from the viewpoint of exploring alternatives to various aspects of our society. You might feel that something very bad is going to develop from a particular trend of technology or social control or use of resources. Maybe you want to make global warming and its effects real, as I did in *He, She and It.* Maybe you want to see what would happen to an information dependent world if some solar or asteroid phenomenon knocked out all computers. Whatever, you need research but you need imagination even more. Suppose fundamentalist Christians took over the United States and could create the kind of theocratic society they long for: Margaret Atwood's *The Handmaid's Tale.*

Maybe you want to envision a more enlightened society, one that offers a lot more of something than our own—equality, harmony, peace, whatever. Utopian fiction is a related genre. It tends to be produced when a number of people believe that things can change. It is a visionary form of fiction but again, whether it works or not depends not only on the quality of ideas and inspiration involved, but in the creation of believable characters in some sort of ongoing action in a setting that we come to accept as plausible and real to us. The vice of much utopian fiction is being too static and far too expositional. All such works have to function as fiction before they can do anything else.

Maybe you just want to play: suppose we had the power to change shapes at will. Suppose we could live for five hundred years. Suppose we had both lungs and gills. Suppose we could read each other's thoughts. Suppose sickness was eradicated. Suppose we could choose special genetic traits for our offspring. Suppose we could freely clone ourselves. Suppose suddenly we learned to communicate with other mammals or birds, one on one. What kind of society, what kind of life, what kind of people and families and jobs and problems would result?

Sometimes writers create fantastic worlds peopled by dragons or talking horses or sentient trees. You can create any kind of world you can make us believe in, provided it is created with consistent, vivid detail and peopled with beings who intrigue us with events and problems and situations that engage us. Loosening your imagination can only help you as a writer, and perhaps some version of these related genres may be your forte.

Exercise:

Invent or select a superhero—probably easier, so long as you are familiar with her or him either from comic books or film—and tell a story in which his or her powers cannot solve the problem with which your hero is faced.

Exercise:

Create an alien and put her or him on Earth. What kind of society does your protagonist come from? What does your protagonist expect from Earth and how are they surprised? What strikes them as good and what strikes them as terrible and what do they find ridiculous? Of course these reactions will issue from your protagonist's own values, the values of her or his culture, interacting with our societies.

Exercise:

Imagine a protagonist in a situation where suddenly she or he becomes convinced that everyone around them is lying. What you are doing in an exercise like this is extrapolating from a common fear or disappointment or kind of everyday paranoia to a more metaphorical form.

MYSTERIES

Books that are shelved with mysteries may or may not concern a mystery. Crime novels are included in this class: we follow the perpetrator rather than the investigator. We know from the onset who done it or rather who is about to do it, but we follow the progress of the crime and then the aftermath, the pursuit, usually but not inevitably, the arrest and perhaps the trial. There have been stories of successful criminals, often a kind of Robin Hood, outside the law but not outside our sympathies. The story of a heist falls into this category.

A similar story concerned with process is the police procedural. This requires a great deal of knowledge of how various police departments operate and how the different types of investigations proceed. There are useful manuals for writers about police methods and forensic methodology, but it would help immensely in making such a book believable and fresh to have some inside knowledge. No type of story so exposes the writer who is faking it as the police procedural. There are, of course, subgenres focusing not on the police but on a coroner or a forensic expert. No matter what kind of procedural you are interested in writing, you must know the field you are dealing with thoroughly.

The classic mystery involves how a crime is committed as well as who committed it and why. There have been many fashions in private detectives over the decades—the scientific amateur who is more observant than any fly (Sherlock Holmes); the gentleman who dabbles in solving mysteries and runs mental circles around the police (Lord Peter of Dorothy Sayers' many novels); the noir private eye originated by Dashiell Hammett; the apparently ditzy old lady who knows human nature and has the brain of a guillotine (Agatha Christie's Miss Marple); the tough young woman (Sarah Peretsky's V. I. Warshawski) or even the very young woman ever up for adventure (Nancy Drew); the able but contemporarily sensitive male (Robert Parker's Spenser). There are hundreds of variations on each of these. Some mysteries have as their protagonist a policeman without belonging to the procedural subgenre. Think of P. D. James's Adam Dalgliesh, who writes poetry.

Another way to plot a mystery is to involve as detective an "innocent," in the sense we use innocent bystander. Someone who accidentally sees a crime or stumbles on the results of it or otherwise becomes entangled uses her or his innate intelligence or their special knowledge (as an insurance actuary, as a librarian, as a whale watch captain, as a landscape gardener) to solve the mystery. The mystery comes to the protagonist, rather than it being her or his profession to solve the problem. Maybe a partner, a lover, a family member is killed or attacked. Maybe something is taken from the house.

Avoid clichés. The hard boiled detective has been done to death, yet every few months at the press, we get a barely updated version. As with any other type of writing, if you want to write detective stories, read detective stories. It might be best to start with what you know. If you work in a flower shop, why not have a florist detective. If you work at the university as Amanda Cross—Carolyn Heilbrun—did, or Lev Raphael, then you might do best to use that setting for your murders or other crimes.

Of course there are crossovers—a number of writers use historical settings for their mysteries. An archeologist sets her crimes in Egypt. A historian uses New Amsterdam. Umberto Eco's *The Name of the Rose* was set in 1327 in a Benedictine abbey. These have a double appeal—to lovers of mysteries and to lovers of historical fiction. Plus with good details and an interesting period detective, they feel quite fresh.

The more individualized the detective is, the more of a past and private life and social ambience she or he has, the more we will be drawn into the story. If the detective does not engage us, it is rare that the plot will. Plotting is more important to the mystery than to any of the other genres we have discussed, but without good characterization, we will probably lose interest; even if we read the book to solve the puzzle, we will forget it five minutes later. We certainly won't go looking for more books by that author.

You must decide whether your detective is a loner, whether she or he has a partner, a sidekick, a superior, a love interest, a competitive rival. Putting your detective into at least a few important relationships often makes him or her more interesting and enables you also to show their character rather than telling us about it. If they have no relationships, then why? Husband tragically killed in a botched operation—or murdered. Maybe the murder was never solved. Maybe a subplot concerns a resolution of that old painful mystery.

If you are going to use court scenes in your story, please, please visit the relevant type of court. Don't base your notion of what goes on in courtrooms from what you have seen on television. Reality is quite different on all levels. I have sat in on trials in Barnstable Court, in Superior Court in Boston, in night court in Manhattan, among others, when I was using these places. It is surprising how many manuscripts we see in which it is painfully clear that the writer has never been in a real courtroom. Don't fake it when it is so easy just to go in and watch and listen. Follow a case through from beginning to end, or sit through a morning or afternoon of minor cases, one after the other. As soon as you get home, take notes. Even if it is far more mundane—a friend who is a courtroom reporter for a large newspaper describes his beat as very routine: bad people doing bad things—the reality is very different than the TV version of justice.

Befriend a lawyer of the relevant type and go to court when they are defending a client or pursuing a civil case. Ask questions. As we recommended in the chapter on research, learn how to interview. Never be hesitant to ask questions. I have had a few informants who stonewalled me over the years, but ninety percent of the time, people are delighted to talk with you about their work experiences. (Here's a conversation starter: Ask them whether they believe TV or movies get it right.)

If you are writing about a specific place, even if you know it well, it would be a good idea to revisit it. If you've never been there, get there. Travel books and guides are no replacement for on-the-spot looking, listening, smelling, touching. The kind of clouds, the kind of light, the architecture, the feel of the streets, the street vendors and their foods, the noise levels at different times of day and night, the kind of vehicles and how they are driven and how they are parked. You may not need more than a day or two in a place, but you need that actual soaking up of sensory details to make your local color work. Readers of mysteries can be truly annoyed if you misplace a building or screw up the orientation of a street or move a park upriver. Maybe you think the copy editor will catch these blunders if you do get your novel published; don't count on it.

In the chapter on Description, we talk about the uses and abuses of description. When a detective is trying to solve a mystery, the details of the rooms and workplaces of suspects are extremely important.

In mysteries even more than any other type of novel, the ending is of crucial importance. Many stories simply trail off. Things stop. We may or may not learn the fate of the characters. But with a mystery, the ending must solve the crime and finger the perpetrator. The end must satisfy. It must issue from the plot, from what we have learned along the way, and it must make perfect sense to the reader. The reader must be persuaded that the solution is a genuine one and answers all the critical questions. If the ending is not satisfactory (the famous cliché, "the butler did it"), then the book did not work as a mystery and the reader is correct to feel cheated. You must persuade your readers that the detective has figured out the who, how and why and that they have laid it out in a manner that convinces you.

We should as readers not be able to guess quickly who did it and/or how, or whatever the mystery is, but we should have a fair shot at figuring it out. We should feel that the clues were there and that if we missed them, it was our fault and not the writer's. In other words, either we guessed correctly or we feel we could have if only we had been more alert. That satisfies the reader. A wild card ending does not. You cannot introduce a new character or one who only appeared on page 70 as the unmasked perpetrator. Whatever your ending, it must be plausible. If, at the end, we find out that there was no murder but Katherine fell down the steps because she had a brain tumor and lost her sense of balance, we must feel that that, too, was a possible, if improbable, outcome; and the clues to that situation have to be carefully planted.

Clues are extremely important. You want to figure them out before you begin so that you can drop them along the way, not too obviously but fairly. An interesting device is the clue that apparently points to one suspect, but upon much closer examination or future development implicates another.

Now whether you are writing a police procedural or a detective novel, you have to deal with motive. You cannot simply beg the question. "Otis killed Pamela, we have proved that, but who can say what he was thinking of." No way. You, the author, have to know Otis through and through and you have to make his motives and his actions plausible to us, so that once we come to understand Otis, we believe him capable of bludgeoning poor Pamela; or we see why he believed himself in a situation so tight and hopeless, the only way out was through Pamela. Or we see that his world view was such that he held Pamela responsible for everything bad and disappointing in his life. It won't work to present him as sane and responsible and then on page 301, have him revealed as a mad psychopath who killed Pamela because he felt like doing so.

So you had better figure out a great deal before you sit down to write a mystery: What is the crime? How is it discovered? Who did it? What were the criminal's motives? Where did the crime occur? Who was close enough and with enough apparent motive to be one of the suspects? Who witnessed what? What other clues do you want to insert into your narrative at what points in its unfolding? What is your detective like? What brings them on the scene—their profession, their connections, their relationship to the victim or to one or more of the suspects, simple curiosity, fear, anger? What leads will prove to be red herrings or dead ends? Which might appear to point one way initially and then later implicate someone else? How will your detective figure out the perpetrator? How will she or he confront or arrest or otherwise bring the criminal to justice? Are you going to stop with that discovery or go on into trial?

Thus the mystery is one of the least improvisational of forms. The historical novel is grounded in research; the mystery may well be also grounded in research, but plotting is far more important than in any of the other branches of fiction we have discussed. You need to know exactly where you're going before you begin so that you can bring the reader along with you all the way to your denouement when the truth is revealed.

The justice meted out at the end has to satisfy our sense of justice. There are occasions when the detective will uncover the perpetrator but will let him or her go. Sherlock Holmes did that several times. He appointed himself judge and jury and gave a sentence of exile. That was because he did not believe justice would be served by punishing the perpetrator; in some sense, he felt the crime was justified. This is unusual but not unheard of. What is universal is that whatever end the perpetrator comes to, we the readers should find it just.

Exercise:

Invent a detective. She or he should be a fresh take on the role. Is your detective a professional or amateur? What time period do they live in? Historical or contemporary? Where does the story take place? Write a short scene in which your detective is set into action questioning one of the suspects or nosing about for clues. Reveal your detective's character by their action in the scene, by the questions they ask, and their attitudes towards others.

Exercise:

Attempt to approach someone in the crime profession to ask them questions about their work. Some may be suspicious but others are proud of what they do, feel underappreciated and are happy to talk about their expertise. Often they feel that no writer has ever captured the reality of their profession. Try a couple of cops, or a coroner. (Ira used to strike up conversations with the local medical examiner at the post office and was invited back to his office and shown decades of files and morbid snapshots of crime scenes. The old Doc was eager to share his knowledge and prove his expertise.)

12

Writing Short Stories

Inexperienced writers often ask where a published writer's inspiration comes from, as if expecting to hear that if you take a certain chemical or say a particular mantra or read a certain how-to book, an angel or muse will appear and hand you a story to complete. If you become a published writer, you will find that people ask you, inevitably someone at every reading, "Where do you get your ideas?" Where stories come from doesn't matter.

Ideas come from the evening paper or the six o'clock news. Ideas come from scraps of conversation overhead in restaurants and airports. Ideas come from people we observe who look intriguing, little scenes we witness whose meaning we often cannot even guess but that we use to build stories around. I once wrote a short story prompted by the drawing of a woman on the cover of a paperback of no other interest. I still have no idea why that drawing caught my attention but I began at once to create the character that would inhabit her and the story that grew around her.

Ideas rarely come from the stories people insist on telling you at parties. "You want to write about my Aunt Edna," they say, buttonholing you by the hors d'oeuvres. "You should write a book about her. Her life is so fascinating. She married the same husband three times."

I always suggest they write the story themselves. We are all drawn to certain stories and simply not led to enter others willingly. Trying to forcefeed someone a story is useless. I cannot remember a single occasion in all my years of writing novels and stories when such an insistently told anecdote resulted in anything but mild or excruciating boredom, but even if the story proves interesting to hear, it does not follow that it would make a successful short story for me—or you.

One source of course is the great storehouse of received tales, legends, biographies, fairy and folk tales, and myths. I have dealt with several myths, including the golem, the artificial being of kabbalah. It was a story told to me by my grandmother when I was a little girl and it stuck with me. It is a tale rooted in Jewish history and ghetto storytelling and came to me already trailing centuries of connotation and meaning. Stories you heard in your childhood, whether of people in your family or imaginary beings, tend to have a particular resonance that bears exploring.

Some stories may not come from our own heritage but still speak to us. Perhaps Faust has meaning for you and you can do something entirely new with it. You have a new angle on selling your soul to the devil, not an uncommon deal to imagine in a society obsessed with wealth. Perhaps *The Picture of Dorian Gray* speaks to you about contemporary vanity. Maybe you just have a new take on Dimmesdale in *The Scarlet Letter* or what one of Hemingway's women was thinking.

Now while the tale of the buttonholer's Aunt Edna and her repeating husband may be flat as old seltzer to you, your own Aunt Edna is someone else again. Family stories are a rich mother lode of goodies to mine, whether you are writing memoir or fiction. All those stories told to you as a kid or overheard while the adults were gossiping are made of gold and someday you will probably use at least some of them. If you can get people in your family to gossip again to renew your acquaintance with those tales, that can be useful, but it's the way that you remember them that counts. Maybe you got the stories mixed up. Years ago I conflated two stories I had heard about men in my then partner's place of business. I turned them in my head into one man and wrote about him. The product was good, but it came from misunderstanding. Finally that doesn't matter, if the way you remember it is what speaks to you, means something about foibles or forgiveness or the role of accident or the terrible cost of revenge. Whatever made those stories stick in your brain like golden burrs, they are yours and you need them.

In many ways, short stories have more in common with poems than they do with novels. I cannot imagine a phrase sticking in my mind (say, Passing headlights lit the rain spangles in her hair) and writing a novel. Novels require more of an architectural sense, a theme, strong and well-understood major characters, a well defined setting. But poems and short fiction could easily be ignited by such a phrase and proceed from there. Anything can spark a poem or a short story. I remember one poem that came from mishearing a phrase in a Talking Heads song, realizing I had changed it, and then taking the new phrase I had invented and writing a poem with it.

You mine your own life as well as those of people around you for incidents that might make a good short story. Years after the fact, I found a story in a small event of betrayal from a teacher I had trusted in high school—two decades afterward when I could see his point of view as well as my own resentment. I could make a good story of it because I no longer wanted to confront him, strangle him, turn him to dust. That's why Wordsworth recommended emotion recollected in tranquility. If you are still so angry at someone you want to hurt them with your story, you will seldom produce a story worth the time and effort of anyone else to read.

Often writers who haven't read much in the way of contemporary short stories have the notion that a story is supposed to end with a surprise, a twist, an ironic coda. They probably read O'Henry in high school. While Maupassant and O'Henry wrote in that manner, the modern short story issues out of Chekhov and is not as concerned with plot as it is with character or ambience. It may well have a plot, as Hemingway's fine short stories tend to. The most primitive short story is the tale. Once upon a time there lived a prince, but he was very poor and lacked everything a prince should have. Tales often have little character development. Often there are stock characters we are to take on face value—the kind old lady with the magic potion, the evil step-mother, the talking horse or cat who will serve as a helper. How can Puss in Boots talk? Because he is Puss in Boots—that's all the answer you will get.

In some of James Tiptree, Jr.'s short stories (James Tiptree, Jr. was the pen name of Alice Bradley Sheldon, who felt her science fiction would be best served with a male face on it), it is the situation and what happens because of it that forms the meat of the story—a spaceship of aliens arrives, but they are all women. How do the government and the media react?

A little tale well told often can work because of the narrator's strong voice. We read on just as we listen when a raconteur is telling us a story. The voice, the language, the style are far more important to catching and holding our interest than the stuff of the tale itself. But a good tale told by a fine narrator (Twain's jumping frog) will always get our attention.

A short story might present to the reader an unusual character. But however unique Eudora Welty's characters may strike us as being, they are firmly embedded in a place, in a social context. They have a past that impinges on the present; they have relationships and opinions and desires. Characters are most interesting to us when they are not stationary but rather in some kind of motion, internal, external or, preferably, both. Simple eccentricity may suffice for a dinner party anecdote, but it will not hold the reader's attention in a short story.

Many stories center on a particular slot of time in the life of a protagonist—anything from the moment before and the moment during a traffic accident to a family meal, a power breakfast or a business luncheon, a walk on the beach with an ex, a shift at work—a fireman's shift or a plumber's day. It might be a weekend getaway for a family in trouble or it might be the first weekend together of a tentative couple.

Most short stories use a single viewpoint. It's cleaner and less complicated. We know whose head we are in and, after all, we have a limited amount of time to spend looking out through their eyes and trying on their clothes and walking in their shoes. Occasionally you may find a story that alternates viewpoints—say, the experiences of each member of the couple who are trying out that ski weekend together. Occasionally you may find a story in which the viewpoint keeps shifting, following a particular arc of events. Perhaps you are writing a series of vignettes centered around the particularly hideous vase that is given as a present in situations requiring a gift where none is truly heartfelt. The vase makes its way from anniversary present in honor of a miserable marriage to a gift to a hated mother-in-law to the wedding of a former lover, and so on. Each character introduced should be linked to the one before and the one coming up next. It's a bit artificial, but it has been done countless times with various objects.

But basically you are going to write a short story in one viewpoint. It might be that of your protagonist or it might be someone more peripherally involved. The viewpoint character may be viewing a disaster happening to someone else, as in the story "Rose," by Andre Dubus, in which a man tells the heartbreaking story of a woman who frequents his neighborhood tavern. If you want humor in a disastrous situation—a wedding that is mismanaged from beginning to end—you may want the distancing of someone who is neither the bride nor groom nor other partner. The most common choice is that of the major character, but that's a decision you need to make and make correctly for the story you are relating.

A perfectly ordinary workday or Sunday morning can be the focus of a short story. There need not be anything extraordinary happening, although there can be. "My God, Ruthie, there's a tiger in the vegetable garden." That will certainly get our attention, but where you go from there had better be convincing. Drama occurs whenever there is conflict or tension or unfulfilled desire. Simply watching a spouse chew cereal can arouse a towering rage in a partner who is already fed up. There can be powerful angst or festering resentment at that breakfast table. Every so often you read in the paper about someone murdering a family member over a TV program or a taco eaten that was being saved for lunch. Money is always good for a struggle. Sex withheld or demanded or unsatisfactory or just plain boring causes a lot of friction. Sometimes you need only get two characters together and let them go at it. Much of what they will be angry or upset about will not be the matter of what they say to each other. They may argue about who left the milk out when they are really arguing about whether one loves the other any longer.

So a particular time slot can be an organizing factor for a story. The setting can also be an important factor in a short story. We are on a plane during heavy turbulence when a passenger gets out of his seat and begins screaming. Now this is only interesting if we have established something else going on. The protagonist is flying out for a crucial job interview. She needs the money badly, but she really doesn't want to do that type of work. She actually enjoys teaching and would much rather do that. Somehow the crazy passenger and the other passengers' responses and our protagonist's actions or failure to take action will relate to her dilemma.

An event may serve as the foundation for a story. Again, the event is not the story but the setting for the story—a setting, yes, but at best a very active setting, one that channels, interferes with, facilitates the action of the story. The event could be a birthday party, a wedding, a funeral, a celebration, a retirement party, a political meeting or town meeting, a demonstration, a hearing, a trial, a fundraiser, a bake sale, a shower, the visit of relatives from Poland or San Diego, a recital, a soccer match, a dance. Sometimes a story is about what does not happen rather than what does.

A young woman spends an inordinate amount of time and money she does not have for an outfit to wear to a fundraiser for a local animal shelter where she is hoping to hook up with a young man she is convinced is interested in her as much as she is in him. It is how this does not happen that is the meat of the story—whether it is because she has been misreading his cues, because he turns out to be someone she doesn't want to become involved with, or because she flubs the occasion so totally that she alienates him or makes a fool of herself. The events of the fund raiser should help precipitate what happens and what does not happen.

James Joyce called the moment of insight that a short story may deliver an "epiphany." It is a moment of Aha! for the character or for the reader. The protagonist may never understand what we grasp, or may do so. But whatever you do, do not call attention to that moment of enlightenment or understanding by labeling it or explaining it. It has to happen from the events in the story and not from your explanation. It might be a moment of sublime connection. It might be a totally cynical moment in which everything turns to crap. It might be a moment of personal insight: I am not the person I thought I was. Things are not going to be as I expected. It might be an insight into a relationship that the protagonist is in or has been in—the sudden feeling that all along the protagonist was fooling herself about the nature of the connection—or a terrible sense of loss over something easily discarded or broken off. There is a precipitating incident and that is the crux of the story.

Beware, in the story of an epiphany, that the character does not change immediately. We all have insights that perhaps should change our lives but that at the most modify our usual behavior a tiny amount. His friend, Bob, with whom Jake has strongly identified for years, drops dead suddenly of a heart attack just as they are rising from their standard Saturday afternoon barbeque. Jake recognizes in that moment that since they have the same habits and lead very similar lives, this may be his fate. Now he may resolve to change his life completely, but he is unlikely to stop drinking with his friends at the bar where they always meet after work, or to begin working on the triathlon. He sees his fate and might make some modification of behavior, but a complete change of lifestyle is unlikely. Scrooge may change completely, although some of us may suspect that within a year he will be back pinching his pennies until they bend, but don't rely on that. Nobody is going to believe it these days.

Some stories come from taking someone and sending them through a quest or journey—the basic Joseph Campbell myth distilled into a short fiction. It might be physical. It might be emotional. It might be spiritual. But the protagonist goes from A to B or at least attempts to go from A to B, even if B is not defined or understood beforehand. There are obstacles. There are interruptions. But in a short story, there cannot be too many of these. I think in general the quest is best pursued in a novel or a novella, at least.

Perhaps Charley goes in search of the strange, or perhaps the strange comes in search of Charley. There is a knock at the door. Someone comes into the tidy house of Charley's life. The nanny arrives, and she is not at all what the couple expected. Mary Poppins or the seductive young woman who turns the house and the marriage upside down or simply a judgmental outsider who forces the protagonist to see her or his life in a different and perhaps disturbing way. The salesman comes to the door selling love potions. The fortuneteller beckons the young woman into her tent at the fair and gives her images of a totally different future. The hitchhiker changes the fate of everyone in the car. An intruder creates a crisis for a family—an escaped convict, a fugitive, a lost child, a runaway, a battered wife—even a stray dog or a deer caught in a shed.

A story does not have to follow a continuous narrative. You might decide to write a short story about a marriage in which you give moments over a fifteen-year period. They are a single take at a single instant, but incidents and moments that are suggestive and reveal the tensions and the direction the relationship is taking. I can imagine a story about a house in which there are the moments of occupation and desertion, of moving in and moving out of renovation and decay. There are many ways to structure a story. A series of quick takes over time is one of those ways.

One thing to beware of in any short story is too much: too many incidents involving your protagonist that make essentially the same point; too many minor characters; too many settings; too much of anything, including "fine" writing. Keep it clean. Keep it directed. A first person voice in a novel can launch into riffs and digressions that, if well done, can charm the reader and give us insight into the speaker and the world of that speaker. But in a short story such digressions are usually fatal. Decide early on how many characters you actually need. Don't put anyone in "because they were actually there" or because you think they're a cute or fascinating character. Again, the novel has space for exploration of cul-de-sacs and scenic viewing areas, but the short story does not. Keep to the number of characters you truly need. The short story is a little box into which nothing that does not function should be placed. Not a great metaphor, but you get the point. Keep out what isn't essential.

Another type of short story is the parody. Maybe you are really fed up with a particular writer—you've had it up to here with the writer of the moment who is the darling of all the critics (this year) or the endless admirers of Dashiell Hammett or the later Doris Lessing leaden science fiction novels. Writing an entire novel of parody is a lot of time to put into what is essentially lighthearted but trenchant literary criticism. You may even be parodying a television series. Whatever it is, a short story is the perfect length for making your point. There is no point parodying something few people have seen or read, but anything common to the canon or to pop culture is fodder for good parody.

I have warned you about cramming too much into a short story, but there is also the problem of too little. We see stories in which nothing happens in a boring manner. Three college buddies are drinking together and talking of How Life Sucks and they can't get paid for doing anything they want and they can't get laid. Now such a story sometimes attempts to make a point by dragging in a one-legged, blind orphan to show them how lucky they are or how plucky she is, or maybe they just go on and on philosophizing in a manner that that the author thought full of depth and insight. Either way, it isn't life that sucks, but the story certainly does. If you want insight in your story, build it in—don't have Joe tell Harry about the bright continuum that is all of sentient and nonsentient life.

Now in general I stopped being willing to put up with epistolary storytelling about the time I finished reading Richardson's *Clarissa*, but there are always writers who can breathe fresh life into a tired form. For some years now e-mail has replaced the long-awaited arrival of the postman. There has to be a strong voice and you have to be willing to put up with narration all the way, rather than the creation of scenes we usually insist on. A classic example of the form is "Address Unknown" by Kressmann Taylor, a story consisting of the letters exchanged between two business partners, an American Jew and a German-born Aryan who returns to Weimar Germany.

Most short stories are basically realistic, but they don't have to be. Kafka's "Metamorphosis" is one of the most famous and successful short stories ever written, but you won't find a lot of your acquaintances waking up as cockroaches (however many had families who made them feel like lower forms of life). You must establish character strongly and quickly and you must create a setting and situation we believe in, even if it is on Beta Omicron 4 and in a hive of paper wasps or suburbia where James Thurber's character looks out and sees a unicorn in the garden one morning. William Gibson's "The Gernsback Continuum" is the story of a photographer who penetrates "a fine membrane, a membrane of probability" and finds himself living in the future that was projected by designers and media futurists of the late1930s, where fleets of zeppelins whiz overhead and people eat by means of pills containing all they require. This is an example of a short story that begins with an idea: What if you took all those long exploded projections of the future and made them real and put a confused contemporary into that world? Because the protagonist is believable and the world is vividly created, the story, although idea-driven, works.

Characters have to have pasts as well as current desires, fears, angers, habits, hobbies. We can be given the past in an image that has a brief memory attached to it. When Gwen saw the hammer Bernie had set on the window sill, a wave of cold slid through her. Her father's large hand grasped the hammer and swung it over her mother's small pale hand. Or we can do a full flashback. When Gwen saw the hammer Bernie had set on the window sill, she felt a chill creep through her. She was in the kitchen of the third floor apartment in the triple-decker in Dorchester where she had spent her first ten years. She smelled bacon scorching on the stove and toast burning. Her father, huge as a house to her, had a hammer in his hand. He had been driving nails into a loose doorjamb. Now he was screaming at her mother, who had let breakfast go in her fear and cowered in the chair, her hands clutching a napkin on the table. And so forth.

You have to decide how important it is to set the full scene in a flashback or whether you simply want an image to jog an instant's memory. It depends on the pacing of your story and on how important what you are transmitting in the flashback is to the reader. But do not, in a short story, get bogged down in flashbacks. I read an unsuccessful story recently in which there were flashbacks inside of flashbacks, like endless parentheses enclosing other parentheses. I could not follow the story or get any sense of forward momentum. With every step forward, we seemed to slip three steps back.

Sometimes in a short story the setting is merely sketched. It is a kitchen in a railroad flat in Chicago. We are given a few choice details—the El roars past at eye level, the waterbugs are climbing the wall by the sink—but that's about it. In other stories, the setting is far more important, at least some aspect of it. If a protagonist is cold or hot and that matters to the story, make the reader shiver or sweat. It is hot in the first paragraph, it is hot on page 2, it is hot on page 3, and so forth. You keep the heat on with details, not with labeling. The asphalt is sticky underfoot. The leaves on the elm are drooping. A dog lies stretched long and lean to the earth of the yard to extract what coolness it can. Sweat runs down your protagonist's back and pools at the belt of her shorts. Her hair feels lank and limp. Her glasses keep sliding down her nose. A drop of sweat gets into her eye and stings. The back collar of her camp shirt is clammy against her neck. The more sharply you observe, the better and the more convincing your details will be to the reader.

If there is a storm going on in the story, make it continue, make it increase or lessen, make it bang on the events of the story. Do not forget once the events in your story move forward and your characters are in conflict that you still need whatever setting you gave them to go on doing whatever it is doing: burning, blowing, snowing. Think of the use of snow in James Joyce's "The Dead," "silver and dark, falling obliquely against the lamp-light," all through the story, until the very last sentence, "falling faintly through the universe and faintly falling, like the descent of their last end, upon all the living and the dead."

Be sure when you pick a setting that it is appropriate. On-site research never hurts. I once set a story in a part of France with which I am not familiar. I had a landscape painter fall in love with the area. My surprise and my chagrin were neck in neck when I visited and discovered the area has all the charm of Gary, Indiana or the Meadowlands of New Jersey as viewed from the turnpike. Fortunately I was only in third draft, and I moved my story to a more appropriate landscape.

When you are told to write about what you know, it doesn't mean you cannot write about death if you haven't died yet, or childbirth if you have never bred, or murder if you have never committed it. Surely you have imagined doing so, unless you are far more saintly than I am. We all find in ourselves myriad characters and we know ourselves to be capable of far more than we have had the opportunity or the necessity of living out. It means do your research. Combine empathy with imagination and observation. Make real and believable characters, see first-hand what you can, read up on the rest. You are not writing a guidebook or a how-to manual. You want your details to work to create verisimilitude. Often a few well-chosen details are better than pages of humdrum description. But they have to be accurate and telling details. They should persuade us that you know what you are writing about, that those little factoids are accurate, and they have set the mood of the story, its ambience.

When you begin, you need to let us know where we are and who is acting or talking; we need to have a clear sense in whose viewpoint we are operating. We need a sense of the era—right now, one hundred years in the future or in the past, ten thousand years ago or last year, in the 60s or in the 80s or in the 20s. We need to know whether we're in Center City Detroit or in Rio or in Dakar. We have to know whether we're among Neanderthals or giant grasshoppers or soccer moms. Surprising us at the end of the story that these characters were giant grasshoppers raising their young is not a great idea.

Finally, there are no rules for writing short stories. You learn best by reading lots and lots of them and asking yourself as you go through each one, what makes this story interesting? Why do I care about the protagonist? How do the diction and the narrative style add or detract from the flow of the story? Do I believe in these characters and their problems? Why or why not? Do I believe in the ending? Does it satisfy me?

Exercise:

Think of a family story that you remember from your childhood. First write it as you understood it as a child. Then tell the same story as you understand it as an adult—with sexuality, if involved, or financial aspects and the motivation of the relevant characters. Which story do you find more interesting? Can you tell the story from the child's point of view but indicate by indirection and what the other characters do, say and don't say, what is really happening as you see it from your adult understanding?

Exercise:

Go out and sit in a public place. Eavesdrop. People watch. When something you hear or see intrigues you, write a story about what you imagine that conversation or that little vignette you observed came from and led to. People the scene with a character or two of your invention and create a scenario of your own.

Exercise:

Take a long narrative with which you are familiar such as *The Odyssey* or *Don Quixote* and fashion a short story from one of the adventures of the protagonist. Perhaps you want to change the viewpoint. It is a different story from Circe's standpoint.

13

Titles

Titles are the first thing a reader encounters in a short story, while looking through the table of contents of a magazine or a review or anthology. A title is what the prospective buyer sees when browsing titles in a bookstore or a library. A catchy title is important to an author because often that is all a reader retains from a book review, whether favorable or unfavorable. Weeks or months later when that reader is browsing thousands of titles in a book store or desperately looking for something to read to get through a layover in an airport, she'll think, Oh, I've heard of that one. A title is name recognition.

Think, would you, when picking up a magazine, turn to a story with the title "Summer Encounter" or one called, "Daddy and the Hammerhead Shark?" Your title is a handle, an introduction to your story or book as well as an advertisement for it. Read me, I sound interesting, I sound intriguing.

Titles that are too bland or that sound just like a slew of other titles are a mistake. *Time And Time Again. Once Upon A Time. From Time To Time.* But a clever twist on a bland phrase can be intriguing. *Once Upon A Mattress* was a Broadway musical based on the fairy tale "The Princess and the Pea." Like anti-histamines, reading a book entitled *Transformations* should probably be avoided before operating heavy machinery. If you are not writing historical fiction, avoid archaic sounding titles: *Time's Winged Chariot*; *The Wretched of The Earth*.

Your title might come from the Bible, *The Book of Ruth* by Jane Hamilton; *Dogs of Babel*, Carolyn Parkhurst; or Bartlett's Quotations, or from another piece of literature quoted. *For Whom the Bell Tolls*, Ernest Hemingway's title, is from the last lines of a poem by Donne. Seek not for whom the bell tolls / it tolls for thee. Or Salinger's *Catcher in The Rye*, an intentional misquotation from the Robert Burns song "Comin' Thro' the Rye:" If a body catch a body / need a body cry?

Sometimes a title is fairly literal and a description of the book's subject: *Of Cats and Men* by Nina de Gramont. *Sister Age*, M.F. K. Fisher. *The Book of Laughter and Forgetting* by Milan Kundera. *The War of The End of The World* by Mario Vargas Llosa; Gabriel Garcia Marquez, *Love In A Time of Cholera*; Laurie Colwyn, *A Big Storm Knocked It Over*; Doris Betts, *The Sharp Teeth of Love*; *Bastard Out of Carolina* by Dorothy Allison.

Sometimes a title is catchy with a hint of surprise: Grace Paley's *Enormous Changes At The Last Minute*, or Susan Lang's *Small Rocks Rising*; Joanna Russ's *On Strike Against God*. Edward Hoagland, *The Courage of Turtles*; *The Famished Road* by Ben Okri; James Tiptree, Jr., *Up The Walls of The World*: Elizabeth Inness-Brown, *Burning Marguerite*; "The Crystal Crypt" by Philip Dick; *The Monkey Wrench Gang* by Edward Albee; *The Beet Queen*, by Louise Erdrich; *Amnesia Moon*, by Jonathan Lethem; *The Hundred Per Cent Black Steinway Grand*, by Laurel Speer; *My Year Of Meats*, Ruth Ozeki; *Interpreter Of Maladies*, Jhumpa Lahiri; *Hand In My Bra*, Joan Leo: *Oranges Are Not The Only Fruit*, Jeanette Winterson.

A Heartbreaking Work of Staggering Genius by Dave Eggers is an outlandish hyperbolic boast. You want the idea to catch in your reader's brain like a burr so that she remembers the title and her curiosity is aroused.

Sometimes a title is a pun or close to one: *Bee Season* (about spelling bees and kaballah and its mystical association with the chanting of letters) by Myla Goldberg. *The War At Home* (about domestic violence in the family of a World War II veteran) by Nora Eisenberg.

Sometimes a title attracts attention because it is much longer than titles generally are: *I Love Myself When I Am Laughing . . . And Then Again When I Am Looking Mean And Impressive*, by Zora Neale Hurston; Samuel R. Delaney, *Stars In My Pocket Like Grains Of Sand*; Ursula Leguin, *Buffalo Gals And Other Animal*

Presences; Deena Metzger's short story called "The Woman Who Slept with Men To Take the War Out of Them;" Angela Carter's *The Infernal Desire Machines Of Dr. Hoffman*; *Three Elements Of Random Tea Parties*, Felicia Lemus. *The Electric Kool-Aid Acid Test*, Tom Wolfe. How about Arthur Kopit's absurd farce, *Oh Dad, Poor Dad, Mamma's Hung You In The Closet And I'm Feelin' So Sad*.

A title might make a pop or cultural reference or allude to a famous person or subject: Manuel Puig's *Betrayed By Rita Hayworth*; Suzanne Ruta's Stalin *In The Bronx*; William Gibson's *Mona Lisa Overdrive*; Oscar Hijuelos's, *The Mambo Kings Play Songs Of Love*; *Crouching Buzzard, Leaping Lion* by Donna Andrews. Or a title might seem a paradox: Helen Prejean's *Dead Man Walking*; Jose Saramago's *The Stone Raft*.

The title might suggest a body of myth or legend. *The Mists Of Avalon* is Marion Zimmer Bradley's take on the King Arthur stories. *The Red Tent* is Anita Diamont's exploration of the story of Dinah.

A title might feature a place as in Michael Chabon's *Mysteries Of Pittsburgh*; or *The Far Euphrates*, by Aryeh Lev Stollman; *A Werewolf Problem In Central Russia*, stories by Victor Pelerin; Cristina Garcia's *Dreaming In Cuban*.

Some titles take a common or ordinary phrase and use it in a surprising way: Nina Berberova, *The Italics Are Mine*. *See Under Love*, David Grossman. One of Simone De Beauvoir's late memoirs is called in English *All Said and Done*. Abby Hoffman's memoir was titled *Soon To Be A Major Motion Picture*. Doris Lessing has a short story "One Off the Short List." Ann-Marie MacDonald's *The Way The Crow Flies*, Billie Letts's *Shoot The Moon*, and James Hynes's short story collection *Publish And Perish*, all illustrate common phrases or variations on them, as does *To Say Nothing Of The Dog*, by Connie Willis.

A title can be both literal and metaphorical: Virginia Woolf's *To The Lighthouse*; *American Blood*, John Nichols; Helen Dunmore, *Talking To The Dead*; *Crocodile Soup* by Julia Darling; *The Mammoth Cheese*, Sheri Holman; *The Fifth Book of Peace*, Maxine Hong Kingston; *Women With Big Eyes*, Angela Mastretta; *Shadow Theater*, Fiona Cheong.

Now to reality: I always title my poetry books, and I get involved early on in the process of cover design. But with my novels, five times out of six, I will come in with one title and the publisher or sales department or editor will insist on renaming the book. Half the time, they ask me for endless suggestions and then take something completely different someone on staff suggested. Sometimes a publisher will come up with a better title than the author's—Lev Raphael's novel *The German Money* was called *Fieldwork In The Land of Grief* before we suggested a change and Theodore Roszak's *The Devil And Daniel Silverman* was *The Cold Front*—sometimes not. I hated the title *The Longings of Women*, but titling is a marketing decision and, depending upon your contract, your opinion may hold little weight with the publisher. It was originally called *Boxes of Comfort and Pain*. Vida was called *A Common Act of War*. *Three Women* was called *The Price of The Body*. Still, you do the best you can both to attract attention in the pile and—in the best of all possible worlds—to supply the title that the marketing department will fall in love with. So you give a title that you consider a strong one and then it is out of your hands. I keep lists of my rejected titles. I have recycled some of them for another book and occasionally one will turn into a poem. Sometimes, if you publish in Great Britain, you will find that the same title will not go in both places. *He, She and It* was so titled in the U.S., but in Great Britain and Australia, it was called *Body of Glass*. There was something unseemly or obscene to the British ear in the American title, so it had to be changed. It's been very confusing.

There are fashions in titles as there are in hairstyles and body art. A few years ago, titles had to be two words, no more, no less, to please some editors. Some writers fancy one word titles: Cherry Muhahji's *Her*; Jonathan Franzen's *The Corrections* (we don't count "a" or "the"); Nicola Barker, *Behindlings*. Joyce Carol Oates's *Them*. But two or three word titles are far more common.

Titles of poems, books, and stories cannot be copyrighted. How many things over the years have been called *Bedtime Story*? In the year Ira published *Going Public*, there were two other novels with the same title, one reviewed in the same issue of *Publishers Weekly*. A title I gave a collection of poems, *Available Light*, I learned had been used a number of times before and after my volume. It's probably better to go with a fresh title, but if the one you have chosen has been used before, unless it is currently in print or in stores, don't let that worry you—unless it's a famous title like *A Christmas Carol* or *Gone With The Wind*.

Titles are handles, ads, come-hithers, and the best titles give the impression of being catchy and inevitable at once. You will undoubtedly revise your titles as seriously as you revise your prose; and you will probably have to take your title through many revisions before you get one that satisfies you and your publisher. The important thing to remember is that your title is a critical decision. You take it lightly at your peril. Give it the thought it deserves.

Exercise:

This is fun because it's pure conjecture: no work to do, no writing involved. Like our first exercise in the chapter on Beginnings in which we asked you to come up with a beginning with no end, in this exercise the object is to come up with a title with no book, that is, a title so intriguing that it would make someone reach for it before any other in a library or book store. There are writers who claim to have started a project with a great title, the way poets are lured into writing a poem after encountering a simple phrase. Sometimes you'll hear an intriguing snippet of conversation and just know it would make a good title. Marge's memoir *Sleeping With Cats* was titled in this way. Try it in the car or on a walk. Bounce weird titles off your friends. You never know. You may come up with a keeper.

14

Writing Humor:
Learning Survival Techniques

Why are a lot of fat kids funny? Because they have to be. Not funny in their physicality but in their wit, their use of language, their ability to mimic or to milk humor from a situation. Their ability to attack before being attacked. To control the situation, to provide the subject of comedy before they become the subject.

There might be natural comedians among high school quarterbacks. There might be a runway model who does the comedy club circuit on weekends. But most funny people begin by perceiving themselves as losers, physical outcasts, social misfits. Of course, perception is key here. You don't have to look like Quasimodo to feel like a hunchback. Having a parent who is ashamed of you and treats you like an outcast is quite enough. "She's quick," you might describe the kid from the violent home; quick to defend herself; quick to get out of harm's way; or quick-witted: quick to make her father laugh before he grows restive and sends her across the room with the back of his hand. Ditto the lunchroom clown who sticks a straw up his nose before the conversation turns to the dodge ball that smacked him in the face in gym class. Or the heartbroken single woman at a dinner party who tells hilarious stories about her last disastrous date so all the married couples at the table won't show their pity for her. Humor is serious stuff. Humor is survival. Humor often finds it roots in pain.

Every newspaper in the country has a humor column that addresses the foibles of families and the annoyances of daily life: of pets, of kids, of computers and in-laws and guests who overstay their welcome. It's fun, it puts us at ease, when we identify. This is what went wrong in my house/life/family, how about yours? But there has always been a deeper need of the humor writer, to reveal false gods, to question what society commonly accepts as normal, righteous, perfect, beautiful; or decries as immoral, stupid, worthless. Comedy can be a writer's effort to tell a painful story by pointing out its absurdity, to expose a society's hypocrisy, to illustrate a situation too dangerous to discuss openly. The master (also read: teacher, boss, clergyman, parent, commanding officer, etc.) thinks he's smart but he's not. I am as smart as everyone else but they see me as stupid. The slave might feel this way; so might the immigrant, or the servant, the child or the secretary. Something is wrong here, things are not what they seem (or, things are not what everyone says they are). Or, everyone is making a great fuss over nothing. Comedy is trying often to evoke more than laughter.

But not everyone can make us laugh. I have a friend who is a talented and successful oil painter. He can paint a bowl of fruit that can bring tears to your eyes. But to hear this guy begin a joke is like entering an elevator that stops at every floor. You stare at your feet, at the walls; you steal a furtive glance at the woman next to you, who is also attempting to tolerate the wait. This friend can take five minutes to a tell a knock-knock joke. He has no timing, no sense of language, no feel for character, or what information is simply pointless to include. The laughs he gets are due to the embarrassment of his listeners.

There are no inherently funny subjects. There have been very funny books written about war (*Catch 22*) and sexual obsession (*Portnoy's Complaint*); about painful divorce (*Heartburn*) and impoverished serfs (*Dead Souls*) and overdosing drugs (*Fear and Loathing in Las Vegas.*) A Sunday newspaper column about our exasperating problems with computers can be amusing if written by Dave Barry and harrowing if it details the consequences of identity theft. There is humor in any situation. It's all in the writing. Can you gain enough distance from the subject to see the foolishness in it? Joseph Heller served in World War II but it took him years to fully capture the absurdity of war in *Catch 22*, the story of a sane man attempting to prove he's crazy in order to get out of combat, only to discover that everyone in charge is insane. Can you get beyond your own embarrassment in order to name and exaggerate the details? In *Portnoy's Complaint*, Philip Roth goes into hilarious detail to describe the scene of Alex Portnoy locking himself in the bathroom to masturbate. Are you too worried about hurting your family to find the universal insanity in their foibles? Are you so angry with fundamentalists that you can't envision the potential for humor when someone with enlightened scientific views trades ideas with someone who believes in the literal interpretation of the Bible?

When I was in my early twenties I could not write about having been an overweight child. It took many years to find a voice that could tell the story without casting blame, without self-pity; to develop a sensibility that recognized the obsession involved (the methods of losing weight) and the twisted logic (the strange diets I would go on) and the physical comedy (like the poses I'd adopt in the mirror) and the cast of characters involved (the diet doctors, my parents, my friends); in short, to be able to apply technique. Nor could I write a funny story about sexual jealousy while my girlfriend was sleeping around any more than Joseph Heller could write about World War II while he was serving overseas. You can have a humorous take on any subject, even a painful subject, if you're distanced enough from it to apply technique.

Once you're beyond the pain you can exaggerate it; you can recall the events in a voice that captivates the reader; you can add characters to complicate the story and comment on it; you can pile on ridiculous images; you can set up repetitive occurrences and confusing situations; you can create expectations in the reader's mind and reverse them; you can even add jokes.

Truly funny books are rare and then, of course, not everybody finds the same things funny. There are, however, certain devices that recur in humorous writing, devices that can be identified and applied. (Joseph Heller said that when he wrote *Catch 22*, he plagiarized shamelessly . . . from techniques he stole from Shakespeare.) While the following list makes no pretense to covering every technique used by humor writers, they are devices that have continued to delight us.

VOICE

Just as a painting can be about color, or texture, or simply about paint, humor can depend a great deal on language and style. Sometimes the voice of a particular writer amuses us with the peculiarity of its cadence, its strange logic (the conclusions it draws), its use of dialect and phrasing. To read the stories of Damon Runyon is to enter a stylized world of tough guys, murderers with a heart. Runyon's Broadway mobsters attempt to sound more educated than they are. They employ descriptive monikers for one another. They use understatement and repetition. Countless writers have introduced us to violent thugs, but few did it quite this way:

"One evening along about seven o'clock I am sitting in Mindy's restaurant putting on the gefillte fish, which is a dish I am very fond of, when in comes three parties from Brooklyn wearing caps as follows: Harry the Horse, Little Isadore and Spanish John . . . I hear that many citizens of Brooklyn will be very glad to see Harry the Horse, Little Isadore and Spanish John move away from there, as they are always doing something that is considered a knock to the community, such as robbing people, or maybe shooting and stabbing them, and throwing pineapples, and carrying on generally."

The voice in many of Grace Paley's stories has a similar affect. Paley's voice, also a stylized derivation of downtown, New York City English, speaks to serious and tragic issues while sounding maternal, sympathetic, and wise. Mark Twain takes on racial injustice with the voice of Huckleberry Finn, a country-raised, uneducated naïf commenting on the inequities of his society. Kurt Vonnegut charms us with an avuncular voice that embraces everything from mass murder to universal Armageddon. So it goes. None of these writers depend on jokes to amuse us but each voice wins us over with its own rhythms, insight, inner logic, and odd juxtapositions. There is a compelling originality and a unique likeableness to each of these voices and all of them, no matter how serious the material they present, appear to withhold judgment.

You may not think you have a unique voice but if you pay attention to the way you sound when you're relaxed, when you're talking to friends, or when you're fired up about an issue, you may have discovered the distinctive voice you're looking for. The trick is to catch it, to figure out its peculiar cadence and syntax, the phrases you repeat to signify emphasis, the stresses as well as the silences, any dialect that you may however unconsciously find yourself speaking, and then to harness it to tell a story using its own distinctive images. One way you may know you've found it is when it's going too fast for you to write it down.

IMAGES

Images such as simile and metaphor can be used to great comic effect:

> Mom is still a perfect size two, still consumes no solid food except Sarah Lee cake. Her every vertebrae is as distinct as a swollen knuckle and as I envelop her in a welcoming hug I imagine a skeleton shellacked with hair spray.

Some writers have extended the use of metaphor to encompass an entire story or novel. Everybody at one time or another feels as lowly and despicable as a bug. Kafka's famous "Metamorphosis" is the story of man who wakes up as a cockroach. What Kafka has created is an image that rings true, however ridiculous, and he exaggerated it, taking every detail to its logical conclusion. In *Gulliver's Travels,* Jonathan Swift satirized the politics of eighteenth-century England by turning people into horses, giants, and tiny midgets. During the Bill Clinton impeachment hearings, Theodore Roszak was alarmed by what he perceived as the influence of Christian fundamentalism on government. His response was the novel *The Devil and Daniel Silverman* in which a gay, Jewish liberal from San Francisco finds himself trapped in an evangelical Bible college. The novel is an extended metaphor for Roszak's perception of American secular humanists as "trapped" in an alien America, challenged by fierce religionists, constantly having to defend ideas they'd thought Western society had taken for granted since the Enlightenment.

EXAGGERATION

Exaggeration and overstatement make people laugh because after a while too much of anything becomes absurd. Some writers pile on the details.

In his story "The Country Husband," John Cheever introduces

us to a corporate executive who survives a plane crash and flees home to his perfect suburban family, only to be confronted with warring sons, a pouting adolescent daughter, and an overworked wife. Argument after argument, complaint upon complaint is piled high, until he's left sitting at the dinner table alone with everyone having gone off in a snit, so angry with each other and filled with their own resentments that they don't give a damn about the fact that he almost died. What Cheever has created is a gross overstatement of contemporary family life that turns a very sad situation into a very funny one.

In *Portnoy's Complaint,* Philip Roth piles on the various methods an adolescent boy can use to masturbate—with a piece of liver, with his sister's bra (I don't have to go on)—and illustrates him attempting to do so while locked in the bathroom, his mother banging on the door demanding to know whether he has diarrhea, his father loudly lamenting that his own bowels are hardened.

In Hunter S. Thompson's *Fear and Loathing in Las Vegas,* a four-hundred-pound Samoan lawyer named Dr. Gonzo on a colossal LSD trip begs, cajoles, and dares Raoul Duke to throw a plugged-in radio into the tub in which he is taking a bath, electrocution being the only possible high he can think of that will add to the "two bags of grass, seventy-five pellets of mescaline, five sheets of high-powered blotter acid, a salt shaker half-full of cocaine and a whole galaxy of multicolored uppers, downers, screamers, laughers. . . . A quart of tequila, a quart of rum, a case of Budweiser, a pint of raw ether and two dozen amyls" they have already consumed. This might be the most exaggerated, and hilarious, drug trip in American literature.

But you don't have to go bigger, louder, grosser, to exaggerate. You can diminish your character, exaggerate your shortcomings. In many of David Sedaris's brilliant stories, he paints himself as the world's most ineffectual patsy, doormat to the world.

Diminishment perhaps has never been taken to greater extremes than in Kurt Vonnegut's famous satire "Harrison Bergeron." Satires take ideas or trends in society and exaggerate them to nightmarish conclusions. Satires can be harrowing as in Margaret Atwood's *The Handmaid's Tale*, in which Christian fundamentalists have taken over the government, or ridiculously funny. Vonnegut's story takes place in the year 2081, a time when it is decreed that everyone should be equal in all ways and by law no one is to be better than anyone else. These laws are strictly enforced by the Handicapper General of the United States. Fourteen-year-old Harrison Bergeron, a genius and exceptional athlete, is jailed for being too talented and good looking and therefore a risk to society. He is shackled with earphones to disrupt his thoughts and forced to wear thick, wavy glasses to make him blind and give him headaches. He is also harnessed with three hundred pounds of scrap metal to handicap his strength and made to wear a red rubber ball on his nose to offset his good looks.

COMIC SITUATIONS

Again, no situation is inherently comic. In fact, situations that are inherently horrifying will turn out differently in the hands of different writers. In the Doris Lessing story, "One off the short list," an actress meets a BBC journalist friend at her apartment where she is forced to have sex. In the David Sedaris story, "c.o.g.," Sedaris accepts a dinner invitation from a friend at an Oregon apple packing plant who attempts to have sex with him against his will and the situation is hilarious.

Circumstances in which characters have differing intentions and desires are charged with conflict. You can turn that conflict in a humorous direction with comic technique: you can pack it with ridiculous details, smart dialog, surprise turns-of-events, reversals of expectations, jokes that comment on the action, characters with embarrassing or recognizable obsessions. Situations that involve characters who have differing expectations, or who do not understand each other, who want different outcomes, or do things at inappropriate times, give you a head start.

Long-distance bus trips don't strike one as interesting comic settings. People are grumpy, inactive, mostly staring out the window or sleeping. But what if one passenger on a packed bus wants to be a good guy and offers to give up his seat for awhile to a woman who is standing in the aisle . . . and she won't give it back? Now you're dealing with characters who want different things. What if the other passengers forget it was his seat to begin with, and castigate him for suggesting the woman give him his seat back? Now you've added a reversal—instead of a good guy, he's now seen as the bad guy. What if a large, surly passenger switches seats in order to sit next to her, and those two begin to have sex—yes, right there on the bus. Now you've added a surprising turn-of-events, and in the hands of David Sedaris this incident in the story "c.o.g." is a hilarious take on a good deed gone terribly wrong.

DETAIL

In the date rape scene in Sedaris' story "c.o.g.," the naked hero grabs a coat from the closet before escaping into the freezing night. What he ends up with is the fluffy pink parka belonging to the would-be rapist's 80 year-old paraplegic mother. In a closet full of coats, why choose a ladies' pink coat? Because it's a totally ridiculous detail that the author uses to infuse humor into a horrific situation.

Names stick with us as humorous details even in works not considered strictly humorous. In Saul Bellow's *The Adventures of Augie March*, Augie's family's nickname for their landlord is Five Properties, because the guy never introduces himself without bragging about his real estate, spreading out five fingers and boasting, "I have five properties." A small humorous detail, but a memorable one.

Details that embarrass us are funny. In *Crazy Salad: Some Things About Women*, Nora Efron details her fascination with her growing breasts as an adolescent. In *The Kitchen Man*, I talk about getting naked with a lover for the first time. There's a lot of risk involved in detailing our embarrassments. You may be labeled immature, you may reveal secrets, you may tell the world you once did something considered shameful, you may "out" your family as imperfect, or show your disrespect for something you're supposed to honor. The upside is instant recognition with readers. Even if they haven't experienced the specifics, they'll love you for it. Indeed, one of the rewards of literature is the ability to observe others experiencing those things too personal to admit to in public.

The piling on of details, sometimes called snowballing, creates a cascade of imagery. Like the scene in the film *Hannah and Her Sisters* when Woody Allen, investigating various religions in a quest to find meaning in his life, decides to convert to Catholicism, and sets out on a table all the things he thinks will be necessary—a crucifix, rosary beads, white bread, mayonnaise—you set up your reader for surprise.

Here's an example of snowballing details from *The Kitchen Man*:

Wellfleet.

The art gallery town. On any given Saturday evening in summer this tiny salt marsh hamlet becomes the Filene's Basement of objets d'art. Happy hour begins at five when tourists following the centerfold map in the local paper wind their way from Main Street to the pier, drinking white wine, snatching crackers and cheese, searching to fill that empty wall over the couch with the largest and least expensive painting that matches their color scheme. By six there isn't a litre of Folonari Suave left in town. The streets teem with sunburned collectors, slouching on to the next temple of art and then the next. . . . There are New Yorkers who dress up and Bostonians who dress down and local artists in faded blue oxford shirts who stand around politely answering the question, "You mean you live here *all* year?"

August in Wellfleet.

When the razor edge of the dune grass crinkles brittle brown. When the sun burns a tired heat and the nights are long and cool. . . . Paradise. Unique in all the world. You come here if you possibly, possibly can. Unless. It is a rainy . . .

August in Wellfleet.

When the divorce rate for vacationing couples hovers at thirty-nine percent. When the bed sheets never dry and the dog smells like a compost pile. When the Sunday *Times* grows very, very boring by Wednesday. If you can get one.

Long, languorous breakfasts when you begin to notice that your husband chews his granola like a Clydesdale. Afternoons when the trees drip like bad pipes and you wear the humidity like a wet pea coat. Nights when you retire early only to bash your shins on the bicycles in the hall that will rust if they get wet. Neighbors in the cottage on the right who fight until three A.M. and neighbors on the left who screw, grunting the passion of wild pigs.

Reversals of Expectations

A late-night subway train pulls into an empty station. A young woman gets off on a deserted platform. The train pulls away. She hears footsteps. She walks faster. So do the footsteps. She stops. The footsteps do, too. She runs. Her pursuer keeps pace. Turning, she glimpses a large man in a leather coat. She breaks for the stairs. He's hard at her heels. Halfway up, she stops. She turns. The man's face is inches from her own. "Don't worry," she says. "I'm not going to hurt you." The man doubles over in laughter and she walks home with no incident.

This is an urban folk tale. This is also a reversal, a surprise turn of events. Screenwriters use them all the time. They are required elements in all thrillers. The fatherly police captain turns out to be . . . (oh shock!) the criminal mastermind. Reversals are also very handy to the humor writer because comedy is often about the unexpected, the last thing you would have thought of, the unlikely response, the opposite of conventional wisdom.

In the novel *Going Public,* Corey Richardson and his much-younger girlfriend are spending the weekend at Corey's daughter's prep school in order to see a production of the school play. Also up to see the play is Angela, Corey's ex-wife, the mother of his child. He assumes Angela will be the possessive, frumpy housewife he took her for when he left her. But she's done quite well for herself, she looks fabulous, and her date for the weekend is a former pro athlete. When the desk clerk mistakenly gives Corey the keys to Angela's room (she has kept her married name) he's shocked to find some wild sex toys. Big surprise for Corey. Major opportunity for unexpected complications. There has been a reversal. Corey is now the jealous one.

Transposition of Expectation

A different kind of reversal occurs when a character thinks he or she experiences something that is in reality something else. In *The Kitchen Man,* we meet a character early on in the novel who is a masseuse whose specialty is the hand-release (a euphemism for masturbating her clients to orgasm). In the last chapter of the book, the character is glimpsed with a man in the back room of a crowded party. She is shaking her arm up and down. It is assumed she is performing the hand-release on a party guest when in fact she is innocently shaking down the mercury of an oral thermometer. Gotcha.

Another example occurs in *Going Public*. Having spiced Angela's vibrator on his first trip to school, Corey, when occupying an adjacent room during graduation later that year, hears a buzzing drone coming from Angela's room and assumes it's the vibrator. In fact it's a hair dryer.

Both of these examples depend on a staple a of humor writing, the repetition of events.

REPETITION

We love to see characters "doing it again," repeating the same mistake, harping on the same obsession, getting in trouble once more. (In the examples above, the viewpoint characters are acting on some previous knowledge—about the masseuse, the vibrator—expecting a repetition of events and getting something else. Not only the character is fooled, but the reader as well.)

Repetition is fun for readers because they have inside knowledge of events, information they've received previously, so they are surprised and delighted to see it come up yet again.

Here's an example of comic repetition in dialog from *The Devil and Daniel Silverman* in which Silverman, a failed writer, tries to pitch a new book to Tommy Sutton, his New York literary agent:

> After three novels bombed in a row, Tommy Sutton gave Silverman clear warning that he was in trouble. But not to worry, Silverman told himself. He was sure his next book would turn things around. That book was *Deep Eye*, the perfect concept: *Moby Dick* retold from the whale's point of view.
> "The whale," Sutton interrupted. "Moby Dick there—he's doing the talking?"
> "Yes, but we don't call him Moby Dick. We call him Shirook Han Omura. That's his name in Whalish, see?"
> "Whalish?"
> "The natural language of the whales. He speaks in Whalish."

"The whale is speaking Whalish? Which means like what? The book is written . . . in not English?"

"Of course it's in English," Silverman snapped, letting his impatience show. *Christ! Wasn't the man listening? Just because I'm a minor client, he can't rent me ten minutes of attention?* "As I said, there's an author's note that explains the book is translated from the Whalish."

"Not good," Sutton said woefully.

"What—not good?"

"Author's note. That's a killer. It tells you right up front this is a hard read. I never buy books with notes from the author."

"Well, maybe we can do without that. The readers will catch on. The important thing is the footnotes about the semiotics of the animal mind, see?"

"Oh." Sutton had an *oh* like a rabbit punch. It knocked the wind out of you.

"What 'oh'?" Silverman asked, tense now with frustration.

"Footnotes."

"Yes, footnotes."

"A novel with footnotes. That's worse than an author's note."

JOKES

Generally, we watch comedians on TV to hear jokes. The humor in literature, however, often emanates from character: the ways people fool themselves and/or try to trick others; the absurd lengths we'll go to get what we want; unexpected or ridiculous things that come out of people's mouths. The joke, the short, formulaic story with set-up, development and punch line is difficult to find a place for in literature—unless you are using it to comment on the story. In the movie *Annie Hall*, Woody Allen starts with a Groucho Marx joke: I never wanted to join a club that would let me in as a member. That's the plot in a nutshell, a movie about a guy who never wants what he can have. If you can find a way to use a joke to set up or comment on the action, it can be great fun. Here's a scene from *The Kitchen Man* in which Gabriel, who has a crush on Cynthia, desperately wants contact with her, but admits:

I feel like the stable hand in the old joke who doesn't know what to say to a girl he's been wanting to meet for months.

"What's the big deal," his buddy tells him. "Just start talking. Relax. Be yourself."

"B-b-but I don't even know how to begin."

"Girls like a guy who's unique. Tell you what. Paint her horse's tail pink. When she comes in she'll ask you, What happened? The you make something up and you're talking."

The stable hand dips the horse's tail in a bucket of pink paint and waits. That afternoon, when the girl comes to the stable, she runs up to him and gasps, "My horse's tail, what happened?"

His big chance is at hand. He takes a deep breath. Steps forward. This is it. "I painted it. Wanna fuck?"

As the scene progresses Gabriel concocts a ridiculous scheme to ingratiate himself to Cynthia, a theater director, by removing a bunch of women's purses that are left unguarded by the door of the rehearsal hall. He assumes the women will think he's thoughtful and sensitive for keeping the purses safe from someone who might wander in and steal them. But when he grabs up an armful of purses, he is spotted and taken for a thief. Someone yells. He is chased. Then tackled. Everyone is upset. The rehearsal has been ruined.

"What do you have to say for yourself," Cynthia asks.

"I painted it. Wanna fuck?"

Now, the most important for last.

Character

The most effective comic characters are not hastily sketched buffoons but carefully created personalities with obsessive needs, unobtainable goals, recognizable weaknesses, fanatical fixations, odd ways of perceiving the world, and a myriad of strongly held human foibles. Some of the great comic characters in literature are powerfully motivated even in their impossible pursuits. Think of Candide, the incurable optimist; Yossarian, butting his head against the wall of illogical military bureaucracy; the over-sexed Portnoy; the love-sick Bridget Jones; the unscrupulous Gulley

Jimson. Many comic characters have become archetypes of human folly and beloved to us because they are doomed, because they represent the human condition for all of us, our constant attempts, and failures, to get what we want.

If comic characters are to be memorable and effective, they must be created with the careful attention we talk about in the chapter on Characterization. You'll want to imagine *all* the aspects of their lives. Focusing merely on their obsessions will give you nowhere to go with your story. Bridget Jones has friends and a work life, an odd family and a kooky internal world. If she was only about her obsession for one man, if she thought about him exclusively and paid no attention to her society, her diary would be a very dull book.

It's often how an obsessive character interacts with the world that brings us pleasure: the odd minor characters they are surrounded by, their strange take on events; the memories of their former selves. The more you know about your comic characters, the more you imagine them in your dossiers, the more activities you create to engage their strange personalities, the richer your work will be. David Sedaris's comic memoirs are beloved to many readers because he unleashes his sarcastic, well-meaning, insecure, self-deprecating, somewhat elitist and very gay personality not just on his family life, but in various work capacities, sexual situations, schools, and so on. In short, he's out there in the world, giving himself many different opportunities to meet people, screw up and get into trouble. Even though he is writing about himself, Sedaris's character dossier is wholly imagined. If you are writing about yourself, if you are your main comic character, imagine yourself in many situations, mundane and bizarre; surround yourself with many minor players who can bring out the best and worst in you; figure out your longings, those that you outwardly crave as well as those you desire in fact (*e.g.* I attempt to seduce someone not necessarily because I want sex but because I'm lonely); in short, make a character dossier on yourself. Comic characters are well-developed characters. Ask of yourself (or your comic persona) what you would do in many different situations. If you do your characterization work, you may discover weird and curious traits you'd never dared imagine before.

DIALOG

Comic dialog is one of the joys of reading. Even in books not intended to be humorous, writers often find their comic wings and treat us to a flight of the ridiculous or the unexpected, a reversal, repetition, a sarcastic taunt, a wacky detail. After all, almost everybody is funny sometimes, so of course any character *could* be. If you study these witty snatches, you'll find that at core they're simply well-written dialog following the loose set of rules in the Dialog chapter. Often they're short exchanges. Humor tends to have a cadence. The speakers are well defined. It's not funny to have to count lines to see who's speaking. If there is dialect involved—some writers use a form of pidgin English to get laughs—it doesn't get in the way of understanding what is being said. Humorous dialog can define character by what the speaker says and to whom. (Remember Eddie Haskell? Obsequious to adults and nasty to Beaver and his friends.) Humorous dialog can also build character. You can use it to show relationships changing, people teasing each other, or double entendre between lovers (briefly, however, because this becomes too cute if it goes on too long). Humorous dialog also lends itself to the techniques we mentioned above:

REPETITION IN DIALOG

From *The Kitchen Man:*

> "Mom, how are you?"
> What do you care?"
> "I do care. I love you."
> "No, you don't." Understand, this can go on for half an hour. I do, you don't. I do, you don't. My mother's keenest pleasure is the affirmation of other people. To that end she demeans herself to everyone. The dentist. The dry cleaner. The plumber. Lady, you need a new hot water heater. It's my fault. No Lady, it's not. It is. It's not. It is. What does he care at sixty dollars an hour? The only way to stop it is to wait, pause; you don't disagree with her, she can't disagree with you. "So," finally she goes on, "how do you like your new apartment?"

"We love it, as soon as we're settled you'll have to come over."

"You wish I never called, don't you?"

"Why do you say that? Of course I don't."

"You do."

"I don't."

"You do."

Detail in Dialog

From *The Kitchen Man:*

"Pouilly-Fumé." Geller holds each bottle up to the light. "One third, not bad. And this one, Chateauneuf du Pape, about half full. That table left in a bit of a hurry didn't they, Gabriel? Les Clos Chablis. A Grand Cru, the very wine our führer drinks. Just a glass left in this one but I kept it cold. And, the pièce de résistance, a bottle of William Duetz Brut, 1974. Two-thirds full. My sister-in-law's favorite."

Mary kicks off a shoe, massages a dangling foot. "You know if one of your customers drives into a wall on the way home some night you're going to have to live with that."

"Fair is fair," Geller says. He sells more wine than Paul Masson. His customers stagger out the door. He pours full glasses for everyone and then approaches the drunkest customer with the empty. Nine times out of ten the big spender hiccoughs, "One more!" and Geller has the bottle open before anyone at the table can object. His tips are twenty percent of enormous tabs and there is always wine left over for us.

Exaggeration / Snow Balling / Weird Images / Character Development

In the following scene from *The Kitchen Man*, the desperate playwright Gabriel has been summoned by the mad director Petrushevsky. It includes many of the elements of comic writing:

". . . I'm afraid I can offer you nothing here." Nothing? His eyes are too powerful. I have to turn away. But why did he write me? He has to work with me. If he doesn't who will?

"Nothing. . . ," he hisses, his spine rolling toward me like a snake's until his face, crooked teeth the color of old newspaper, breath of cigarettes, spreads wide angle before my own, " . . . nothing except work, the work of facing yourself for the first time in your life. Is that why you came to me, Gabriel?"

He laughs, he knows it is not. "We believe," Petrushevsky continues, "in the many working as one. Unless you are a genius. Are you a genius, Gabriel? Are you Shaw? Are you Shakespeare? Are you Artaud? Artaud who said, 'if we could feel, then we could feel the pain, and if we could feel the pain, it would be so great we would end it.' Are you Artaud?" Petrushevsky presses, "Are you a genius?"

"Of course not," I mumble.

"What?" his voice makes me jump.

"No," I say.

"What?" he shouts.

"No!" I shout.

"No!" he stands, "we are none of us geniuses. We are workers, workers in the theater, not the theater of plush and gold but the theater of pain and sweat. We are communards, each member pulling his weight, shoveling the shit of his life, working until the play is ready. If the play is not ready?" He pauses. "We do not perform. We are not cows, Gabriel, we do not squirt plays like milk, we are not turtles, we do not drop our plays like eggs in the sand. We are artists working toward perfection and truth."

"I understand."

"You understand?" This amuses him. "Then I shall tell you why I wrote you. I wrote you because your play is . . . almost very good."

Not every writer wants to write humor. No humor writer is funny all the time. All of us, however, encounter humorous moments in our writing, and moments of humorous potential, whether it's a strange conversation, or an odd grouping of characters, an unexpected turn of events, or a situation that might be exaggerated. Knowing the techniques of humor writing can help you recognize these moments in other writers' work, analyze what makes them funny, and apply them to your own.

Exercise: A Very Bad Day

Ever had a day when everything went wrong? Record it in a story. Event by event, from the moment you step out of bed . . . onto a warm dead mouse the cat laid beside your slipper. Into the bathroom where the toilet's backed up. Downstairs where the heat has cut out. Lay it on, detail after detail. Have no mercy. Do not stop. Read it aloud. It would be the cold audience indeed that did not find this funny. Why? Because we identify. Because we vicariously revel in those universal domestic misfortunes that on any day of the week can fall on our heads.

Exercise: An Extended Metaphor

It's ninety degrees outside and the humidity is ninety-eight percent. You feel like a dishrag. Write a story from the point of view of a dishrag. You have just finished the hardest project of your life; you are totally worn out. You feel like a mule. Become that mule, the way Kafka became a cockroach in "Metamorphosis." Or maybe your co-workers are pigs; your boss is an ass. Make your office a barnyard. Make each person the animal they most resemble in behavior and temperament, as Orwell did in *Animal Farm*. Maybe your character feels as alienated and misunderstood as a bear who plays the saxophone. Check out Rafi Zabor's *The Bear Comes Home*. The object is to bring the image to life.

Exercise: Repetition in Dialog

You may have friends whose brains are somewhat fried, or elderly relations with very bad memories; or you may know people who simply don't leave room for others to speak and who continually repeat themselves: telling the same story no matter how many times you've heard it; reiterating the same phrase again and again; or, like the mother in the example above, deriding herself over and over in a search for affirmation. The object of this exercise is to create a dialog between two (or more) people in which at least one of the speakers constantly repeats a story, or a phrase, no matter how ridiculous or unrelated. Make us see them "doing it again."

Exercise: Finding Your Voice

This exercise may involve other people. Or, it may involve being far, far away from other people. For some, it may take your favorite stimulant. Or relaxant. What you're trying to accomplish, by whatever means, is a state in which you are most completely yourself. A state in which you are not attempting to impress anyone, but feel free to let loose.

Think of a ridiculous story or situation in which you were involved. By ridiculous, I mean absurd, out of the ordinary, unwinnable, embarrassing. Perhaps it was hair-raising at the time, but in retrospect it was bizarre, off the wall. I can't tell you more than that. We all have these kinds of stories. I remember a time I was invited to the Emmy Awards ceremony in New York City. I thought I was going to meet television stars who would discover me or advance my career; in fact, I ended up getting drunk and passing out. We all have ridiculous stories. Marge tells one from her destitute days as a fledgling writer in Chicago when she woke up in a cheap rooming house and found a rat in her bedroom with its head stuck in a mouse trap. She battled it with a broom, threw shoes at it, grabbed it by the tail and, not knowing what to do next, tried to flush it down the toilet. Those kinds of stories.

Now the idea is to tell it in all its ridiculous detail. Take all the time you need. If you're telling it to someone else, take note of where they laugh (but also, where they doze off). If you're nervous at first, keep going. If it's a story worth telling, it will begin to tell itself at a certain point. That's your voice. That's the story speaking, not the embarrassed adult or the person who is attempting to use language to impress. However you can, take note of what you leave in, what you leave out, the characters who inhabit the story, the phrases that you use, and especially the rhythm.

I could tell you to use a tape recorder, but some people freeze up before a tape recorder. But you need to capture the story and the telling of it however you can, in notes, in memory, or maybe constant retelling. Some people freeze up in front of an audience. I like to wake up very early in the morning, drink strong coffee, begin the story in my head and capture it all while furiously writing on a legal pad. Sometimes I'm thinking and writing so fast the pages rip as I turn them. Most times I can't read my own writing and I almost always lose parts of it when I try to transcribe it later. Occupational hazard. The idea is to capture a stream of consciousness rant. Once you've caught it, that's your voice. And then the real work begins, the editing: the crafting of the language into an artifact that makes sense to readers, the locating of the repetitions, the choosing of details.

Exercise: Creating a Satire

Can you think of a trend in our society that drives you crazy? The newspapers are full of absurdities every day. Can you narrow one down to a sentence?

Try to fill in the blank: I hate it when _____. (Go ahead: indulge the inner curmudgeon.)

Vonnegut placed his warped notion of reverse discrimination 120 years into the future (he published "Harrison Bergeron" in 1961). Voltaire used the kingdom of Westphalia to illustrate his disdain for a popular philosopher in his day named Leibniz who preached "everything is for the best in the best of all possible worlds," advocating people's meek acceptance of their fate.

Is there a philosophy that drives you nuts? Or a development in our society that you find ludicrous? Write a short piece in which the inevitabilities of that idea, or the logical conclusions of that societal trend become the norm or the law of the land. Make them ridiculous rather than horrific. Pile on the details. (Think of Vonnegut's 300 pounds of clanking junk, the red ball for a nose and heavy glasses with wavy lenses that Harrison Bergeron was forced to wear in order to bring his natural born talents down to the level of everyone else.)

15

A Scandal In The Family

Every book has a story behind it that is usually as interesting as the book itself. Whether it's the adventures of the author's research trips or the fights with her editor; the funding that was cut at the last minute by the National Endowment for the Arts or the shipment of galleys we received from the printer—missing all punctuation—I never tire of trading these stories at sales conferences and writers' workshops.

Because with every success recounted—and a published book, no matter how disappointing its sales may be, is a success—I take away hope for publishing another. The story of *The Kitchen Man* has been interesting to writers in our workshops who have faced issues of writing about people they love or in some cases failing to write because they could not face these issues. In some workshops, I'm asked to read the offending material, so I've included it in Appendix I of this book.

In the winter of the year I turned thirty years old, I was drinking a great deal of bourbon and listening to Bessie Smith albums every night upon returning from a job building a house. For one hour every morning, long before first light, I would climb out of bed, make a pot of strong coffee, feed the cat Jim Beam, whom I'd named after the bourbon, and work on a novel about a waiter. It was called *The Kitchen Man*, named after the Bessie Smith song. I had been a good waiter (I judge this by my tips, which were sizable) but a complete failure at the building trades (I judge this by the number of times I was ordered to re-make windows I had framed, and once, a sleeping loft, which seemed to sway in mid-air like the gang plank in a Popeye cartoon.) My mind was occupied. I was thinking about the novel all the time, stopping to scribble jokes on scraps of wallboard, muttering conversations I would assign, the following morning, to my characters. In this way I managed to complete and revise a four hundred twenty-five page draft in a little over a year. It was accomplished enough to get me a good New York agent, which I defined at the time as someone who had at least one client who had written a best seller and took me to lunch in a restaurant with a wine list.

For the next two years, the book made its way to twenty-four mainstream publishers. In those days there were many more New York publishers. Their rejections ranged from the condescending ("Mr. Wood is a writer whose next book just might be good.") to the absurd ("I cannot publish this book because I hate the protagonist. He reminds me too much of myself.") I was aware too of a disjointedness of opinion that I could not dismiss. Many people who read the novel—I am talking here about other writers, some quite famous ones, and avid readers, as well as audiences who heard excerpts at readings—liked it very, very much. I kept being told how the book spoke to them of families like their own, of body types and neuroses like their own, of what they always feared went on inside pretentious restaurant kitchens, of people they recognized from life but not literature. So, I kept sending it out.

I was aware at the same time that although I was a moody, envious, border-line alcoholic, given to pitiful, stentorian sighs (literary biographers will note that my wife's output, prolific by any standard, increased greatly when I got an office outside the house), the fact that I was not published saved me from a confrontation with my mother and father who were realistically, if not sympathetically, rendered characters in the book. It was certainly the case that the guilt I felt about what I had written had fed my ambivalence about seeing it in print. When the agent gave up on the book I refused to follow my wife's advice to submit it to an independent press that might have been open to something quirky and not recognizably commercial. I told myself it was either a big time New York City publisher or nothing.

After a year and another draft in which I cut a hundred pages, I did send it out to two small presses or, rather, my wife dared me to shut up and stop moaning about it and send it out. Within a month I received an acceptance letter from The Crossing Press, then in Trumansburg, New York, and a few weeks later a contract. I was real. I was to be a published novelist, and if it was with a publisher many people outside the business had never heard of, this fact might work in my favor. My parents, who encountered books mostly in airports and suburban malls, were never likely to come across it. When my mother and I spoke, I never denied that it was going to be published, I just never mentioned it. I was working as an artist-in-the-schools at this time and as a sixth grade teacher phrased the question in the fetid confines of the faculty lounge as I announced its publication to my colleagues, "Who the hell's gonna care about a book published in a place called Trumansburg?"

At least one person did. The publicist. He had two essential qualities that elevated him, in my mind, to the best publicist I have ever worked with: he loved the book and he was fearless on the phone. At that time there was no Oprah's Book Club but if there were he would have tracked her to the ends of the earth. He sent it everyplace—*The New York Times, The Washington Post,* the *Toronto Globe and Mail*—followed up doggedly, and it worked. The wacky small press novel about an overweight gourmet waiter was widely reviewed. Not long after pub date, I got a call from my mother. "Why didn't you tell me your book came out?"

"You mean *The Kitchen Man*?" Duh. "I don't know, Ma. I must've forgot."

"There's a big review in the Sunday *New York Times*."

But my parents only read the *New York Post*. I had thought I was covered. "How did you know?"

"Your aunt called from Arizona. I'm going out now to buy the book."

"Don't do that!" I said. "What I mean is, a mother should never have to pay for her son's book. I'll send it to you." I had bought myself some time.

Up to that point, I had never had a conversation with my parents about the pain I had felt growing up, about their treatment of each other and their verbally poisonous fights. Looking back on my life now, coming of age as a suburban fat kid whose struggling parents were ashamed of him seems a humorous footnote, but at thirty years old the attendant anger was still so much a part of me that in writing my first autobiographical novel, I had to include it. There was no way to write about myself otherwise.

It took me a week to decide to send the novel and during that time I came up with the scheme of using a razor blade to neatly delete chapter four. But the publicity man was doing his job, capitalizing on good reviews to get even more print media attention. The book was gaining momentum. Paperback reprint offers from the large New York publishers were coming in. Movie producers were calling; so were the relatives. Before I got around to sending the book, my mother called to inform me that she had bought it. That she was liking it.

"Really! How far did you get?"

"Just up to chapter three."

I did not hear from her for some weeks after that. When I did finally force myself to call on Sunday morning, her response was predictably cool. "Oh, I got really busy. I stopped reading it," she said.

"How far did you get?"

"Chapter four."

"Is that him?" I heard my father's rumbling behind her. He took the phone.

"Hi, Pop."

"Hey, I read your book."

"What did you think?"

"Well, you didn't treat me too bad."

"I didn't?"

"But you really socked it to your mother!"

The conversation ended. The momentum of the book continued. A paperback sale was negotiated. And a movie option. I agreed to be represented by the William Morris Agency. I signed a deal to write the screenplay for Universal Pictures. I still was avoiding speaking to my mother about the book. It hurt me that my success had caused her embarrassment. But it also hurt to feel that my experience was not mine to write about. Was it not my side of those years together? Didn't the right to tell the story of my own life belong to me?

My mother and I continued to have shallow, careful conversations until in one of them, many months later, she said, "Did you really feel that way about us? That we were so bad to you?"

I did. And yet I didn't. That is, they were my parents: I loved them and recognized that we had gone through some tough times together. I understood that my mother had married in her teens, and that my dad was just twenty years old; that they themselves had difficult parents, that finances never ceased to be an issue. I understood all the reasons why they were the way they were. Because she had brought up the question, I was able to tell my mother that yes, it had been bad for me, but that I honestly felt they had always tried to do their best. I believe she heard that. I cannot say that we patched up all differences and became a tight mother and son. I can say that it was a start. From that point forward we stopped lying about the past; we acknowledged there had been some good times but by and large those years had been difficult for all of us.

My father read and re-read the book and bought copies to give to friends. He was not a man who had a vocabulary to express such things, but I believe that seeing himself in print made him feel his days on Earth had been documented and were therefore more important, that I had rendered his life as art. My brothers were amused by what I had written but not particularly moved. Years younger, they did not have the same experiences or, because my folks had managed to solve many of their problems and change over the years, the same parents. My writing was in no way prescient. Neil Simon, Phillip Roth, and hundreds of other writers had been lampooning the Jewish-American experience for years. Still, my mother became very proud of her son the novelist and began to send me articles by children who had written about their families, often with a note that said, "Oh, what you wrote about me is nothing compared to this one!" She even redefined our cheap relatives as those who took my book out of the library but wouldn't buy a copy. I have had the feeling, moreover, that my mother has been somewhat disappointed in my subsequent books because she was not in them.

I'm not about to revise the experience and pretend it was pleasant, but neither can I say I'm sorry. I wrote what I had to write. It was the truth of my side of the experience. It may have hurt my parents to read it, it may have embarrassed them, but it did not kill them. It did not cause them to suffer nervous illness. It did not make them lose their jobs. It did not cost them any friends. Growing up together was not easy for any of us. The novel bore witness to those difficult years. In the way shared tragedy sometimes does, it brought us closer together.

Writing about my family with emotional honesty and seeing it through to being published was my choice. Since every family is unique, I would never advise someone else to take this risk. In all our classes, and in the relevant essays in this book, we emphasize the various distancing techniques that writers sometimes use to write about those close to them. But simply changing a person's name or disguising their appearance and details about them is not always sufficient protection from charges of libel. You cannot make false or defamatory statements about living people. You cannot subject a person to undeserved publicity without permission. The law is complex and we readily admit our ignorance. In all our workshops, we warn participants about the possible legal implications involved in writing about real people. We mention the advisability of seeking out attorneys who specialize in intellectual property issues, libel and/or invasion of privacy. We offer the titles of books that can inform you about these issues and we strongly advise people to consult them.

But having mentioned the risks, there are certain things I've discovered for myself:

1.   We live in a society in which the most heinous and embarrassing human behaviors are merely fodder for sitcoms and daily talk shows. What you may agonize about revealing might make the average reader yawn.

2.   Revealing the truth as you see it might explain a person's life in a way that makes their behavior far more explicable than covering it over would.

3.   Sometimes people really don't mind being written about because you are enabling them to see their lives in a new perspective. My father read and reread my novel many times; my mother gives away copies as gifts. Some people thought my parents were treated very callously in the book. My parents ultimately felt that I had helped them to understand their own lives, and our most difficult years as a family, from a useful perspective.

4. Your job as a writer is to make people real. Cartoon characters and walk-ons don't make a story breathe. You've got to allow the

reader to see a well-rounded picture of your important characters and that includes the contradictions in their personalities, all the surprising but often not very flattering dualities that make each of us interesting and unique.

5. Most important to me is that by telling your truth, you help readers accept the truth about themselves. By admitting that your family might have had problems, you're helping others out of their shame and isolation. You're helping them understand that their lives might not be perfect, but neither is anyone else's. There's a great backlash today about our confessional society. I admit, daytime TV talk shows and all the dependency literature we've endured have us wondering whether people shouldn't keep their sordid histories private. But to my mind, it was worse "back in the day" when the archetypes of the solid American middle class family bore no resemblance to the problems and the tensions I walked into when I came home from school, making me feel my family was a shameful secret.

6. There are many ways to view any experience. How you experienced a particular incident may be very different from someone else who was there.

7. In your memoir or your novel, you are writing, not for now, not for the evening news, or the weekly magazine, but presumably for years and decades to come. You are attempting to distill experience into art. What is tender and emotional now may not be so in time. You are banking on the fact that it is the rendering of events and emotional truth that is important; that the identities of the actors is less important than the play itself. You are attempting to fill the facts with meaning.

One last footnote on the publication history of *The Kitchen Man*. One might have thought that twenty-four rejections would have made me skeptical about large conglomerate publishing companies being the proper home for a comic literary novel. But the year after it came out, I was flush with all the attention and thought that a writer of my stature would be best served by a large New York publisher. Although the Crossing Press would have gladly brought out a paperback edition, I pressed them to sell the rights to a major paperback house. Over the years, the book slowly gained a following. I was being invited to read at colleges. In fact the book was being taught at some. One day my new editor called to tell me that she was sorry (she actually was) but she had just received notice that the book had been recycled and was no longer in print. Yes, it had been selling; but not enough to justify keeping it in inventory.

It's a strange experience to see a book of yours go out of print, to have two or three years of your life pulped. It's listed in your résumé. Academics mention it when they introduce you, but it's a little like a story you tell that you can never prove, or a deceased friend that exists in your memory only. When we started Leapfrog Press, we brought it back into print as our first book—partly because there was a continuing demand and partly because we were just learning how to publish and decided our early mistakes should be on our own work, not somebody else's.

By the way, no one was more upset when the book went out of print than my mother who, by that time, was buying five or six copies for friends every holiday season, and now had to begin the tedious search to find copies in used book stores.

16

Work And Other Habits

In talking about barriers to creativity, we are also talking about daily life and daily habits and how we live our lives in general and in particular, and also how we can help each other overcome these barriers.

One way to begin breaking down the inner barriers to creativity is in small local groups, in collectives, in workshops, with other writers who come together to try to keep each other working, productive, sane, alive, and who try to help.

What's most important in a workshop, whether a formal one or one you put together from an ad in a coffee shop, is being committed to helping each other do what that writer wants to do, not what you want to do or what you think that writer should want to do.

Let's say you're in a workshop with other fiction writers. You write tough laconic prose and you like things to be dry and clear and crackly. Someone in the group writes about their childhood sexual abuse. This is emotional stuff and it is written about in an emotional way. It's everything you would never do on paper. Your natural response may be boredom, sarcasm, embarrassment or the intellectual equivalent. But that helps nobody. What you have to do is to distance yourself from your distaste and figure out how the writer can do what she is trying to do and do it better. It isn't anything you would ever write or even care to read, but you aren't *Everyone*. If the other writer can pull it off, some people will want to read it. Your obligation in any workshop is to offer comments in good faith about how the writer can do what she wants to do, not what you want to do.

Another example: you loathe violence and are strongly for gun control. You can't imagine why any sane person would want a gun in the house. Another person in the group writes a cop procedural that has a lot about firearms in it. You would never pick up this book, but here you are listening to descriptions of how to bring down a suspect without deadly force and with it. Nobody is asking you to join the NYPD. But you owe it to your fellow participant in the workshop to listen carefully or read carefully and give that writer the feedback that will enable him to write a better police procedural, not an anti-gun tract.

We can help each other in small and undramatic, daily, weekly, monthly ways. We can help by being ready to listen. We can help by reading each other's manuscripts. Often it is easy to get friends to read something in print—everyone wants a copy of a book, not understanding the author is limited to a small number of copies depending on the contract—but very few are really willing to put the time into a manuscript. (They may insist that they are, but just wait and see how long it gathers dust beside their bed.) Yet that is the one important time for input. After a book is printed, criticism is interesting but not useful for improving the object. When a book is in manuscript, it can still be altered. Then is the time that criticism, that the willingness of others to read and to be generous with their time and involvement, is most meaningful.

We can help when another writer has trouble working. In Vermont, several women I know formed a small group. They worked together in the same house, so that each kept the others working, prevented the giving way to temptations or interruptions. It was a fixed time for work and nothing else. In addition, they read each other what they had written at fixed intervals and gave each other vital feedback.

In Chicago, when I was completely unknown and quite invisible, I joined other unknown writers, African-American and white, in a small group that met regularly and gave each other criticism and hope. Without that small group, I don't think I would have stopped writing, but I would have written more slowly.

Parents can form a playgroup with other writers who have children. This would free up certain days for work at the cost of perhaps one day a week. Where there is a willingness to help each other, a commitment to midwifing each other's creativity, we will find ways.

I feel guilty if I don't write, but I observe that sometimes writers who view writing primarily as self expression may feel that writing itself is an indulgence. A person may even feel guilty about writing. Nobody asks you to do it to begin with—to create something new. You're solely responsible for the content, which may be revealing and contrary to how you're told you should feel. But most important, when you sit down to write, you imply that what you are saying, what you choose to take the time and space and resources to say, is more important than anything else you could be doing at the moment in service to others. Tillie Olsen has written eloquently about the long silence of women—about the heartbreaking times of trying to combine mothering, working, and writing and how she lost much of what she wanted desperately to create. Time, time, unbroken chunks of time.

We may be taught only certain emotions are permissible to express. When we begin to write, we may find those old inhibitions and prohibitions now internalized as a censor, changing the work in revision or else stopping it before it can get out. The inner censor sets limits to what I dare to say of what I feel and know and see and think. Self censorship for all writers has similar roots. You are afraid that people will say, that's ridiculous. Nobody acts that way (except you). No one else feels that way toward her child/spouse/lover/mother. You have to have a commitment to the truths wrung from yourself as well as the truths already made public by common struggle or history.

For women, many of our experiences were dumb to us, unnamed, unpossessed because misnamed. I had insights at fifteen that I would seize again at twenty-six and lose because I had no intellectual framework in which they might fit and be retained. As writers we are always asking in public through our work whether our experiences and those of other people with whom we empathize and from whom we create, are experiences common to at least part of the population, or whether the experiences we are working with are singular, bizarre. There are inner censors that make shallow or imitative or tentative or coy the work of a writer, often through fear.

Voices speak in our heads that tell us we are brazen to admit

certain things, that we should be ashamed. We may fear to of-
fend those with power over us or hurt those we wish to love us or
those we wish to please. We may fear what those whose politics
or religion we share and whose good opinion we rely on may say
about work that deals with a contradiction in our mutual politics
or religious values, and the contradictions between ideology or
belief and action. Yet such contradictions are rich to writers. Often we grasp our characters most firmly in those moist irrational
interstices between intention and delivery, between rhetoric and
greed, between image and fear.

Shame can get in creation's way. We all have notions of what
we should be. A writer had better have considerable tolerance
for that gap between what we would like to be and what we are
in a daily way; at the same time, I think it helps a writer to have
experience of how extraordinary people can be in situations that
stretch them utterly. Sometimes we are ashamed of what moves
us or how much we are moved; at other times we feel we ought
to have been moved and we try to pretend. We don't only fake
orgasms; people have faked orgiastic appreciation of many things
that bored and even affronted them, from the Grand Canyon to
their party's heroines and rhetoric, to the current literary fad or
lion.

As a poet and as a novelist, I have to believe that when I go
into myself honestly to use what I find there, that it is going to
speak to you. Some of our experiences are similar and some are
different, but the naming of both liberates us. The recreating of
the experiences, the use of the feelings that may be different feels
more dangerous to me, as if I may stand alone in saying those; yet
I think these experiences are important too for us. So much of
our lives have been lived in the dark, in ignorance of what others
think and feel and experience. Many of our notions about what
others' lives are like are simplified images from the media.

Exercise:

Often we ask participants in a workshop to sit in silence and think
about their lives and what they have written about, and then to
think of something that made them ashamed or afraid, that they
have never written about. Something they were reluctant to share

with others. You might want to make a list of subjects about which you have never written—not lions and tigers and earthquakes and space travel, but things inside yourself, the hidden or secret side of yourself. After you have finished a short list, read it to yourself and imagine what or how you might write about one of those items on the list. Do you need to employ one of the distancing techniques we spoke of in an earlier chapter? Fictionalizing it? Using third person? Creating an alternate universe? Do you need to seek permission to tackle it from someone you love? From yourself? Do you feel you might need legal advice?

Suppose that a person writes what she must. That is only the first step in being a writer. The work must survive the moment of its creation. It must get out to an audience. She or he must dare to show the work. She must risk ridicule, misunderstanding, scandal, condemnation, and what's often worse, none of the above: silence. No attention at all.

Many people do manage to write, but then hide their writing. This is writing as self-expression, but not as communication. There can be no feedback, no sense of success or failure, no sense of outreach, of impact on the world. This is to act, but to pretend not to have acted and take no consequences for one's act.

Occasionally the supermarket tabloids run a story about parents who have a baby and then shut up that child in a room. (I know you would only glance at these papers while standing in the checkout line, of course!) The headline reads: "Diapered 23 Year-old Found in Cleveland Apartment, Chained to Playpen." I suppose it comes from not cutting the umbilical cord.

Once the work is done, it's ready for its own life. Your art is not you. It exists on its own. Others will take it, use it, abuse it, carry it off. It is their right to do so. There is a necessary letting go in artistic production, a point when you permit what you have made to depart from you and begin its own history. You will hear from it, or more accurately, hear about it from time to time in a fan letter, a hate letter, a review. However, it's not *you* but *it*. There must be some mental discipline to make this distinction, a very important one for preserving sanity.

Writers who meet together to support and criticize each other's work can easily spawn readings—anyplace, at bookstores, at coffeehouses, at schools, in nursing homes and hospices, in restaurants, at universities and libraries, in galleries, at festivals. Often groups or cooperatives of writers can get readings that would never be available to any one particular unknown or little known writer. Some groups have also published their own anthologies or started magazines. The number of writers who first published themselves is larger than you might imagine, but it is sometimes more effective to self-publish as a group and often achieves more visibility and better distribution.

You may get frustrated by the size of a small audience, but believe that even the best selling and most respected writers are sent on tours and into malls where six people show up for a reading, half of whom wandered in by accident. It's part of the business and you can never predict whether the date you scheduled six months before turns out to be game seven of the World Series or, as one of our writers discovered the day he did the "Fresh Air" show and expected a large crowd at a popular suburban bookstore, the final episode of "Survivor." However, in a group of five or six, each writer can generally bring (coerce) five or six friends to come and listen. That makes a sufficient audience for beginning readers to practice on.

If reading to an audience gives you stage fright, practice on each other. Shout, yell, let go, emote, sing your work. Borrow, share a tape recorder and listen to yourself. If you find yourself dull, an audience will wither. Learn to get inside the poem or the story. Think of the work, not of yourself, and make it shape itself on the air. Make people hear it. Practice and practice some more. Readings are one of the best ways for you to reach an audience and to discover for yourself whether the work has merit. If you have published something, readings are one of the best ways to get people to buy it. People will seldom pick up a book by an author whose name does not strike a familiar chord, but after a reading, if people in your audience have enjoyed it, often they want a book as a souvenir of the experience, as a way of revisiting what moved, amused or stimulated them.

You want to write, but you might be having trouble doing what you want to do; perhaps that's what drew you to this book. In a workshop, there is a point on the last day when I ask participants to think critically about their situation. How is your time organized? Could you get up early in the morning and write? Could you write late at night when everyone else is asleep? Could you find some block of time on the weekends?

Do you have a place where you can really write? Is there a door that shuts, or at least a partition setting off that space? Many people get hung up on their equipment. Is the computer functional and the screen easy to read? Do you need a more up-to-date word processing program? It's easy enough to say that many great writers have had no more equipment than a legal pad, but no publisher we know would accept a submission of three hundred hand-written pages.

Sometimes the problem is eliminating a time-consuming ritual, or even harder, a small pleasure. Do you need to stop subscribing to the morning newspaper or at least stop reading it with your sharpest mental energy every morning? Should you swear not to turn on the TV certain evenings or during the day on weekends or other days off? Should you disconnect the phone? Can you give up jogging or going to the gym on certain days to have time to write? You cannot do everything, so you must prioritize and, if you really want to write, you have to make time for it. Perhaps you need to give up a social activity or a meeting or two. Perhaps you have to decide, okay, I'm not going to take off that ten pounds, but I will get my book written instead. Which means more to you? That's what it comes down to. It is always a matter of priorities. Many people ask how much time it really takes to write a book and they're surprised to hear us say, quite honestly, that one solid hour of concentration everyday may be enough. Think about it. A page a day, 365 days a year, is certainly enough for a first draft. Sometimes the worst thing you can do is allot too much time—time for fussing over individual words, time for rewriting perfectly functional sentences, for dallying on the Internet or in the dictionary, in the bathroom, in the kitchen. One hour with your best energy every day can force you to focus, to get your sentences down on paper because there is no more time. It may be the one most productive hour in your entire day, the one you think about and make notes for. One hour. Before everyone else wakes up; or after they go to bed; or while they're all out to lunch.

Ira tells the story in workshops of the woman who came up

to him after we had finished presenting and asked him how she could change her life so that she could find time to write. He said, "How about getting up earlier in the morning?"

She said, "I already get up at five."

"Nothing wrong with that."

"But I meditate. Then I run for an hour."

"Okay, after that."

She said, "I have breakfast, shower, get dressed and go to work."

"How about on your commute?"

"I have to drive."

"How about on your lunch hour?"

"I eat at my desk and then I go the gym."

"How about when you get home from work?"

"I have therapy on Monday, my quilting group on Tuesday. . . ."

You get the idea. Her life was blocked out and she was not willing to relinquish any of her activities.

"Then you're screwed," said Ira.

We've all learned long ago that nobody can "have it all." Nobody. It's a myth. Writing, like a good relationship, time with your kids, a fashion model's body, a Ph.D., a vacation in Maui—you name what turns you on—takes sacrifice. What are you willing to give up for that one hour a day?

What we ask people to do in workshops is to think seriously about how you organize your time and your space and to come up with one change that would enable you to do more of the writing you want to do. Not a vast change, such as *I am going to quit my day job*. Rather, a small change that you have some hope of carrying out. We ask them, as we're suggesting to you, to write down this intent on a piece of paper and put it in the corner of a mirror you use every day. In a month, you take it down and replace it with another intent, that can carry you a little further.

One of the major advantages you can carry away from a writing workshop or a writing course is simply a stock of questions to ask yourself, both before you begin on a piece, and while you are in progress, when things go wrong. Am I beginning in the right place? Does my beginning seduce the reader into wanting to continue? Do I know enough about my main characters? What are their longings? Are they motivated and convincing? The more conscious you are of the possible variables, the more control you have over what you are doing. You can avoid wasting large amounts of time and, more importantly, your writing energy, on false starts that do not produce viable work by learning to do enough preliminary figuring out. You can also learn what to ask when you realize your narrative is not succeeding.

It is equally important not to begin a long work prematurely as it is not to delay starting it for too long. If you start too soon, you will waste a lot of time and energy writing from the wrong viewpoint or in the wrong person (first when it should be third, for instance), writing stuff that belongs in the dossier but not on the page. You have to allow time before beginning a longer piece, but you do not want to delay your launch until you have talked about it too much and lost interest in what you are doing. We all know people who were going to write a book about some subject dear to them but never in fact get around to doing it. You can talk out a book or a piece and lose the necessary momentum. Discussing a work you have not written may be necessary if you are seeking funding or an advance, but it is dangerous to do too much of it. Many a writer has had to repay an advance because by the time they got to actually writing the book they had been shopping around, they lost interest in the whole project. You also run the serious risk of being discouraged by other people in the early stages, when you are most vulnerable to criticism or simply a lack of enthusiasm.

When you have finished—usually not the first draft but what you imagine to be the last, although it may well not be—you need to plan to protect yourself from postpartum depression. It is an extremely real and menacing state which I have witnessed not only in myself but in many others, apprentice writers, those being published for the first time and writers in mid career. I try to have another project on hand at that point—for me usually a book of poetry I am putting together, or some essays I meant to work on. Perhaps reviews I have been promising I will get to. A short article. A short story. My only play was written at such a time. Whatever you select, it is important you have something in the wings.

I try out manuscripts between third and fourth drafts on my agent for her feedback on whether the novel is ready to try to sell and her estimate of possibilities. Up until this time, no one at all will have seen the book except Ira Wood. I may have sent an excerpt to a magazine or read a chapter to an audience somewhere, but the novel has not been seen by anyone, certainly no one in publishing. This is also the time I seek criticism and feedback from friends, colleagues, other writers whose opinion I trust, experts in something I'm dealing with and also from people I regard as good general readers—people who read a lot and can critique what they have read.

I wait that long to share what I have written with my agent partly because I do not want anybody telling me I can't tackle a particular subject or that something isn't commercial or sexy or fashionable or whatever before the work is essentially in place. It may need some tightening, some tidying, some trimming or perhaps some expanding, but it stands.

You must learn, once something is completed, to hustle for your work. You would not hesitate to push a little for a child or a lot for a business. Your work is an "other," once it's completed, and it deserves the same attention. It may be an unfortunate reflection of our times, and it is certainly ironic, given that writing attracts people who enjoy working in isolation, but a writer today has to be something of an entrepreneur, ready to market one's work, if not oneself. This certainly means submitting it, again and again. It may mean getting yourself readings, writing query letters, learning to deal with rejections and, on occasion, insults. It may mean writing reviews, for print or online media, to make connections, to make deposits in the favor bank and to get your name known by readers and by publications who will be more likely to review you. As foolish as it may feel to spend half an hour yakking with a talk show host on a local cable channel who may or may not have read your book, or a radio disk jockey who certainly has not, you never know who is listening, who may become curious now or five books from now. It's well to remember that close to 125,000 books are published every year. You have to separate yourself from the pack by reading and signing books in libraries, in schools, at conferences; in mall stores where you may be asked to sit behind a stack of books at a card table, of no more interest than the parakeets in the pet shop window. Do it; then laugh about it with other writers. If you push your work collectively, you will feel less shame, less guilt, which is another reason to have a group.

A writer must have the support of some kind of community in writing about her experiences, or she will feel crazy. A person who believes she is crazy will not write or will write, perhaps, but in a code. She may destroy what she has written because it is, she believes, bad—bad in not measuring up to standards she has been taught usually based on the work of men who grew up in the 19th century or bad in a moral sense—wicked. A strong woman is still widely seen as a bad woman. A woman who internalizes such judgments—as to some degree all women raised in sexist societies do—will punish herself for her strengths as well as her weaknesses.

Similarly, a man who writes may feel he is less of a man because he deals with feelings, emotions, the epiphenomena of the interior and daily life. Or simply because he does not go off to a job every morning as other men in his family have done. He may feel the need to counter the image of himself as wimp by acting twice as macho or writing twice as offensively as anybody else. He may accept the judgment that he is less of a man, less of a person, and thus less deserving of respect. For this he may blame himself, his mother, women in general or some woman who personifies the sex to him. We have seen examples of writers who've done all of the above. We all have emotions and inner lives, whether we choose to put them into a particular work or not. It is wise for a writer to accept that we all have strengths and weaknesses, virtues and vices, failed intentions and shameful fantasies as well as simply silly ones. We are all bundles of variant selves we may never have a chance to live out in the external world—and often for good reason.

Now, a work must be able to be conceptualized before it can get past the inner censor and be written. We are limited to what we can imagine. What we do is partly determined by desire, partly by what we think will be the consequences, and partly by what we imagine are the possibilities we can choose among. We need to read widely and critically to study the craft of other writers. We also read because when someone has written about a particular subject or in a particular vein, it may prick our imaginations into new possibilities—not an imitation but a new direction that the other writer has opened up or simply rendered imaginable.

Basically, good writing is done because it has to be done, because the person doing it cannot be dissuaded, distracted, ignored or punished into silence. It always happens against the odds. But you don't start back on square one. If art demands a long apprenticeship, it also offers the rewards of mastery, of what was once inconceivably difficult becoming second nature, and of there always, always being something more difficult and demanding asking to be tried. Our imaginations, our abilities may fail, but never the possibilities before us.

17

Fame, Fortune,
And Other Tawdry Illusions
Marge Piercy

My name is not a household word like Drano or Kleenex. Mostly people have no particular reaction when they meet me, although you can never be sure. My gynecologist "knows who I am" because his receptionist Audrey read one of my novels, as has my accountant. However, from time to time people recognize me on the street or in odd and disconcerting circumstances like in a shopping mall when I was trying on a skirt, or another time in a restaurant when Woody and I were having a bloody if moderately quiet argument. I am not so bad about accidental recognition as I used to be. I do not try to crawl into my own pocket or pretend if I don't move a muscle or breathe, I will wake in my own bed, but I can't say I ever behave more gracefully than a sneak thief caught.

Publishing books, especially about women, brings letters that can break your heart: women losing custody of their children, women shut up in mental institutions because they rebelled against being an unpaid domestic or took a female lover, women in all shapes and colors of trouble.

> Women dyeing the air with desperation,
> women weaving like spiders from the gut
> of emptiness, women
> swollen with emotion, women with words
> piling up in the throat like fallen leaves. . . .
> — from "Women of Letters"

You also get flattering letters from women as well as some men who tell you what your books have meant to them. You also receive hate mail, if you have any visible politics.

The admirers who do not give pleasure are those who call up, generally when you are sleeping or writing, making supper, entertaining friends and say, "Hello, I read your book, I happen to be in town, and can I come over?" There is no way to satisfy such a caller. When I was younger, I was so astonished and grateful anybody had read anything of mine and liked it, I would invariably say yes. Dreadful, dreadful scenes resulted. Worse than that, whole boring evenings and days and someone who felt they had the right to invade again at will and at some point would have to be dealt with forcefully. People who want to invite themselves into your house to meet you generally are pushy and sometimes more than a little nuts, and nothing less than letting them move in or letting them have at least an arm or leg of their own will satiate a baseless hunger. Now I make excuses, unless I know the person in some way, unless a genuine connection exists so that we can hope for two-way communication.

Every week several books and at least one manuscript arrive with requests for blurbs, criticism, help of some sort. I used to try to respond to all those requests, but I got further and further and further behind. The books I now put on a pile in terms of when they arrived (I am currently a year and eight months behind) and the manuscripts I promptly return, if the authors provided postage. I do not attempt to read manuscripts at all, unless it is for someone I know or submissions to Leapfrog Press. They are screened anyhow by our first readers. All the books I do finally glance at or skim at least and a certain number I read, but I feel haunted, snowed in by them. I remember how long I was utterly unknown. I feel guilty, but I know rationally that if I were to read even a quarter of them, I would do nothing else; and I do not have a lot of time to read in the first place. Unlike academics, I don't have long vacations or often any vacations longer than overnight. To make a living at writing, I have to hustle and have to work six days a week.

I travel a lot giving readings, and there the weirdness flourishes in some pockets like mold. People go through ego dances before me that I find confusing and bemusing. I do not have the middle class patina and I am not much good at making gracious casual conversation. I like best to talk to people one on one, not necessarily about me. Women who go about giving readings are expected to act like ladies, like mommies, or like tough dykes, and I don't fit into any of those standard roles.

Joanna Russ says it's my body type and my style that gets me in trouble. Nobody tries to make her play mommy, or at least not quite as often at first glance. She's tall as the Empire State Building, lean and elegant, and dresses tailored. I am five feet four (almost), zaftig, and dress more or less peasanty.

I remember back in the seventies, I was wearing my standard Women's Liberation army garb, slumped way over so my boobs wouldn't jiggle too much because I wasn't supposed to wear a bra, dressed in about thirty pounds of denim, when I thought to myself, Why do I have to wear male drag to talk to and about women? I went back to skirts or comfortable pants. I dress the way I feel good. And I always read in a dress: Let there be no mistake I am a woman, proud of it.

What do people want from somebody they have heard of? It is not even, frequently, a matter of having read your work and formed expectations, for I have gone through upsetting *pas de deux* with individuals who had no idea what kind of work I produce. I was pure celebrity to them, some kind of superperson because a published writer. Of the people who have some familiarity, many are attached to one particular novel and express resentment that I do not resemble physically or in character Vida in *Vida*—that I am not a native speaker of Spanish, like Consuelo in *Woman on the Edge of Time*, or a systems analyst like Miriam in *Small Changes*, have never been homeless like Mary in *The Longings of Women* and do not live with a daughter and a stroke-enfeebled mother like Suzanne in *Three Women*. I have had fans become hostile when I tried to explain that a novel was not autobiographical. The hostility seems to divide into those who feel put upon (I thought it was true and now I find it's just a story!) and those who suspect you're trying to keep the truth from them; all novels are thinly disguised autobiography and you're just trying to cover up being a lesbian or being a mother who has lost custody of her children, or whatever.

Readers of the poems tend to have somewhat more accurate expectations, although one of the first things always said when I get off the plane is, "I/we expected you to be taller" or "I/we expected you to be bigger." I intend to write a poem soon about being four feet tall, and then everybody will say, "Oh, but we expected you to be smaller." All microphones are preset as if everybody were five feet ten, and the podiums are sized accordingly.

Once in a while you arrive into a situation in which somebody has decided beforehand you are their sex object. You land and are visited with this great rush that has nothing whatsoever to do with you, and which seems to assume you have no commitments, no attachments, but are really a figment of their sexual imagination capable of fitting right into the fantasies they have worked up. I find that so off-putting I don't even feel flattered. Mostly men do this, but sometimes women do it. There may even be the implication that they got you this real nice gig, paying more than they think you or any woman is worth, so you should thank them by rolling over belly up in their bed. That happened a lot more when I was younger, of course, but even at my age, it still happens sometimes.

Occasionally you walk into a situation in which the brass of the department didn't want you. You are the sop to the younger faculty or the small contingent of feminists or radicals. I was once introduced in Illinois by the head of the English Department in this way, "Our speaker tonight is Marge Piercy. I never heard of her, but the younger faculty made me invite her." End of introduction.

My advice to the struggling young writer is, never thank anybody sexually, and never use your body as payment or prepayment for help. Fuck only people you want and then, no matter what goes wrong and how you get clobbered emotionally, at least you will have catered to your own sexual tastes and you will not feel victimized. You have been your own free agent and will be stronger for it. If you are honestly turned on by someone who can help you, clear sailing. But if you are a woman, you have to be especially careful you don't get known as X's girlfriend, because then you can write *Four Quartets* and still people will say you got published because you were X's girlfriend.

Every writer has some groupies, and how you deal with them is your own decision, within the law. You can sense that a great many of them would not like you as you are, as opposed to the idealized or otherwise fictional image they are toting around; or what they offer is a come-on for expecting you are going to be for them what Joanna Russ calls a magic mommy: solve all their problems, make them happy, get them published or produced or whatever, make the world right—for them—and have no real needs of your own to be satisfied. Since writers are generally pretty needy beings, such encounters are programmed for disaster.

On the other hand, one of the possible relationships that may work out for a woman writer is a relationship with a younger person who does know who you are and what you do and who genuinely admires that before getting to know you—but does get to know you. Such an intimacy can contain a lot less bloody gut fighting than somebody, particularly a man, your own age.

Oftentimes women who have achieved some small success find that the man or woman they lived with beforehand can not adjust to what they view as an unnecessary fuss about somebody they knew back when. Fame loses you lovers and friends, as well as bringing people flocking closer. It does, however, make it easier to find new relationships. You can pick and choose a little. That doesn't mean you'll choose any more intelligently than you did when you were seventeen and still squeezing pimples or twenty-five and invisible as a grain of sand at the seashore, but you may have learned something.

Many men and many women cannot bear success even of the most limited and partial sort coming to someone they married or whose life they have been sharing. They may feel they cannot hold on to their lover with all the new competition, real or imagined. More often they resent what they feel is the shift of emphasis from themselves as center of the marriage or life, to the other person who was supposed to dance attendance on them, not to be rushing off to Paducah to give poetry readings, not be signing books, making speeches, or giving interviews. Certainly they should not be on radio or television or be photographed grinning no matter how foolishly.

You will, as a traveling woman, find all too often that a welcoming fuss, however minor, also infuriates local men who feel that you are after all just a cunt and they've seen better, and why isn't everyone fussing about them? Similarly you will find as a traveling woman that frequently academic women in universities who may write a poem or two a year or always meant to write someday will look at you with annoyance and just about say to you, why all the attention on you? You're just a woman like me. Why should they pay you to come in here and read, lecture, pontificate?

People also commonly confuse three things that are quite distinct. As an American poet you can achieve a certain measure of fame, but you don't get rich and you don't acquire power. The Bush family is rich and the Bush family is powerful. Bill Gates is very rich. Allen Ginsberg may have been famous, but he didn't own half of Venezuela or even New Jersey and he wasn't consulted on the national defense budget or our policies toward South Africa. Morris the Cat enjoyed far more fame than any writer I know, but you didn't imagine him as wielding power.

Few writers are rich. If they are, maybe they inherited money. When you hear about a $100,000 paperback deal, the hardcover publisher usually takes $50,000, the agent $7500, and the writer's share on paper is $42,500 except that she got a $15,000 advance to finish the book, so that $15,000 is taken out of her share. That gives her $27,500 minus taxes. Let's say it takes her three years to write a novel, I would think a decent average of what people need. My shortest book took two years; the others, all longer. That gives her about $9,000 a year income for the next three years. Happy $100,000 deal!

For a writer, having some fame is surely better than having none, since if people have heard of you they are likelier to buy your books than if they have not, or at least take them out of the library; but it doesn't mean you're drinking champagne out of crystal goblets while you count your oil revenue shares, and it doesn't mean you have any choice about how the world is run and what happens in the society you're part of. Similarly the writer above with the $9,000 coming in for the next three years is immensely better off than she was when she wrote for an occasional $25 or $50 fee from the quarterlies, or when she did a reading a week for twenty weeks at one hundred bucks per reading, ending up sick in bed and worn out with no writing done and having earned a total of $2,000 after her expenses on the road are deducted.

Make no mistake: I like applause. I adore being admired, I even like signing books, which I understand some writers don't. I'm tickled somebody is buying them. I work hard when I give workshops and try to give honest and useful answers when students question me. I like having my books discussed; I passionately care to have them read. I even like giving workshops where I read lots of often incoherent or sloppy student writing—I do enjoy trying to teach them how to make it all better.

But I resent jealousy, especially when beamed at me by people who have made as clear choices in their lives as I have. I know how invisible I was to the kind of people I meet around universities and other institutions in my non-famous life, when I was poor and subsisting on various underpaid part-time positions. I know how they treat their secretaries, waitresses, telephone operators, cleaning women, store clerks. I was living in a slum, eating macaroni and wearing secondhand clothes (not then fashionable) and chewing aspirins because I couldn't pay a dentist while I wrote the first six novels before the one that got published.

I can never forget how little respect or understanding I received from other people when I was a serious but largely unpublished writer, not yet sanctified by the fame machine. It's hard getting started in the arts, and one of the things that is the hardest is that nobody regards you as doing real work until somebody certifies you by buying what you do.

Another kind of irritation I provoke in resident or visiting male writers is drawing larger audiences or selling more books than they do, whereupon they are careful to inform me it's because I "jumped on this feminist bandwagon." I'm fashionable, but they're universal. Universal includes only white men with university degrees who identify with patriarchal values, but never mind even that. If they imagine it helps me to be known as a feminist, they have never read my reviews. The overwhelming majority judge my work solely in terms of its content by a reviewer who hates the politics and feels none of the obligations I do when I review works to identify my bias and try to deal with the writer's intentions. Such reviewers also seem to have failed to notice that the women's movement, while touching the lives of a great many women, no longer has access to the media, and enjoys little money and no political clout. To try to bring about social change in this country is always to bring down punishment on your head. My grandfather, a union organizer, was murdered. At various times in my life I have had my phone tapped, been tailed, been beaten very, very thoroughly with a rich medley of results to this day, gassed, had my mail opened, lost jobs, been vetoed as a speaker by boards of trustees in Utah, been heckled, insulted, dismissed, refused grants and positions that have consistently gone to lesser writers, and they imagine there is some bandwagon I am riding on. A tumbrel, perhaps.

Then there are local politicos. A phenomenon I have noticed since my anti-war days is how rank and file in American movements for social change treat those who have assumed, perhaps fought for or perhaps had thrust upon them, some kind of leadership. Frequently the mistrust with which your own treat you is sufficient to send people into paranoia or early burnout, away from political activity damned fast; it certainly contributes to crossing over to the Establishment where at least you can expect that people will be polite to you.

If you are effective at anything, you will be sharply criticized. The real heroes of many people on the Left and in the women's community are failures who remain pure according to a scriptural line and speak only to each other. Also, lefties may harbor fantasies that you are rich. The creeping desire I suppose is to believe that if you sacrificed a principle or two and perhaps actually spoke in American rather than in jargon, you would instantly be pelted by hard money. At every college I visit a feminist will demand to know how I dare publish with New York houses rather than the local Three Queer Sisters Press—as if the point of feminism isn't to try to reach women who don't agree already, rather than cozily assuming we are a "community" of pure souls and need only address each other. Often women who have some other source of support (husband, family, trust fund, academic job) will accuse you of selling out if you get paid for your writing or for speaking.

Feminist presses have an important function, as do all small presses. With the New York publishers almost to a house owned by large conglomerates, they are the one hope for freedom of expression and opinion. The all-pervasive electronic media are not open to those of us who do not share the opinions of the board of directors of Exxon-Mobil, of Rupert Murdock and Anaconda Copper. What was true in the days of Thomas Paine and what is true today is that you can print your own pamphlet or book. The printed word is far more democratic than television or radio. You do not need to be a millionaire to acquire and run a publishing enterprise. My partner, Ira Wood, and I have a small press of our own that publishes many serious writers who can no longer get published in New York.

Just as a small press does not take much capital to set up and run, owners of small presses whether collective or individual can and do take chances on books that will make little money, that appeal to a small group. Most of the important writers of our day were first published by small presses and some such as James Joyce were published by small presses for their whole professional lives.

Conglomerate publishers may not be interested in a book because it is too original. They may be offended by its politics. I found out with *The High Cost of Living* it is still impossible to write a novel with a lesbian as a protagonist and have it reviewed as anything but a novel with a lesbian as the protagonist—nothing else is visible behind that glaring and overbearing fact. A book in fact may appeal to only a small audience, quite honestly, but appeal strongly to that audience and thus remain a good backlist item for a small publisher who can keep that book in print.

Fame has a two-edged effect on the character. On the one hand, if you suffer from early schooled self-hatred, then fame can mellow you. If you like yourself, you may be able to like others better. Naturally I apply this to myself, believing myself easier-going since the world has done something besides kick me repeatedly in the bread basket. However, I would also say that fame—like money and probably like power—is habituating. You become so easily accustomed to being admired, that you begin to assume there is something inherently admirable in your character and person, a halo of special soul stuff that everybody ought to recognize at first glance.

Fame can easily oil the way to arrogance. It can as easily soften you to cozy mental flab, so you begin to believe every word you utter is equally sterling and every word you write is golden. There is a sort of balloon quality to some famous men—including famous writers—and you know they may never actually sit alone in a room agonizing and working as hard as it takes to do good work, ever again. You may even come to regard yourself as inherently lovable, which is peculiar given how writers actually spend a lot of time recording the bitter side of the human psyche and our utter foolishness. Having a fuss made over one leads to the desire to have more of a fuss made over one, and even to feel that nobody else quite so much deserves being fussed over, or that any fuss, any award, any prize, is only a tiny part of what the person truly deserves.

We can easily confuse the luck of the dice and the peculiarities of remuneration in this society with inner worth. I recently overheard an engineer who writes occasional poetry berating the organizer of a reading because he felt he wasn't being given a prominent enough spot in the line-up. "My time is worth something," I heard him announce, and he meant it: He considered what he was paid by the hour and day as an engineering consultant somehow carried over to his poetry and meant that his poetry was to be valued more, since the time he spent writing it was worth more an hour than the time of other poets. A fascinating assumption, it launched this particular observation about the confusion between what the pinball machine of financial rewards and public attention spews out at any given moment, and the assumption that the subsequent money or attention reflects some inherent superiority over the less lucky.

Once in a women's workshop at a writer's conference, several of the mothers were talking about feeling guilty about the time they took to write, time taken from their children. I asked one woman who had been published a goodly amount whether being paid for her work didn't lessen her guilt, and she agreed it did. Finally, the group decided that if enough people seemed to value your work, whether by paying for it or just by paying attention to it, if some people showed that they read or listened to your work and got pleasure and/or enlightenment, something real, out of what you wrote, then you felt less guilty. You could begin to justify demanding from the others in your life the time and space to write. Certainly attention paid to your work seems to validate your effort and make it easier to protect the time necessary to accomplish something.

I suppose the ultimate problem with the weirdness I encounter on the road is that it makes me wary. It's hard to respond to people I meet sometimes, when I am not at all sure what monsters are about to bulge up from under the floorboards of the suburban split level where the reception is being held. I also find demands that I provide instant intimacy, or the idea that I should walk into rooms ready to answer probing questions about my life and my loves patently absurd. The books are public. They are written for others. They are written to be of use. But I am not my books. I never doubt that:

> the best part of me (is)
> locked in those
> strange paper boxes.
> —from "The New Novel"

But I don't believe that people who have bought or read the books have a right therefore to sink their teeth into my arm. I had an unpleasant experience at a fancy Catholic school recently where a group of women made demands on me I found silly. I gave a good reading, worked hard to make the workshop useful, went over their work. Then I was castigated because I was not "open emotionally." One of them quoted to me a phrase of mine from "Living in the Open" which apparently meant to her that you must "love" everybody you meet and gush and slop on command.

For some people, admiration of something you have done easily converts into resentment—disappointment you are not Superwoman with a Madonna smile, or resentment if you do not bear obvious scars. They can forgive accomplishment if the woman who arrives is an alcoholic, suicidal, miserable in some overt way. To be an ordinary person with an ordinary life of ups and downs and ins and outs is not acceptable.

That admiration that can sour into hatred is frightening. Bigger celebrities inspire it far more than small fry, for which I am merciful, but I would rather not inspire it at all. You meet an occasional person who, if you do not work a miracle—light up their life, change things, take one look at them and say, Yes, you are the one—they feel they have been failed in some way.

If what people want in a place is a good energizing reading, a useful workshop, an honest lecture, answering questions as carefully and fully as I can, then they are satisfied. If what they want is a love affair with a visiting Mother Goddess, a laying on of hands to make them real, a feeding of soul hungers from a mystical breast milk fountain, then they are doomed to disappointment. For that act, I charge a whole lot more.

18

The 10 Most Destructive Things Writers Can Do

(to Destroy Their Careers or Never Get Started)

Whatever You Do, Don't. . . .

10. Hold Out For Random House

Big Presses are often looking for Big Books and Brand Names. If an author approaches us with a fantasy of getting rich, I always encourage them to try to get an agent. We can't satisfy anyone's fantasies and everyone has the right to shoot for the moon. Indeed, people have hit home runs with their first books. *Cold Mountain. A Girls Guide To Fishing and Hunting. Prep.* Sometimes they become one-book wonders; the literary equivalent of Wang Chung or Milli Vanilli. But many times, as in the cases of John Irving or Jonathan Franzen or Annie Proulx (who all seemed to appear out of the blue) you'll find out that your "overnight success" has been laboring in the trenches, putting out mid-list or small press books for years.

If you have written something quirky and original, a small press might be right for your book. It'll need time to catch on, to develop a reputation, and a small press will keep it in print long enough to do that. Also, there are far more small presses than big ones so you have a greater chance of attracting an editor. There have been many writers who would not consider small presses, which is akin to guys who are holding out for a woman who looks like a movie star and won't consider a woman who loves sex, has a great job, a terrific sense of humor but is ten pounds overweight. Where do they find themselves? Often chasing their own fantasies.

Don't hold out for Random House. You certainly owe your work the time to take a shot at an agent and a big advance, but if it doesn't happen, don't be too prideful to consider an alternate route and don't wait too long. Books do become dated and small press editors who receive submissions of novels set in 1998 with a letter that says, "I just finished a novel. . . ." are no fools.

9. Fake It

The old adage says, "Write what you know." That works pretty well for a first book (everybody on the planet has an autobiographical book in them); or for authors who lead "high concept" lives like homicide cops, criminal psychologists, ex-forensic scientists and courtroom lawyers; for weird, neurotic types like Harvey Pekar, and those rare observers, like Anne Tyler, who have a special talent for squeezing insights and humor from the mundane. But most writers lead pretty dull lives and need to do research in order to give depth to their writing. Don't fake the research. Don't watch cop shows on TV and imagine you know enough to reproduce a portrait of life on the streets. "Writing what you know" is misleading. Successful writers understand that writing is only a part of their work; equally important is the quest to "know" more.

You cannot decide to fake a best seller. You think you can knock off a Danielle Steele or a Sidney Sheldon? Good luck. No matter your opinion of the quality of the work of writers whose books sell in drug stores and in the millions, those writers are passionate about what they write. They don't fake it. They are not writing down to their readers, they are the voices of their readers' inner souls.

8. Quit Your Day Job (Create an All-or-Nothing Schedule)

Believe it or not, you can write the first draft of a book in a year if you give it just one hour a day. The trick is to find your *best* hour; the one in which you are writing in that state during which you are totally engaged. Don't wait for the *perfect* schedule to start, or the *moment of inspiration*. It rarely turns up. Thousands of writers have "stolen" the time to write. But you have to find the best time for yourself, be it at five in the morning before work, or late at night when the world is asleep. No one can tell when the best time is, but if you give yourself too much time, you're likely to waste it fussing and get frustrated and quit.

7. Imitate Trends

Trends last for a season or two. If we think back to what was hot in the last few years, memoirs, spiritual books, anything having to do with angels, movie star bios, minimalist fiction, the short story revival, magic realism, dysfunctional family sagas, political books (left *and* right), chic lit, manga/anime, we invariably find that the market has become saturated and they are no longer the "in" thing (which does not mean that a good book concerning any of the above will not be published, only that publishers are not attempting to scoop up every book). You can't copy trends. While there is a type of book that is released on the heels of disaster, it is generally either written by a journalist who has simply gathered facts, or a compendium of news articles. Rarely does such a book engage the mind and the emotions or rise to the level of literature. There have always been books that seemed to have been in the right place at the right time, well-written books that shot to the tops of the best seller lists and were exactly what the public seemed to want to read the moment they came out. Erica Jong's *Fear of Flying* appeared when many women were discovering feminism and Robert Sabbag's *Snowblind* complemented an entire generation's discovery of cocaine. Roger Kamenetz (*The Jew in the Lotus*) and Mitch Albom (*Tuesdays With Morrie*), even Alice Sebold *(The Lovely Bones),* all to a greater or lesser extent touched on a national interest. But none knew, years in the writing, what that interest would be. You have to write your passion, whether or not it is "in" because you will have to live with the process for years. Marge's agent and I encouraged her to write a memoir and she threw herself into the task. But by the time she submitted it (and she is one very fast writer), her editor said, "A memoir? But they're *out*." Never mind, it was very favorably reviewed and made its way. If you have a passion for a subject or genre that is not "in," or will be "out," continue with it, figure out how to communicate your passion to a reader, how to present the material in an original way. You're a writer, not a department store buyer or a party planner whose career depends on the next new thing.

6. Fail to Write About People You Know Because You're Afraid it Might Hurt Them

If you have a great story to tell but you're afraid of hurting people, don't fail to write. Rather, learn to deal with that material. First novels are often autobiographical novels. There's nothing wrong with writing the intimate story of your life; the difficulty is in overcoming the fear of doing so. The trick is to learn the techniques of distancing. Do you need to write in third person? Do you need to interject yourself into a genre? Fictionalize the material? Or, dare we say it, get permission from those involved? Too many people stop themselves from writing because they can't bear to hurt people in their family. But, you can learn to disguise the material so that the story matters, not the identities of those concerned. You'll be using your innermost feelings but the characters won't resemble your loved ones. Moreover, in dealing with the material, you'll be healing yourself. Is writing therapy? No, but it helps.

5. Hide (Fail to Publicize Yourself)

The frustrating contradiction of writing is that writers, who need to be the most aggressive artists to get noticed, are probably among the most reclusive of artists, more comfortable behind a computer screen than on the telephone or in front of an audience. But you have to develop a new attitude; you have to become an entrepreneur.

This does not mean that you have to put boxes of books in your car and visit bookstores around the country (the way Wayne Dyer turned himself into a best seller *long* before New Age books became the rage). You can be a reviewer, a great performer, a book chat commentator; you can be a cable talk show host; you can run a reading series or interview famous writers for the newspaper (thereby increasing your chances of making contacts and getting blurbs). The idea is to be out there. To distinguish yourself from the pack. To get your name in the papers. To do favors for others so they in turn will owe you favors when your book is published. The day of the solitary poet in the garret is long gone. Garrets rent for a lot of money. You can write, but if you want to be read, you can't hide.

4. Fail to Read

People are always asking us the best books to read to teach them how to become writers and we tell them to read what they're going to write. You wouldn't want to be operated on by a heart specialist who only read *The Way of the Surgeon* and you don't want to read a writer who's only studied *how-to* books. Writers learn their craft by reading good books in the genre they want to write in, not by seeing the movie version of a books they're too lazy to read. If you want to write mysteries, read a hundred of them. If you want to write your life story, read memoirs. Your best teacher may be your librarian or your bookseller. You don't have to reinvent the wheel or the novel.

3. Burn Bridges

The world of publishing is surprisingly small and underpaid. An editor or publicist at one company may very well turn up at another. Moreover, when you're in the process of submitting a book, you want as many editors and publishing houses open to you as possible. Venting one's frustrations on someone in the industry may feel good at the time, it may even be warranted, but it is a poor strategy for survival. Wallace Sayre's Third Law of Politics states: "Academic politics is the most vicious and bitter form of politics because the stakes are so low." The same might be said about publishing. The vast majority of us—writers, publishers, editors, publicists, sales reps, reviewers, booksellers—are in this business because we love books, not for the remuneration. Because the number of readers is declining, and the number of books published is rising in inverse proportion to the newspaper column inches dedicated to books, we all have to say NO to each other a lot. NO I can't publish you, review you, blurb you, and so on. Unfortunately, disappointment is all too frequent in the book business, and it's well to realize that if you write a nasty letter to your publisher (as I once did), you may not remember it in three years time when you are hawking your next book . . .

but he bloody well will. Every word.

2. Get Jealous

It's easy to get jealous of other writers who have had some success while you are still struggling but it's far better to take a wider view: The more people who read a book, the more they are likely to read other books. If they have a good experience with a novel, if it got them through a long, uncomfortable airport layover, or a bout with the flu, or a sleepless night; if they learned something that will change their lives or were genuinely entertained by a book, they will go out and buy another. Successful writers are not siblings getting the attention *you* deserve, they are business people out there building their customer base.

It is much better to flatter than seethe. The irony is that few successful writers feel successful. The majority of them have been working long and hard in obscurity and know that one well-received book does not guarantee another. They are one and all receptive to flattery, and may even be able to help you with contacts, blurbs, readings, and more. Far better not to boycott the reading of the writer you're envious of if they're doing an event in your neighborhood. Better to get a seat in the front row and applaud like mad. Even buy a book! Have them autograph it! It's not sucking up, it's networking!

1. Give Up

It takes many years to succeed as a writer. Some quite famous but mediocre talents have succeeded simply because they have hung in and gotten better over time, or long enough to be taken seriously, or outlived their contemporaries. There are many ways to succeed, from big presses with large advances, to small advances and big awards, to small presses and great reviews to bad reviews and fans who adore you. If you love to write . . . hang in. Nobody is going to beat the bushes to find you. The world has too many writers. You have to hang in and make yourself visible. It only takes one good match, one publisher who understands your vision, one important review, to begin a career. We published a genuinely brilliant young writer who took his own life exactly three weeks before we called to say we were publishing his first book. Were there other frustrations in his life? I'm sure. Would publishing his book have ended all his problems? I doubt it. The only thing I do know is this: The one sure way to fail to become a writer is to give up trying.

19

Practical Information

Once you have finished a piece of work, whether it is a memoir, a novel, a short story or a poem, what do you do with it? You've written it, revised it, perhaps tried it out on your writing group or a friend or ten friends. Now you're ready to test your luck at getting it published in some form.

First, some information that's almost too obvious to include, but you'd be surprised to learn that perhaps fifteen percent of writers who submit to our press and all the various zines and journals we have edited over the years don't include a Stamped Self-Addressed Envelope, a SASE. It does not matter if you want your manuscript back or not. If you do, be sure you include an envelope with sufficient postage for the weight of the manuscript. Don't guess. If you don't want it returned, you still want to know whether the work is accepted or rejected. Always include a SASE. Some editors simply discard such unaccompanied manuscripts unread. If the writer isn't savvy enough to include a SASE, they are unlikely to pass muster in their work. Considering that even the smallest presses receive twenty to thirty manuscripts a week, you should not find it difficult to figure out why the SASE is a prerequisite to being considered. No indie press or zine can afford return postage, not to mention the extra office work involved, on all the manuscripts that come to it. The easier you make it for them to give you an answer, the likelier you are to receive one.

We also see a great many manuscripts that do not put the writer's last name and a running short title at the top of every page. Apparently these writers, too, do not understand the volume of submissions all editors receive. The stuff falls on the floor. The cat knocks it over or it gets moved aside to make room for lunch. A wind blows through an open window. The ceiling leaks. Use your imagination. We have also received manuscripts that were unnumbered. How they expected anyone to keep that manuscript intact and in order is anybody's guess. If you make it difficult to read your submission, then the editor will be in no hurry to read it and may not bother at all. After all, you are in a pile with sixty to one hundred others. If yours offers particular problems, it will often go unread or be given only grudging attention.

Do not put your manuscript in a fancy package, use blue paper or pink ribbons or draw pictures unless they are part of your text. It is a turn-off to see a gussied-up manuscript. The editor suspects the manuscript needed that ribbon or that lavender paper to stand out.

Be sure your printout is clear and dark. Again, no editor who has been reading manuscripts for six hours is going to bother with one that is hard to read. Don't imagine you can make the manuscript look shorter by using a smaller font. Every editor knows that trick and resents it. If your editor's eyes are tired, she will not give your manuscript the reading you would desire. As we have said in the chapter on Beginnings, you can count on an editor reading perhaps two pages of a short piece and perhaps ten pages of a long piece. If you haven't grabbed the editor's attention by then, you will not have a second chance.

An increasing number of editors are accepting e-mail submissions but they want them on their terms. For instance, at Leapfrog, for reasons of computer security, we automatically delete any unsolicited attachments and, due to the sheer enormity of the number of e-mail submissions, we do not respond unless we have some interest in the book the author is pitching. That is, we'll accept an e-mail query and if we're interested, we'll ask to see the first forty pages in hard copy. Some New York editors we know welcome e-mail submissions but they will not read any that do not come from an agent. Always do your homework to find the editor's submission guidelines. This information can usually be found on the publisher's web site.

Unless the editor asks you to, do not call the publisher. Frankly, it marks you as something of a pest. The U.S. Postal Service may not be perfect but it usually works. If you want to know whether your manuscript arrived, enclose a post card addressed to yourself or send an e-mail. If you have not heard from a publisher, it is more than likely because they have not read your submission yet and will not be able to until they have the time. Once they have read it, you can be sure they will get back to you. If they like the book, they're excited about the possibility of signing it. If they don't, there is no advantage to keeping it in the office. Publishers do know how much of an author's time and self-esteem go into a book. But authors should also know what goes into publishing a book. There is an irony involved in the schedule of publishing that may account for the fact that many publishing offices are in a state of constant catch-up. Books are signed and announced a year or more ahead of publication. While one book is in the acquisition process, others are being produced and released so that the publishing staff is almost always in a state of completing work on projects they had contracted many months ago and which are approaching deadline—writing catalog copy, presenting to the sales reps, overseeing jacket copy, cover design, internal design, printing, galleys, sending out galleys, marketing, writing advertising and publicity copy, trying to get the book reviewed, sending out complementary copies once the book returns from the printer, trying to get readings and booksignings and interviews for the author. It's a costly and time-consuming process for large, independent and very small presses alike. Once a book is accepted, it goes to the head of the line and grabs the available attention, as it should. The manuscripts waiting to be read have to wait some more.

The best writer is one who meets deadlines and then does readings, interviews and other publicity. A book doesn't sell itself. Readings add value to a book; they give the bookstore and the potential buyer an evening of free entertainment. They add a personal dimension. In anticipation of a reading, a bookstore may order thirty or more copies of your book, display and advertise it. (They will not keep more than a few copies of the book in stock after the reading, however, unless they feel your reading has generated some excitement; *i.e.,* potential sales.) Two writers can be equally good. One will give as good a reading to the three people who show up on a snowy night in January as to a packed house of one hundred. That same writer will solicit readings for herself and not simply wait for the publisher to do it or for lightning to strike. That writer will sell books. The one who sits home will not.

Some publishers and zines state that multiple submissions are fine with them; others state quite clearly that they are not. With these, you have to follow your own conscience. I know we used to permit multiple submissions, because as writers as well as editors we were sympathetic to the length of time it takes to get word back on a manuscript. Then we got stung. We read a novel, spent the time to critique it—and we are talking now about an investment of days, not hours—only to find that the writer had submitted elsewhere and had already sold the book, without telling us. No, we're not going to have the writer arrested for stealing our time; but neither are we likely to forget his name.

Always keep a record of where you send your work. Years ago I sent a submission to the *Minnesota Review*. The rejection slip came back with my poems, and the notation on it, We did not care for these poems the first time we saw them and our opinion has not changed with time. I was embarrassed and I had wasted my time and postage. Always keep a chart on the wall or a record on your computer of where your work has gone. If an editor rejects your work but sends an encouraging letter, do not send more work immediately. Wait a month or so and then send more, reminding them gently that they had encouraged your submission. Do not wait a year. The editor will have long forgotten your work; in fact, there may even be a new editor reading manuscripts.

Try to learn the name of the editor—perhaps by using one of the resources we recommend next. Address the note that accompanies your work to the right editor. Don't send fiction to the poetry editor or vice versa. Get the spelling right. Editors can be quite put out if you misspell their names. If you have been published or won any awards, mention them. However, do not include workshops you have taken. Everybody in the business knows you can take a workshop with almost anyone, and it means nothing. Furthermore, you may be saying you took a workshop with George Fadoodle, and the editor hates him and has ever since Fadoodle wrote a bad review of his work. So you have put a strike against yourself when you needn't have. If you are submitting poetry, do not bother to say you had an article in *The New England Journal of Medicine*, no matter how prestigious that is in the medical field. Do not mention your articles in *Golf Digest*. Only literary work matters when you are submitting literary work. You can mention work in another literary genre than the one you are submitting this time—a poet writing fiction, for instance, may promise an above average style—but that's all that counts.

For book-length fiction and memoir, in our experience, over-long cover letters, like packages that have enough tape on them to withstand a category three hurricane, mark the writer as an amateur. The function of a cover letter is to introduce yourself and your credentials and to provide a brief overview of the work. Your previous publications are important, but nothing you say in the cover letter will convince the press to publish the manuscript. The work will stand up for itself. It will get read, if only the first few pages. There really is no reason to give a long, detailed synopsis of the manuscript. The flap of a hardcover book is designed to arouse enough of your curiosity to make a purchase. Flap copy is approximately two hundred fifty words long, and is usually a good example of a well-written synopsis, but too long for the synopsis of a cover letter. Have confidence, they will read it eventually no matter what your cover letter says. But a short, three-to-five sentence synopsis is far better than a three-page single spaced outline of every chapter.

I don't know why, but cover letters seem to adhere to fashion, which once led me to believe that some how-to book was telling writers to include marketing plans with their manuscripts. I never did find out if that was true, but for about a year, manuscripts arrived accompanied by elaborate marketing plans in colorful binders. While an author's marketing ideas are essential once the decision is made to publish the book, especially if the author is serious in their promise to help the publisher carry it out—many authors, already on to their next book by pub date, do not want to be bothered—it seems somewhat pretentious when accompanying a submission. In any event, it is usually discarded.

There are certain things you can include that might give you a leg up. Most important is your publishing experience. Editors like to know your track record. If you have published before, include the books, zines, publishers and dates. Some people without extensive publishing credentials include their education, but this is not necessary. Whereas telling an editor you graduated a famous writing program may offer some hope that the project which is about to consume her Saturday morning does follow some generally accepted conventions—deeply drawn characters, for instance—she may not, unless she has an affiliation with that program, care. Many people who have succeeded in other professions include a detailed listing of their accomplishments—medical doctors are notorious for this—but it doesn't help them get their novel published any more than great reviews of your novel would get you into medical school. Other items writers often include are positive comments from previous rejection letters, writing coaches and former teachers. These kinds of things are often skipped. However, if one of those former teachers is a well-known writer and has given you a positive prepublication endorsement, one that you have their permission to use on the book, this very well might make the editor predisposed to the book. For one thing, someone with authority has given your work their imprimatur; for another, the publisher knows that if they publish this book they will have a valuable selling tool to offer their sales representatives, who can use it when presenting to bookstores. But what if you don't know anybody famous? Have no previous publications? Then what you do have is the work to speak for you—which puts you on the same playing field as all but the very small percentage of people whose names alone will get them published.

There are a number of resources for writers that are invaluable. Those who have been writing and sending their work out certainly know about Poets & Writers, Inc. (72 Spring St., New York, NY 10012 or www.pw.org) but it is an important enough resource to mention. Once you have published a certain amount (you must consult them to obtain the current minimum publications), you can be listed in their A Directory of American Poets and Fiction Writers, a publication updated every two years that is used to locate writers, often by organizations who ask you to do readings or workshops. *Poets & Writers* magazine is the place where almost every writers' conference in the country and many overseas advertise. You can look through the winter and spring issues to find out where an author you are eager to study with is teaching that summer. There are at least one hundred writers' conferences, and the author of your dreams is teaching at one and perhaps five of them. Writers' conferences are particularly useful if you are at the point where you desperately want feedback on work you have done. Not only do you get The Word from an author you admire, but you can share your work with other writers who want feedback on their work as well. Always there are readings and sometimes visits from publishers and/or agents. It makes for a very intense week or so and may really rev you up.

In the back of *Poets & Writers* magazine, there are listings of new journals and what they are looking for, contests you can enter, anthologies actively soliciting material. Often these anthologies are precise in their interests. They may want poems and personal narratives about people with disabilities and their interactions with animals. They might want the stories of lesbian nurses. They might want only writers who live in or grew up in Kalamazoo. If you have something that fits into that particular niche, you have a good chance of getting accepted and into print. *Poets & Writers* publishes some craft articles and interviews, but many writers buy it primarily for the back of the book, all those up-to-date listings and ads and information about possible markets, contests, workshops.

Another important resource is the National Writers Union (113 University Pl. 6th Fl., New York, NY 10003 or www.nwu.org). This is a labor union affiliated with the UAW. The union understands that publication credits do not define a writer and thus they are not criteria for membership, but you must be actively writing and attempting to get published and you must pay dues. The union has locals around the country, which hold conferences with useful talks and panels. Often there are local groups of writers specializing in various genres. Other than a literary agent, it's the only chance you have at finding out whether the deal offered you is the going rate. There are online chats and excellent information about agents available to members. You can get group health insurance and credit cards. If you are mistreated by a book or magazine publisher, the union has a grievance procedure available to you. If you begin to be published, it is highly likely, if not inevitable, that you will have trouble getting paid by somebody sometime, and it's great to have the union in your corner. The union has brought court cases against large and powerful entities such as *The*

New York Times, and won. It has picketed publishers who were abusing writers (and publicizes complaints about publishers on their website). Other unions respect its picket lines. The Writers Union is a real and increasingly more valuable resource, and if you begin to publish, you will use it.

Another resource you need to know about is the Dustbooks (P.O. Box 100, Paradise, California 95969 or www.dustbooks.com) line of directories and other works useful to writers. The most important of these is the *International Directory of Little Magazines and Small Presses*. It lists and updates the 4,000 book and zine publishers of poetry, fiction and non-fiction in every conceivable genre. It gives you the names and addresses of editors and what they are looking for. It's always best and will save you a lot of time if you can find a copy of the publication you are considering submitting to. Sometimes you can't find a copy and the *Directory* will suffice to give you some idea of what a publication will and won't consider. You can supplement this indispensable directory with other resources, such as *Literary Marketplace* (www.literary marketplace.com) featuring listings on 30,000 entities associated with the book trade including publishers, agents, awards, distributors, etc. and the useful line of books published by Writer's Digest Books (www.writersdigest.com), including *Poet's Market* and *Novel and Short Story Writers Market*.

Always put a copyright slug at the end of whatever you send out. This gives you some legal protection. To register a copyright, you must ask for forms from the Copyright Office in Washington (www.copyright.gov) and pay a fee. When you are published in a zine or in book form, the publisher takes care of copyright registration for that issue or for your book.

Sometimes it is worthwhile to submit short pieces in Great Britain, even if they have been published in the U.S. first. You do not include a SASE but a self-addressed envelope with International Reply Coupons included, available at any post office. If you have any contacts in Australia or New Zealand, the same goes. Canadian publication cannot duplicate publication in the U.S. The rights you give for first publication are generally phrased as "North American first serial rights." That, naturally, includes Canada, and vice versa. If something is published first in a Canadian journal, do not then submit it in the U.S.

Publishing online is another way to get your work out, immediate but largely unprotected. You have to consider the pros and cons yourself. For both of us, our web sites are important and we put effort into them constantly. As often as time allows we post samples of our work, figuring that the offers for readings, workshops and lectures that come in, or the ability to reach a new reader, balance the risk of someone not bothering to buy books because they can get the work free online. At least one large conglomerate-owned publisher found many of its titles illegally duplicated in electronic form and for sale on eBay. It is aggressively pursuing the matter in court. But the online booksellers now allow you to read the first chapters of many thousands of books and the Google Print feature is paving the way for Internet searches to include content of all titles in print. It's a frightening world for writers.

Since the first edition of *So You Want to Write*, The New York Times has reported that the number of electronic books sold has risen significantly, surprising a lot of people who gloated over the immortality of "dead tree books" and the cot death of the infant e-book. The resurrection is largely due to the popularity of cell phones, smart phones, PDAs, notebook and pocket PCs, even global positioning devices, all capable of content storage. Apple's iPods have eased consumers into purchasing purely digital content but even stodgy old libraries are getting into the act—although the old favorites die hard: The New York Public Library initially reported that the *Kama Sutra* was its most popular e-title. The e-book's economic impact is yet to be felt for large publishers, independent presses and self-published authors alike. Although in 2004 the U.S. saw sales of 1.4 million downloadable books versus 2.2 billion traditional books, new technologies such as electronic ink are replacing those clunky old electronic readers and promising a brave new world of e-reading experience. For now, if your work is online, or published in e-book format, getting the word out is still the key. If you are serious about building a name for yourself, you have to put effort into attracting readers. What that means is advertising the availability of your work everyplace you can think of, from the return address on your envelopes to the signature on your e-mail. There is little point here listing all the places to which you can submit your poems or stories; no print publication can ever keep up with a search engine. As writers we have to be interested in putting out the best work we can, writing what is meaningful to readers, no matter what technology we use. The most important thing we can say to writers about the Internet is that they will lose out if they are not online savvy.

Most communications with editors are carried out via e-mail. An editor certainly wouldn't reject you if you weren't online, but should your work be accepted, you'd miss out on an intimacy with your editor born of hundreds of small decisions that take place in the publishing process.

I should repeat that most zines and small presses take far longer to read manuscripts than you would like to believe possible. Three to six months is not uncommon. Agents and editors at large publishing houses are not much faster. The submissions outnumber the people who read them by an exponential factor. When I submit poems or stories and they come back, I reread them before sending them out again to see whether I can make them stronger. However, I know that some of my best work was rejected again and again before it saw the light of print or electronic publication. If I believe in the work, I continue to believe in it whether the first ten places rejected it or not.

As a writer, the tendency is to see the publisher as someone who passes judgment on you. A more realistic image of small press editors as well as many agents and editors at large publishing houses is of an overburdened office worker desperately looking for a project they can love and champion, live with night and day for a year. They hope to find a work that come commercial or critical disappointment, they can be proud of. Think how many books you read in a year that you unreservedly love. Probably not many. When you read a book, especially if you've purchased it, you want to like it, but often you don't. So why imagine that an editor is any different? There are always issues of social class, sexism, age and race: Book editors by and large are not representative of the population. There are always economic issues. Even not-for-profit small presses hope to publish books that will find a market. You may be rejected because the editor simply has no ability to empathize with the world or the characters you are writing about, but none of these issues is about you, the author. Editors do not know you, no matter how much of yourself you may have put into the work. Once a manuscript leaves your desk it has to make its own way. The editor who does not want to publish your book does not think of him or herself as superior to you any more than you think yourself superior to the author of some novel you read and did not like. If you can't grasp that, writing is always going to be fraught with disappointment. The writer's ability to accept rejection is as much a part of a writer's job as a quarterback's ability to withstand being knocked down. Sending the manuscript out again and again is as important as the writing itself. If you don't write it, it can't get published; but neither can it get published if it is not continually placed in front of as many editors as possible.

When you are sending around a manuscript and editors give you suggestions to revise it (but are not offering to buy it), take their comments seriously but with a grain of salt. Hardly any editor ever has the time to write a complete and well thought-out critique. They may point out something that gave them pause, which may be the opposite of what another editor tells you. Or, it may be something they simply latch on to which gives them an excuse to reject you. A wise independent press editor once put it this way: The acquisitions function of an editor is not the same as the editorial function; even if it is the same editor. When reading for possible acquisition, an editor does not pay attention to fine details; it is possible, too, that if they did not accept it, they never read the whole book. Better to collect the comments of many editors before altering your vision. If four different editors tell you that Jim, the husband of your protagonist, comes off as a wooden stereotype, you may have work to do. If only one editor mentions it, it may be him, not Jim. I once destroyed a novel that kept almost making it with publishers. I would revise it after every rejection to please the last editor, and the next editor would want something entirely different. Finally my vision was lost and I had to put the novel aside for ten years before I could tackle it and do what I intended, and not what sixteen editors had said off the top of their heads while deciding not to take a chance on an unknown writer. The most honest rejection slip I ever received was from a West Coast poetry zine. The editor wrote, "I like your poems, but I started this journal in order to publish my friends, and I don't publish people I don't know." I never forgot it and never held it against the editor—I often teach one of his poems in my poetry workshops.

Whether the editor took the trouble to write a critique of your work or not, it is rankly amateurish to reply—to argue, to denounce, to plead. You do NOT answer a rejection letter. You may kick the wall or yourself or stick pins in a clay doll, but you do not call up or write an answer.

Finally, what do you do if no one wants to publish your manuscript? There is probably not a writer you can name who does not have at least one book that never made it into print. Then there is the writer who suddenly bursts on the scene to spectacular reviews and a flood of books in print. The medievalist professor John Gardner waited years and years for the acceptance of his first novel, and when it was accepted, they accepted all his rejected books, too.

Often, the work that is most like last year's big hit finds its way into print, but the work that is most original is rejected time and again. Still, the question nags, how do I know it's good? How do I know I'm not crazy? Some people believe that everything they've written is a work of brilliance; some never have confidence in themselves. Many writers are blind to both their strengths and weaknesses. How do you know you're not crazy, that if no publishing company bites, the book is good enough to be published?

Libraries are full of books that some readers love and others despise. If you're serious about your work, if you've studied enough writing to feel that yours stands up, if your readers' opinions are opposite those of your rejection letters, if when you perform excerpts of the work your audiences seem truly moved, you may not want to wait for the publishing world to discover you. The cost of believing in your work is neither as expensive as a used car nor more vain than backing a business idea. Here's a list of famous authors who first published themselves: Leo Tolstoy, Walt Whitman, Charlotte Brontë, Virginia Woolf, Edgar Allen Poe, Stephan Crane, George Bernard Shaw, Ernest Hemingway, Joseph Conrad, Mark Twain, L. Ron Hubbard, Irma Rombauer, Richard Paul Evans, James Redfield, T.S. Eliot, Gertrude Stein, Henry David Thoreau, Elizabeth Barrett, Rudyard Kipling, e.e. cummings, Deepak Chopra, Thomas Paine, Carl Sandberg, D.H. Lawrence, Upton Sinclair, Beatrix Potter. If you believe it is vanity to publish yourself, then you probably believe that no one should go to college unless they get a scholarship. Or that it is vain for Stephen Spielberg to produce his own movies. Self-publishing involves a tremendous amount of work but there are many resources to help you. There's an entire subculture of one and two-book publishers who are passionate about the subject and more than willing to act as mentors. Moreover, there are many choices. You don't have to print thousands of books on a web press, you can print a fraction of that number using print-on-demand technology, or print an e-book or offer it in PDF format on your website. No, you certainly do not want to fall victim to a vanity or subsidy publisher who will overcharge you for more books than you can ever hope to sell and will never get you reviewed. But there are alternatives. The Publishers Marketing Association, with close to 4000 members, is the largest book publishing trade association in the world. It offers invaluable information on printing and marketing to its members, both online and through annual seminars they call Publishing University. On its website (www.pma-online.org) you can access more up-to-date information about the practical aspects of seeing your work through to print and distribution than we can even begin to mention in this book. If you believe in your work, there are more ways of getting it out to the world than at any time in history.

The old paradigm of the pained, solitary genius writing in seclusion and posting her book off to a gentleman publisher is dead. The writer today is an entrepreneur, a person who believes in herself and backs up that belief by publicizing, marketing and if necessary financing the work. Some of today's best selling writers are on the road with every book (and have made themselves best selling writers by doing so). While there are those who are too timid to read to an audience, too busy to tour, too proud to bother with the mundane questions of interviewers, they demur at their own risk. The field is too crowded. There are well over one hundred thousand titles published every year. The writer who holds back is the writer who is forgotten. There are important people to meet when you hit the trail to push your work: other writers who will trade battle stories and connections, bookstore owners and librarians who may stock your work, fans who will remember you the next time around. Seeking the information to publish yourself opens you to an online world of thousands of other writers whose experiences may be similar to your own. Marketing develops community. Once again, there are more ways of getting your work out to the world than at any time in history, and more identifiable niches of readers interested in specific topics, but you must change your notion of the writer as a solitary creator to that of a creative entrepreneur. Once the work is out there, all writers, the famous and the unknown, the highly paid and the self-published, have the same job, and that is to draw people to their work.

20

Frequently Answered Questions

At the end of every workshop, we invite questions. Sometimes the same questions are asked again and again in slightly different form by many people, which leads us to believe that either they didn't like the answers the first time, or that these were the questions they really came to the workshop to get answered. It doesn't surprise us that we are told that other writers give different answers to the same questions. Writers, like critics, are full of prejudices. We freely admit that these are our opinions. Sometimes we don't even agree with each other.

Do I Need An Agent?

You will if you have a finished novel to sell or a non-fiction proposal and you want to be published by a large mainstream publishing company. Some writers who publish articles with large circulation magazines use an agent; some well-known poets who are negotiating book deals do, too. But if you are placing poems and short stories in magazines and do not have a collection to sell, or if you are primarily dealing with a small independent or university press, it's not necessary to have an agent.

Good agents know who is open to publishing what kinds of work; who at the large companies have the power to make decisions; which editors are "hot" and therefore have clout and can garner more marketing resources for your book. Good agents make it their business to keep their ears open to changes in the publishing business and to make connections with editors. Editors are extremely busy, more so as bottom line demands have cut staffing and they are responsible for additional tasks. Many editors today rely on agents to cull through literary magazines, visit writers' conferences and keep abreast of cultural trends. Some agents make it their business to "beat the bushes" of the literary world, to discover talent and cultivate it; some agents are excellent hands-on editors.

We've known unrepresented writers who have gotten their work read by editors at the large publishing houses as a result of some connection (an established writer or a relative) but when the editors were ready to make an offer, they advised these writers to engage a literary agent (who, with a contract pending, was obviously interested in talking with them). Publishing contracts with large publishing houses, and increasingly with independent and university publishers, can be complex, involving the distribution of reprint, foreign, translation, theatrical, and electronic rights and many other provisions including warranties, indemnities, royalties and accounting, discontinuance of publication, and other issues. Some agents are open to submitting to independent and university publishers once they believe they have exhausted their possibilities with the large houses, some are not. When Ira could not get *The Kitchen Man* published, he sent it to independent presses himself—and suffered a standard but not very good contract. When his next novel, *Going Public*, was rejected by the conglomerate-owned presses but accepted by an independent, his new agent at one of New York's most prestigious literary agencies continued to represent the book because, even though no real money was forthcoming from the hard cover sale, she understood that once in print, she would negotiate paperback, foreign, and theatrical rights. It is possible to pay an agent or a lawyer a fee to look over your contract if you don't have an agent representing you. There are also some excellent books on the market that address publishing contracts. *Negotiating a Book Contract* by Mark L. Levine (Moyer Bell) is clear and concise. But while most independent presses will read work that is submitted directly by the writer, it is much more difficult to get a serious reading with a New York editor. One last thing worth mentioning is that some inexperienced writers feel that once they have an agent, a famous agent who represents big-name talents, the road to success is paved. Unfortunately, while an attachment to such an agent may initially give your work some cachet, get it into the hands of editors higher up on the food chain, and get you a quicker reading, it is ultimately the work that counts. A less glitzy agent who believes in your talent and will encourage you through the ups and downs of a publishing career might be a better bet. However, if you are writing poetry or literary fiction, you may want to go to a small press. In that case, an agent is of no advantage in getting published.

How Do I Get An Agent?

There is no shortage of books available that list agents' names and specialties. A simple search for "literary agents" on the internet will yield hundreds of thousands of sources. *A Directory of American Poets and Fiction Writers*, published by Poets & Writers, Inc., however, lists not only the names and addresses of writers but for some, their agents as well. Another variation on this strategy is to look at the acknowledgments page in the books of authors with whose work you feel a kinship. Most authors thank their agents and if your work is something like theirs, you now know the name of an agent to contact who represents that kind of work. But the best experience Ira ever had searching for an agent was made possible by the National Writer's Union. Previously he had relied either on referrals from friends who spoke highly of their agents but really had no idea whether their agents would be a good match for him or whether they had any expertise selling the kinds of things he wrote. Having spoken to so many writers disappointed in their experiences with their agents, he had come to the conclusion that he wanted to know as much as possible before tying up his time, and the agent's, for what is seldom less than a year or more of submissions. The agent's database of the National Writers Union solved the problem.

Far more reliable than any of the available books on agents, and less expensive than a popular service that offers to fully research a small number of agents for a steep fee, the database is now available online for members. It lists all the obvious information—addresses, contact information, specialties (cookbooks, mysteries, children's books, fiction, non-fiction, romance, etc.)—but something invaluable as well: various members' candid experiences with each agent. He could find out who, in various writers' opinions, was really good for non-fiction, for instance, and who was a great editor; who really respected writers and treated them accordingly and who, in their opinion, would be very enthusiastic for the first six months and lose interest when the going got tough. Indeed, visiting the database was like a gab fest with a room full of writers and their very subjective opinions. After a few hours with the database, he had six solid leads, sent query letters to each agent, got a call back from four and visited them in New York. He ended up with an agent with whom he was very happy. We'd like to emphasize the importance of a face-to-face meeting with the agent before you make your final decision. There is often a chemistry involved between you and an agent and that is difficult to determine without a meeting. All new clients are treated well, and why not? You are brimming with potential. It is only after the manuscript is returned a few times that the relationship can be truthfully evaluated. Is the agent giving up on you? Is she returning your calls? Does she sound discouraged on the telephone, or worse, is she beginning to blame you for the failure of your book to find a publisher? While an initial visit can't answer these questions, you can get an inkling of what the future might hold. You can observe them in action. Do they speak dismissively to people on the telephone? Ira once had a meeting with an agent who put him on an extension phone and allowed him to listen as the agent dealt with a publisher condescendingly. Although he felt like an insider at the moment, it didn't take him long to realize that this agent might very well treat him or his publisher like this one day.

Does their office seem disorganized? Is their staff friendly? (You'll be spending a lot of time dealing with the office staff, especially if you are not one of their top selling clients.) Are they forthcoming with the list of clients they represent? Good agents are proud of their client list, which tells you their authors' names, their latest books and with what publisher their titles were placed. Are they open to considering independent and university presses? Make it a point to visit a few potential agents. Just a half-hour chat—an office visit may be better than lunch; you can observe them in their environment—can provide a hint about your potential relationship later on.

Are New York Agents Better Than Those Outside New York?

Many writers do prefer to be represented by an agent with a New York office (or those located in a media center like Los Angeles, or within a quick day trip to New York, in Boston or Washington, D.C.) because it is felt that these agents are more likely to be in the loop, or industry insiders. There are a growing number of good agents who are located in cities around the country who specialize in representing writers from their regions, and others who have worked many years in New York publishing and, having developed their contacts, have set up shop in places that can afford them another lifestyle. Still, there are changes taking place in publishing regularly and you should ask any potential agent how they manage to stay current. Some are on the phone all day every day and manage their contacts with editors on a regular basis. Not all publishers, certainly not independent and university presses, are located in New York. It is easy for someone to call themselves a literary agent no matter where they live. These are sometimes referred to as "business card agents" and they prey on writers. They advertise their services and get themselves listed in many of the books that purport to help writers find an agent. Again, always ask the agent to tell you who they represent and what they have recently sold. Determine whether they are members of the Association of Author Representatives, whose members subscribe to an impressive canon of ethics. Never pay an agent for reading your work, even if they tell you they will reimburse you from the proceeds of your first sale. The job of agents is to read the work of writers. If they take you on, they will attach fifteen percent (twenty percent for foreign rights) of everything of yours that they sell. This is how they earn their money. While you may be billed for postage, copying, bank fees, messengers, and the like, you are not responsible for paying for their reading time.

Publishers Take So Long, Can I Make Multiple Submissions?

This is a question that, as writers and publishers, we fall on both sides of, and can probably be answered best by telling a story.

After Ira had spent two years attempting to get *The Kitchen Man* published in New York, he was impatient. He sent the novel out to two small presses. When it was accepted by one, he took the offer immediately and wrote a courteous note to the other press, stating (untruthfully) that the Crossing Press editor had heard him read at a library, loved the excerpt, offered to read the manuscript over the weekend and called up first thing Monday offering a contract. Total bullshit, of course, but somewhat plausible. He heard nothing back from that other press. Three years later, when he was submitting his next novel, *Going Public*, he received the following note: "Dear Mr. Wood, Some years ago you submitted *The Kitchen Man* to us and withdrew it while we were in the middle of reading it. Good luck with your *Going Public* elsewhere." Did he get arrested? No. Was his career over? Of course not. There are no laws saying you can't make multiple submissions, even if the press explicitly asks you not to. But small presses have long memories and it has always been our habit to attempt to curry friends in the very small world of publishing rather than enemies. If a press says no multiple submissions, honor their request. Agents, however, routinely make multiple submissions to publishers, hoping to use one publisher's interest to spark another's (something is always more valuable when somebody else wants it) and seeking to receive a bid that another publisher must top. It is courteous, in the least, to admit that the book is on submission to another house.

Isn't It Better To Be Published By A Large Publisher Than A Small Press?

If you are looking for a sizeable advance against royalties, you should indeed try to place your book with a large publisher. If the publisher feels the book has significant commercial potential, if their sales force is able to sell-in a substantial number of copies to bookstores (that is, get a large advance order), the big corporate-owned publisher may assign the book a large marketing budget. It may decide to place ads in national newspapers and magazines. It may send you on tour, pay the promotional fees required by bookstores (both chains and the large independents) to insure prominent shelf and newsletter placement, and attempt to arrange national talk show interviews for you. (It should be noted that online booksellers also offer promotional programs, to have your title on the page that pops up when you enter the site, for instance; to link your title with another or to send out e-mails about your title.) You need to be aware, however, that the size, famous name, and wealth of a publisher, no matter how many books it has on the best seller lists, is no guarantee that your book will get that treatment. A large publisher publishes a large number of books. It cannot possibly allot a huge marketing budget to each one. While most large publishers are very good at sending out review copies, and while book review editors might have a certain prejudice for the titles published by them, being published by a New York press is no guarantee of being reviewed. Space for book reviews in newspapers is extremely tight. Many writers are surprised that a publisher would fork out what seems like a very sizeable advance and not back up that advance with marketing support. But again, the large publisher has a lot of titles to market and will throw its support behind those books that have gotten the really big advances (after all, it's a bigger investment to protect), those that have had a terrific sell-in (it makes more sense to support books that are in the stores than the warehouse) and those sleepers that come along and catch fire. According to the "Report to the Authors Guild Midlist Books Study Committee" by David D. Kirkpatrick, the average literary book gets less than $5,000 of total marketing support by a conglomerate-owned publisher, "but just to get a book put on a table at the front of the store in one of the chains can cost $10,000." Writers are also devastated when their books go out of print, a situation that is quite common because large publishers, required by their conglomerate owners to watch the bottom line, have to pay taxes on their inventory. If a book is not selling at a certain rate, it will be shredded.

Independent, not-for-profit presses tend to keep books in print for a long time, and even small presses that don't have not-for-profit status keep enough copies on-hand to make it available for sale years after publication, when a writer's reputation has grown and she is more likely to be asked to do readings, workshops, and so on. These presses tend to publish far fewer books a season, so every title gets more of the publicist's time, if admittedly a smaller budget. Many small presses do send writers on tour and may have excellent contacts with the media. Some small presses are also very good at getting books reviewed. It is not uncommon for a dogged and enthusiastic publicist with unconventional marketing ideas to obtain more visibility for a book than a large and busy publicity department.

How Much Money Do Writers Make?

At a lecture in Flagstaff, Arizona, some years ago, Toni Morrison was asked, "What advice would you give a young person who wants to be a writer?" Without a second thought, the Nobel laureate and best-selling author answered, Don't quit your day job. Tony Morrison was writing brilliant novels long before they began to appear on the best-seller lists. While raising two children, she worked for many years as an editor at Random House, where she not only had to juggle her writing, her career and her family life, but observed countless writers who had to do so as well. I would date it to be some time in the 1980s, but it may have been long before, that the notion of the writer's life became confused with that of the screenwriter's life; that is, that the definition of the "successful" writer was one who was rich instead of widely read. In earlier decades, writers were assumed to be intellectuals rather than personalities, renegades as opposed to millionaires. People might dismiss your latest book by saying, "Never heard of it," but rarely by asking, "Is it a best seller?" as if to insinuate that if it were not, it wasn't worth mentioning. Only a very small percentage of writers reach the best seller lists. Because there are so many titles printed every year, readers tend to opt for the books by authors with whom they are familiar as well as books heavily advertised by the chain bookstores. A perusal of the best-seller lists will yield the same names year after year. Well-known writers are brand names and we are a society that trusts brands. So the rich writers are getting richer and the poor . . . well, you know how it goes. Which is not to say there aren't surprises. New people break in all the time. Publishers have not stopped publishing literary books and, in fact, shelf space for them, as a result of the proliferation of chain mega-stores, has increased. It's just that it's getting almost impossible for them to get noticed. In his

"Report to the Authors Guild Midlist Books Study Committee," Kirkpatrick gives an example of "the best possible outcome for a midlist author." He sites the example of David Foster Wallace's novel, *Infinite Jest*, which sold 30,000 copies in hardcover, and 60,000 in paperback. Mr. Wallace received an $85,000 advance from his publisher, Little Brown (after his agent's 15% commission), and another $42,500 in royalties, totaling $127,500. The book took him five years to write. You do the math. The report sums it up: "Writing books is a losing proposition financially for most writers. Serious authorship is not now and has never been self-supporting, except in a rare handful of cases." In 1981, the Authors Guild Foundation commissioned a report on authors' incomes from the Center for Social Science at Columbia University, which found that the median income for an American writer is about $5,000. According to Mr. Kirkpatrick's informative study, copyright 2000, "That figure has probably not changed substantially." Don't quit your day job.

You Mentioned That You Don't Consider It "Vanity" To Publish Yourself. What Then Constitutes A Vanity Publisher?

Even in the very difficult publishing environment we've mentioned, there are opportunities for writers, especially with publishers who are creative, willing to look at new models. Electronic publishing is an attractive model because an e-book is inexpensive to produce, easy to update, and does not present the costly problems of paper-book inventory and can theoretically then remain in print indefinitely. But few publications review e-books and unless they are best-selling titles, it's tough to get the word out about them. Science fiction sells well and increasingly women's romance and erotic novels. (Privacy of browsing online seems to be an attractive feature.) In spite of a recent upsurge of e-book sales, they have yet to live up to the high expectations predicted for them. A new generation of e-reading devices, supplementing the proliferation of electronic book-ready handhelds may yet drive their popularity. A more promising model might prove to be print-on-demand, in which a publisher or bookseller will literally print a book when it is ordered or print a small number to satisfy anticipated demand.

Some paper-and-ink publishers, as well as publishers who work with the new technologies mentioned above, encourage authors to subsidize the production of their own books and here the author has to be especially careful. Costs can be high; some that I've heard quoted almost double that of producing the book yourself. But this estimate may cover review copies, publicity and marketing. Marketing is the key. If the publisher is going to produce an agreed upon number of books, including bound galleys to be submitted for review, warehouse the book (or print it on demand), include it in their catalog, make it available through national wholesalers, such as Ingram and Baker & Taylor, as well as the online booksellers, then the money you spend might be seen as an investment in your work and your writing career. I would contrast this with what has been known as a vanity publisher, who will produce (or promise to produce) a large number of copies, send you your share, and let the rest rot in their warehouse. Sometimes they never print the books that are supposed to be in the warehouse. The difference, of course, is the commitment to get the work out to the reading public. An honest subsidy publisher will treat your book like any other publishing house. A vanity publisher will ship you a garage full of books. In spite of their promises, that is all you will get.

So What Do I Do If No One Will Publish My Book?

There are as many answers to this question as there are people willing to answer it. Here are some of ours:

1. If you're serious about your writing, that is, if you genuinely enjoy writing and are not under the illusion that it is an activity that will make you rich and famous, you'll forget about the book that did not sell and write another. And if necessary, another. With each book you'll become a better writer and you may come back to that book someday with more insight and skill. You may bastardize parts of it for other novels. If you happen to succeed with another book, you may even sell it later, once you have a reputation. You'd be surprised how many writers' second books were actually their first. You have to look at your first book as apprentice work no matter the disappointment of not seeing it get published. Like any professional, you have to view those first

few years of writing as time put in to learn your craft. It is disappointing, for some writers even heartbreaking, to give up on a project that has taken up two years of your life, but you wouldn't expect to be a doctor or a lawyer after your first two years college. Why underestimate the apprenticeship of a writer?

2. If you have taken a few years to write a book and have been paying attention to the literary world, then presumably you've learned a number of things along the way. You've learned that fewer people are buying books but that there are more books than ever being published. You've learned most writers are disappointed in their careers and only a very few can be considered "successful" by the standards of the business world. This should help dispel the notion that there is something wrong with you; that because your book did not get published, you are some kind of failure. You've learned that writing can be a very isolated life so that if you're going to continue, you need to fortify yourself. Some people get a writer's group together; some attend writer's conferences. Both will put you in touch with a community of other writers. Poets are always sending their work out to magazines (or should be). Smart fiction writers attempt to get excerpts published as short stories. Publications in little magazines give you credentials. Credentials give you confidence. Some writers perform their work wherever and whenever possible, which enables them to understand that what your audience enjoys and what editors want to buy can be two different things. Whatever works for you. What's important is that you retain the pleasure you take in the writing, that you do not hang your selfworth on someone's decision to publish you, which in real terms boils down to investing many thousands of dollars and at least a year of time and resources in your book.

3. It's also important to scrutinize your battle plan for getting published. Have you been submitting to the right agents? Has your agent been submitting to editors who are best for your type of book? Are you beginning to accumulate rejection letters that are saying the same things? If so, do you see any merit in rewriting? Is it time to start sending your book to small presses? Are you researching what these small presses actually publish so that you are not wasting time on pointless submissions? Is your book dated?

Editors can smell a book that's been kicking around for years. Are you still attempting to place a book that takes place in 1997 when the story might seem fresher if updated to the present? Are you yourself getting tired of the process and would you like to get to work on a new project that you're excited about? Do you really want to keep writing or are you putting off a career change?

4. Under certain circumstances, it may make sense to publish yourself. Here are some examples:

The first is a very regional book, a book of interviews of famous and successful residents of a suburban town outside Boston. The author was a retired attorney who had a hunch that readers might be curious about all the entrepreneurs, sports figures, movers and shakers, ex-politicians, many with national reputations, who lived in his town. He interviewed many of these personalities on his local cable show and then wrote an essay based on each interview. Publishers thought his book a risk because the interest was too local, and yet the author believed that there might be a market among residents who were both proud of and curious about their neighbors. Some people might define the success of this venture (for it is a business venture) as selling enough books to cover the cost of his print run; others might define success as turning a profit. If he produced an attractive and well written book and was careful about the costs of production, and if he marketed the book well—setting up events in bookstores and other venues, advertising in and getting himself covered by the local newspapers, perhaps selling bulk copies of the book at large discounts to local charities who might sell it at cover price—he might well make his investment back. And yet he considered the project a success because he felt that he had met some astounding people he otherwise would not have had the opportunity to meet, and that he was giving something back to his community, a historical record. Couple this with the fact that he had become a local celebrity himself and, certainly on his own terms, the project can be termed successful.

The second instance of a good decision to self publish is one involving a novel. Rejected numerous times, the author simply believed in her vision and didn't care whether a publisher saw its merits. In her case it was easy to understand why the book was not attractive to a mainstream press. The story was about a stripper in Hollywood who went off the deep end and ended up committed to a mental hospital. The style was like that of Charles Bukowski, raw, honest, cynical and shocking. The author engaged in a collaboration with a local visual artist who illustrated the book with erotic drawings and paintings. Together they financed the printing of about 200 copies, publicized a local event, and managed to get coverage in the arts sections of the regional newspapers. Thus she assured herself a small readership. When word got out that the local librarian couldn't keep the book on the shelves, that it was continually being stolen by local teenagers, Leapfrog Press got interested, sought out a copy of the book and decided to publish it. It needed a thorough editing job; it needed many scenes added and the time line of events straightened out, but the writing had energy and humor, and, in spite of the dark subject matter, told a fascinating story.

What is the percentage of self-published books that get discovered by publishers? Very small, but it happens. *The Christmas Box* and *The Celestine Prophecy* are the poster children for the phenomenon of self-published books that make it to the best-seller lists. But the number of famous authors who originally self published is surprising. A recent phenomenon is the success of a self-published genre dubbed "urban lit"—the new incarnation of the "street-fiction" popular in the 1970s that told stories about the lives of junkies, prostitutes, pimps, and drug dealers.

Teri Woods was a former paralegal and office cleaner who wrote *True to the Game*, a hip-hop novel about a drug dealer and his hustler girlfriend that was rejected by twenty publishers. With some backing by family and friends, she had 500 copies of the book printed and sold them from the trunk of her car in Harlem—according the *New York Post* "the same car she sometimes had to sleep in because she was homeless." Woods sold thousands of copies and started her own publishing company. Ghetto realism was eventually "discovered" by the mainstream presses but small and self-publishers continue to drive the momentum with many new authors telling their stories about life in prison and on the street.

It's well to ask yourself what you want out of self publishing. Before you make the commitment, try to realistically define success. Are you looking for a few hundred copies to sell at readings? Will you be using the book to complement another project, such as a seminar you give or a class you teach? Are you hoping it will be a springboard for publicity? Do you feel there is something special about the book, such as the inclusion of illustrations, that will add value and thus enable you to sell it? Are you attempting to build a reputation? Does the book have strong regional significance? Would the book be of value to a specific niche of readers? Realistic expectations may result in surprising success.

So what should you do if no one will publish you? Try to judge the responses of the people who have experienced your work. If they're truly moved, it may be a sign that, like "urban lit" it's too original for publishers who are looking for a safe investment, and that others will be moved enough to want to buy it.

Appendix I

Excerpted from *The Kitchen Man*, as referred to in Chapter 15

A SCANDAL IN THE FAMILY

I am a soldier in the service of the appetites of the rich, a waiter at Les Nieges d'Antan. The Snows of Yesterday, the finest restaurant north of New York City, a number one choice in the haute cuisine category of every magazine in which we advertise.

I assume a position of parade rest amid the commingling aromas of pipe smoke and fresh cut flowers. Vowels of contentment . . . aahhhhh . . . announce the presentation of a meal; bedroom groans, Ooh, no! I can't stand it, stop! greet the squeaking wheels of the dessert cart. Saturday evening, we have been fully booked since Tuesday, and all goes according to meticulous plan.

Until I am called to the telephone.

"It's your mother." She announces herself like the finance company, to get the bad news over with, as if she's a burden.

"Mom, how are you?"

"What do you care?"

"I do care. I love you."

"No, you don't." Understand, this can go on for half an hour. I do, you don't. I do, you don't. My mother's keenest pleasure is the affirmation of other people. To that end she demeans herself to everyone. The dentist. The dry cleaning man. The plumber. Lady, you need a new hot water heater. It's my fault. No, Lady, it's not. It is. It's not. It is. What does he care at sixty dollars an hour? The only way to stop it is to wait, pause; you don't disagree with her, she can't disagree with you. "So," finally she goes on, "how do you like your new apartment?"

"We love it, as soon as we're settled you'll have to come over."

"You wish I never called, don't you?"

"Why do you say that? Of course I don't."

"You do."

"I don't."

Pause.

"So, Gabriel, when are we going to see you, the parents who love you so much?"

"Tell you what, call me at my new number. Tomorrow, in the afternoon and we'll make a date."

"I'd rather call you at the restaurant."

At this moment thirty customers are staring at my back, squirming, yawning, dying for another cup of coffee. Some raise one finger to get my attention—very continental. Some smile, the friendly approach. Some brood, Wait until you see your check, Jerk. "It's not good to call me here, Mom."

"You call me back then, Darling."

"Why, what's the matter? Why can't you call me at home?"

"I'd rather not, that's all. You know me. What if *she* answers?"

She is an Obie Award winning playwright, a professor of theater. *She* is the person I live with, the person I love.

"The woman, Gabriel."

"Her name is Cynthia."

"Very nice. But I'd feel funny. So you call me, okay?"

"Mom, what's the matter with you?"

"I don't know if you want me to be honest or not?" Honest, in my family, is synonymous with vicious. To be open with each other is to attack, to unload every unkind, sordid impression. To protect yourself in my family you have to say, "please don't be honest," which undermines the very notion of family and makes you feel like a coward. "To be honest," my mother continues, "She's practically my age."

This is not true. Cynthia is ten years older than me. "And she's practically my wife."

"Gabriel, I don't expect you to understand. You will when you get older."

My mother is a sixty-seven year old size-five petite, an anorexic

Madame Bovary, in love with romance, at war with aging. My mother starved and drugged me until I was twelve years old. Philip Roth had nothing to complain about.

I read about Sophie Portnoy. I dreamed about Sophie Portnoy, balabusta, matriarch, kitchen witch. Arms soft as overripe honeydew folded over a flower print dress, standing above her ungrateful Alex begging him to eat, rooting for his appetite like a ticket holder at a horse race. Please, Darling, the crisp roast potatoes and the warm apple sauce. The sweet nutty *tsimmis* and the *flanken*. The way you like it. Try, Precious. Honeycake for dessert. Raspberry sherbet, too, for my hungry boy.

My mother weighed every item she served me on a plastic scale. She had a local handyman drill a padlock on the refrigerator door. She emptied my pockets for loose change before I left the house and cruised the shopping plaza because a neighbor kid told her I sometimes bought a knish and devoured it by the dumpster in back of the deli. She ran her fingers around the waist band of my pants to make sure they were not tightening (to this day I opt to drip rather than tumble dry, having more than once been the innocent victim of shrinkage). She clicked her tongue in disgust when the clothing salesman led us past the regular sizes to the elephant tent of the children's wear department: the table marked Huskies.

I was weighed four times a week, always showing far above the Metropolitan Life Average Weight for Children (of India? I wondered) and driven bi-monthly to a diet doctor whose lunch clung to his mustache, who pinched my flesh blue and prescribed amphetamines. Before every meal I chocked down a black pill whose street value today is six dollars. My hands shook. My stomach was an express elevator. I was a chronic insomniac at ten years old. Alex Portnoy locked himself in the bathroom and wacked himself silly. With so much speed in me I couldn't even get it up.

But I couldn't blame her, not then, not now. I was grown before my time—tall and broad, the kids called me Haystacks, after a TV wrestler who was buried in a piano crate—and she never grew up. A bobby soxer at thirty, adulthood took her by surprise. Lost in some Andrews Sisters movie, she hummed "Mares eat oats and lambs eat oats" as she primped in her bedroom for hours, discarding blouses, trying lipsticks, just to walk down to Shirley

Avenue for milk and cold cuts. She batted her eyes at every man on every corner and giggled every time the greasy butcher rolled his toothpick on his tongue and said, "You want some meat to-day?" But I blew it for her. A baby boomer stuffed with the seven basic food groups, I exceeded all genetic expectations. I was my grandfather's pride, a brick shit house, second generation grown weed-wild. But she couldn't be the neighborhood flirt with an enormous son in tow.

She was my confidant; I, her only friend. Pals, we shopped together, sipped lemon Tabs, practiced the fox trot and the lindy my father was always too tired to learn. At ten years old I knew all about Howard, the man she could have married, who had acne pimples big as candy corn, but who would have made us rich. I knew she hated her big nose, that it kept her from being beautiful, that she saved quarters and nickels in a jar to have it fixed. Together we sang the song she once wrote that was as good as any on the radio. Silently we wished that one day the car would not turn into the driveway at six o'clock, that one day my father would not clop up the stairs and throw his business problems on the couch with the evening *Post*. Silently we wished to go off, mother and son, the bobby soxer and the brick shit house, in search of a contract for her song, in search of Howard, and a nose job.

"Mom, I want you to meet Cynthia. I want us all to have supper together, I want—"

"Your father and I want to see our son, Gabriel. You don't have to drag along some stranger just because we're too boring to take up your precious time."

"Who said that? I didn't say you were too boring."

"But we are."

"You're not."

"We are."

Tonight we're meeting my parents at a Chinese restaurant: their choice. Then we're all four going to a performance of Cynthia's play: my choice. They were scared. They've never been to the theater. They tried to beg out but I held firm. If we're ever going to be close again we have to bust out of our tired old patterns.

"Jesus Christ." Wearing black pants and a black shirt I am sucking in my stomach in front of the hallway mirror. "I look as fat as a pig."

"Fat?" Cynthia is applying her makeup in the bedroom. "You've been starving yourself for two days and I'm warning you, Gabriel, Chinese food is full of MSG and you're going to get sick."

This brings me to the door. "Promise me. *Promise* me you're not going to start in front of my parents with the MSG in the food."

"What, start? You don't have a body like everybody else? MSG on an empty stomach doesn't make you sick?"

"Please?" I am not above getting down on my knees. "For me. Just this once. Don't haggle about the chemicals in the food. My parents will not understand. They simply will not understand."

"Then why in the world are we eating Chinese food when you knew you were going to starve yourself beforehand?"

"Because my father won't eat anything else." This is a fact. At Gettysburg, at Fort Ticonderoga, at Valley Forge, wherever we went on vacation, my father would never eat supper anywhere but at a Chinese restaurant. In Williamsburg, Virginia, my baby sister yowling with hunger, we drove two hours to find a place staffed by blond William and Mary students in magenta luau shirts. Ditto Amish country. Red checker table cloths. Soy sauce in cellophane packets. You know you're in trouble when the waiter comes to your table with bread and butter in a wicker basket. "And just ignore it when my father starts to speak Chinese."

Cynthia is suddenly impressed. "You never told me your father speaks Chinese."

"He doesn't. So I beg you. Please. Ignore it."

Jimmy Lee's Happy Talk Lounge, Dad's favorite restaurant, is two-thirds empty. My parents are sitting in a corner booth, under a canopy of bamboo and thatch, next to a plastic Mugo pine. The ashtray is overfull. There are two highballs in front of Mom, two Cokes in front of Dad. He never drinks. When mom sees us she pops the pill she's been clutching, bolts down whatever is left in her glass, and waves. Toodle—oo. Dad stands.

I take one last look at Cynthia in her red crepe suit, elegant enough to please my mother, low-cut enough to interest Dad. Knowing my father has a sweet tooth she baked brownies for him last night; knowing my mother is phobic about long hair, Cyn trimmed hers two inches.

"Gabriel, oh, Gabriel." Mom is still a perfect size five, still consumes no solid food except Sarah Lee cake. Her every vertebrae is as distinct as a swollen knuckle and as I envelop her in a welcoming hug I imagine a skeleton shellacked with hair spray.

"My Gabey," Dad says as we paddle each other on the back. He is a tall man for his generation, with a chest like an oak wine cask and a round fluid middle. His name is Sam, nicknamed Samson, all his life likened to an ox. "Gabey, Gabey," he sighs, proud. "How's your car?"

Mom steps back to view me at arm's length. Her hair is red now. It was blonde before the summer. "You look gorgeous. Look at that handsome face. So you have a belly," she goes straight for the bulge over my belt and twists it like challah dough. "When you get older everybody gets a belly."

"Except for Doctor Pincus. Doctor Pincus has no belly," Dad says.

My mother freezes. Her eyes squint warning. "Don't start."

"Oh, svelte Doctor Pincus with his little mustache. He looks like David Niven your mother says."

"He's a cultured, educated man, Sam."

"He's a fairy."

"This is a poor man whose wife passed away a year ago. According to your father he's beating down my door. He's not looking for a woman of sixty-seven, believe me. Nobody's looking for a woman of sixty-seven."

They moved to their present house during my first year away at college. Vaguely, I recall a sign in front of a split-level across the street: I. G. Pincus, optometrist. "He told me my wife had the eyes of a forty year-old woman."

My mother lights up. "When did he say that?"

"I almost sent him to the moon." Dad balls his fist. "He should talk about my wife's eyes."

I smile at Cynthia, a sad but victorious I told you so. For months Cynthia thought I was keeping her from meeting my parents because I was ashamed of her. Now, ignored, foil wrapped gift in hand, she can observe them for herself as they make the entire world their stage. Perhaps in another life they would have become the Lunts.

"Mom, I'd like you to meet— "

"Just a minute, Gabriel. When did Doctor Pincus say that, Sam? I want to know."

"Mom, this is Cynthia."

"Yes, darling, of course, yes." My mother smiles but her eyes do not leave my father's. She kisses Cynthia's cheek. "Hello, hello, Cynthia. Did Gabriel tell you I saw one of your books in the library? I was so proud. But if you want me to be honest, I asked my friends and nobody's ever heard of you."

"It's Doctor Pincus that's never heard of you," Dad says.

There is nothing left to do but eat. Mom seats us. "Sam and Gabe, there. Cynthia and I, here. And you two take these." Mom pushes the little wooden bowl of crispy noodles to our side of the table. "We certainly don't need these, do we?" Mom says to Cynthia. "Not at our age."

"Ah, Gabey, Gabey," dad sighs. He squeezes my knee. "My first and only son. You look terrific." He snaps his fingers. "Waiter!"

I want to evaporate. I want to disappear. If anyone in my restaurant snaps his fingers for my attention, I ignore him. The waiters here do, too. "Chop Chop! Ching Low!" Dad calls.

"Pop," I say gently. "Maybe if you don't make fun of their language. Maybe if you spoke to them with a little respect."

"Oh, I see, I see." Dad slides, huffing, out of the booth. He stands next to the table and bows to a passing waiter. "Oh, excuse me, kind sir. Excuse me for troubling you. But if you do not mind the inconvenience, would you deign to honor us by gracing our table with an order of egg rolls?"

I glance at Cynthia for help, acknowledgement, anything, but my mother is commanding her complete attention. "…and Doctor Pincus says I should not be ashamed to admit that I've had a hysterectomy. It's not uncommon for a woman our age, right?"

I eat and I eat. I cannot hear their voices when I eat. The rice steams in its little bowl, sticky as a snowball, the mustard burns my sinus clear, the charred flesh of the pink sparerib flakes on my fingertips as the hot juice runs down my chin. I eat it all, everything. I refill my plate with the sweet and sour gravy, the shredded mu shu pork, the soggy mattress of egg fu yong, the crunchy water chestnuts.

I eat and I grow young, a child again at my parent's table.

I eat and watch them, huge as dinosaurs, knocking each other over with the thunderous wallop of their scaly tails. I eat now as I ate then, compulsively chewing, swallowing, trying not hear my mother screaming at my father he was too fat to sleep with. I eat now as I ate then, as my mother sobbed through our entire Thanksgiving dinner, her food untouched, her tears falling into her cranberry sauce and making it run in thin maroon rivers. I ate as my mother watched the clock and my father slept off his depression, Friday night to Monday morning, awakening only for trips to the bathroom, fingers digging into the crotch of his wrinkled boxer shorts.

"Look at him eat with chopsticks," my father says with pride. It is the small changes he notices, the gestures acquired away from home. I'll order an after supper *eau de vie*, suggest we watch "Masterpiece Theater" instead of "Sunday Night Football." The small things, each one a wave taking me farther out to sea. "Gabey, Gabey," he shakes my shoulder with love. "How's your car?" It is only when I visit my father that I appreciate engine failure.

"Car's fine, Pop."

"You got enough money, Gabey?" Dad whispers. "You had to bake the brownies, you couldn't buy them?"

"I'm working. No complaints." I take more rice, more mu shu pork.

"How come we never see you?" You don't love us anymore, Gabey?"

"Of course I love you, Daddy." One more egg roll. One more butterfly shrimp. A last ladle of Five Happiness chicken.

"Naw," my father sighs, "you don't love us."

"But I do."

"You don't."

"I do."

"You don't"

Pause.

Her food untouched, glazed and reflecting the yellow light of the Chinese lanterns, my mother shakes her head and sighs. "You don't talk to us anymore. Not like you used to."

I am having momentary difficulty catching my breath. "Sure I talk to you."

"Oh, you tell us all the time what's good. Everything is fine.

You never talk to us like your sister does. You never tell us what's really on your mind."

I am slightly nauseous now. It comes in waves. One minute I feel feverish and about to fall over, the next I start to shiver. No, I don't talk to them now, I don't try to communicate. I blather on like a happy idiot, like an AM disc jockey. The last time I tried to talk honestly, to help them with their problems, I sat my mom down on the couch and held her. My voice trembled. She was crying. She hated living with him, she said, she cursed the day they were married. "Mama, if you are in so much pain, maybe you should separate for awhile. " That evening my father called me at my apartment. "So you told your mother to leave me, you little prick?"

All sound is muted. All lights in blur. I hear Cynthia defending me. I hear her ask my mother why only negative feelings are real ones.

"You don't understand," my mother says with contempt. "You have children and they become strangers and it hurts."

"But I do understand," Cynthia says. "I do have children."

"So you're a success, we're failures," my mother says.

"You're not."

"We are."

"You're not."

"We are."

I have never been so hungry. I am eating the last of the white rice and lobster sauce. I scrape the soggy water chestnuts from my mother's plate.

"Gabe, maybe you should slow down a bit," Cynthia reaches for my wrist.

"Let him live." My father shows his teeth. "Eat, Gabey, eat. It's good here, huh? Remember we used to be so close? We ate out every Sunday. We went on trips together. Remember we went to the Amish country? Oh, we found a good restaurant there."

My throat is dry, so dry I can only nod. I reach for my water glass, swallow it all, then Cynthia's.

"Remember the trip we took to Washington?" Dad continues.

On that particular excursion my father was mute for seven and a half hours, fuming anger like a toaster with crust jammed against its heating coil. Finally exploding, on the sixteen lane highway that rings the capital he said he was only on this goddamned trip because he'd never hear the end of it from my mother if he didn't spend his only vacation schlepping his kids to Washington, D.C. So leave! Go home! My mother wailed. She grabbed at the wheel. He shoved her away. We swerved off the road and my sister lost three teeth when her head rammed sideways into the ashtray.

"We had some good times, huh, Gabey?"

"Leave him, Sam," my mother says. "They get older they go off. They forget all the love."

"Want some dessert, Gabey? Hey, boy! Chop Chop!"

I breathe deeply, I steady myself. When the dizziness passes I will walk calmly to the men's room.

"How about ice cream, Gabey?" Dad says when the waiter arrives. "What you got? Van—ee—ra? Choc—rit? Slaw—belly?"

"Maybe he's eaten enough," Cynthia says.

"Leave him be, let him be a man." Dad burps, one of those intentionally loud, smelly burps, designed to shock.

"Sam!" my mother scolds him.

"So sorry, miss," my father bows to Cynthia. "You're an intellectual, I'm sorry. Maybe you never heard a burp before."

I am on my feet, not aware of having planned to stand up, but lurching to the door for air.

"It's the MSG, the chemicals," Cynthia says.

"Oh, the chemicals, pardon me," Dad says. "We should have eaten health food."

"Go to him, Darling, take care of him," I hear my mother say to Cynthia. "Go!"

In the parking lot I stand spread eagle over the trunk of my car. Cynthia paces, alternately caressing me, stroking my back, wiping my forehead; alternately raging. "What kind of idiot doesn't eat for two days and then poisons himself?"

"I was trying to look nice, to please them, to make them happy."

"But they are happy."

"They're miserable."

"But that's it, Gabriel, don't you see? They're happy being miserable."

"You wouldn't say that if they were your parents. I can change them, Cynthia. <u>We</u> can, together. By taking their minds off their own problems and helping them focus on the world. It's a slow process, I know. Tonight, the play. Next week something else. They're asking for help, don't you see? Who in the world wants to be miserable?"

My mother lights a fresh cigarette from the one in her mouth when she sees us come in. Dad is finishing a dish of chocolate ice cream. "Feel better, darling?" My mother reaches for my forehead. "You should go home and lie down."

"You should, Gabey. We're beat, too. We're just going to go back to the house and watch TV."

"But Cynthia's play…"

"We wouldn't like it, Darling."

"But you don't know that."

"We're too old, Gabey. Your father likes to go to bed early. I like my coffee and cake. We're just that way."

On the way out the waiter stops me, not to thank me for the five dollars he saw me add to my father's tip, but to hand me the foil-wrapped brownies Dad left in the booth.

Appendix II

RECOMMENDED BOOKS

In our tradition, there is a story often told about the great sage, Rabbi Hillel. A Roman soldier, taunting him, said he must recite the entire Torah while standing on one foot. Hillel thought for a moment, standing with difficulty, for he was an old man. "That which is hateful to you, do not do to your neighbor," he said. "That is the whole Torah; the rest is commentary."

Okay, maybe you've read this entire book cover to cover. Or maybe you read writing books the way you read mysteries, so you skipped to the end. Maybe you're standing in a bookstore right now and are trying to see what tips you can pick up without buying the book at all. No matter. We're going to sum up the entire book, everything we have to say about how to learn to write in one sentence, like Rabbi Hillel: *If you want to be a writer, be a reader.*

That's it. That's the whole deal. As we said back in chapter one, if you want to write memoirs, read one hundred of them. Figure out how other writers have avoided making themselves victims or failed to; figure out how other writers with great accomplishments in their middle age managed to solve the problem of keeping readers hooked while recounting a relatively uneventful childhood. If you want to write suspense novels, read all the thrillers you can find and pay attention to how these writers end one chapter and build anticipation for the next, or drop hints early on that will figure into the plot later. Or fail to. Bad writing can be as instructive as successful writing.

Just because you've been reading since you were five does not mean, no matter how interesting your life, that you can write about it in an interesting way. We do not suggest reading books like this one in hopes of finding a formula, but books in which other writers have managed to overcome the same problems of craft that you will inevitably face. *If you want to write, read.* The rest is commentary.

Here are some books you may find suggestive:

Allison, Dorothy — *Bastard Out of Carolina.* New York: Dutton, 1992.

Alvarez, Julia — *Yo!.* Chapel Hill: Algonquin, 1997.
In the Name of Salome. Chapel Hill: Algonquin, 2000.

Asaro, Catherine — *The Last Hawk.* New York: St. Martin's Press, 1998.

Angelou, Maya. — *I Know Why The Caged Bird Sings.* New York: Random House, 1970. (Memoir.)
Singin' and Swingin' and Gettin' Merry Like Christmas. New York: Random House, 1976. (Memoir.)
All God's Children Need Traveling Shoes. New York: Vintage Books, 1991. (Memoir.)

Atwood, Margaret — *Surfacing.* New York: Simon & Schuster, 1972.
The Handmaid's Tale. New York: Anchor, 1998.

Baker, Russell — *Growing Up.* New York: Plume, 1995.

Ballard, J.G. — *Empire of the Sun.* New York: Pocketbooks, 1985. (Memoir

Barrington, Judith — *Lifesaving.* Portland: Eighth Mountain Press, 2000. (Memoir.)

Bellow, Saul — *The Adventures of Augie March.* New York: Penguin, 1996.

Bragg, Rich — *All Over But the Shoutin'.* New York: Pantheon, 1997. (Memoir.)

Brecht, Bertold — *Three-penny Novel.* New York: Penguin, 1972. (Out of Print.)
Threepenny Opera. New York: Arcade, 1994.

Brontë, Charlotte — *Jane Eyre.* New York: Penguin Books, 1984.

Brownmiller, Susan
    In Our Time: Memoir of a Revolution. New York: Dial Press, 1999. (Memoir.)

Burke, James Lee   *Burning Angel.* New York: Hyperion, 1985.

Casella, Casare   *Diary of a Tuscan Chef.* New York: Doubleday, 1998. (Memoir.) (with Eileen Daspin)

Chabon, Michael   *Mysteries of Pittsburgh.* New York: Morrow, 1988.
    Werewolves in Their Youth. New York: Random House, 1999.

Chaucer, Geoffrey   *Canterbury Tales.* New York: Bantam, 1982.

Cheever, John   *The Stories of John Cheever.* New York: Vintage, 2000.

Conrad, Joseph   *Heart of Darkness.* New York: Penguin, 1999.
    Lord Jim. New York: Oxford University Press, 2000.

Danticat, Edwidge   *Krik? Krak!* New York: Random House, 1996.

De Beauvoir, Simone
    Memoirs of a Dutiful Daughter. New York: Harper, 1974. (Memoir.)
    Adieux. New York: Pantheon Books, 1984. (Memoir.)
    The Prime of Life. New York: Marlowe & Company. 1994. (Memoir.)
    Force of Circumstance. New York: Marlowe & Company. 1994. (Memoir.)
    The Coming of Age. New York: Norton, 1996. (Memoir.)
    America Day by Day. Berkeley: University of California Press, 2000.

Delany, Samuel R   *Stars in My Pocket Like Grains of Sand.* New York:Bantam, 1984.
    Triton. New York: Bantam, 1984.

Dinesen, Isak   *Out of Africa.* New York: Modern Library, 1992. (Memoir.)

Doctorow, E. L.   *Ragtime.* New York: Random House, 1975.
    Loon Lake. New York: Bantam, 1981.

Dos Passos, John   *U.S.A. (Trilogy)*. New York: Library of America, 1996.

Dunnett, Dorothy   *The Game of Kings*. New York: Vintage, 1997. (Or any of the books in the Lymond Chronicle Series)

Eco, Umberto   *The Name of the Rose*. New York: Harvest Books, 1994.

Evans, Richard Paul

    The Christmas Box. New York: Simon & Schuster, 1995.

Eve, Nomi   *The Family Orchard*. New York: Knopf, 2000.

Faulkner, William   *Sanctuary*. New York: Library of America, 1985.

Ferrell, Carolyn   *Don't Erase Me*. New York: Houghton Mifflin, 1997.

Finney, Patricia   *Firedrake's Eye*. New York: Picador, 1992.

Fisher, M. F. K.   *A Cordial Water*. New York: North Point Press, 1981. (Memoir.)

    The Gastronomical Me. New York: North Point Press, 1989. (Memoir.)

Fitzgerald, F. Scott   *The Great Gatsby*. New York: Scribner, 1995.

    Tender Is the Night. New York: Scribner, 1996.

Flanagan, Mary   Cream Sauce. In: *Bad Girls (stories)*. New York: Atheneum, 1985.

Fowles, John   *The Collector*. New York: Little Brown, 1963.

    The French Lieutenant's Woman. New York: Little Brown, 1969.

Frank, Anne   *The Diary of Anne Frank*, New York: Doubleday, 1952. (Memoir.)

Garcia, Cristina   *Dreaming in Cuban*. New York: Knopf, 1992.

    The Aguero Sisters. New York: Knopf, 1997.

Gibson, William   *Count Zero*. Westminster: Arbor House, 1986.

    Mona Lisa Overdrive. New York: Bantam, 1988.

    Burning Chrome. New York: Eos Books, 2003.

Godwin, Gail   *The Good Husband*. New York: Ballantine Books, 1994.

Goldberg, Myla   *Bee Season*. New York: Doubleday, 2000.

Goldman, William   *Marathon Man*. New York: Delacorte Press, 1974.

Gomez, Jewelle   *The Gilda Stores*. Ann Arbor: Firebrand Books, 1991.

Gordon, Mary   *The Shadow Man*. New York: Random House, 1996. (Memoir.)

Graham, Toni   *Waiting for Elvis*. Wellfleet: Leapfrog Press, 2005.

Hammett, Dashiell
   Maltese Falcon. New York: Knopf, 1930.

Heller, Joseph   *Catch 22*. New York: Simon & Schuster, 1996.

Hellman, Lillian   *An Unfinished Woman*. New York: Little Brown,1969. (Memoir.)
   Pentimento. New York: Little Brown, 1973. (Memoir.)
   Maybe. New York: Little Brown, 1980. (Memoir.)

Hemingway Ernest
   A Farewell to Arms. New York: Scribner, 1929.
   The Short Sweet Life of Francis McComber. In: *The Complete Short Stories of Ernest Hemingway*. New York: Scribner, 1998.

Herlihy, James Leo *Midnight Cowboy*. New York: Penguin, 1990.

Hijuelos, Oscar   *The Mambo Kings Play Songs of Love*. New York: Farrar, Strauss, Giroux, 1989.

Hinsey, Ellen   *Cities of Memory*. New Haven: Yale University Press, 1996.

Hoffman, Abbie   *Soon to Be a Major Motion Picture*. New York: Perigee, 1980. (Memoir.)

Hogan, Linda   *Mean Spirit*. Atheneum, 1990.

Homer   *The Odyssey*. New York: Noonday Press, 1998.
   Iliad. New York: Penguin, 1998.

Houston, Pam   *Cowboys Are My Weakness*. New York: W. W. Norton, 1992.

Jackson, Shirley   *The Lottery*. New York: Popular Library, 1949.

Jaffee, Annette Williams
   Adult Education. Wellfleet: Leapfrog Press, 2000.

James, Henry   *The Spoils of Poynton*. New York: Dell, 1959.

Joyce, James   *Portrait of the Artist as a Young Man*. New York: Modern Library, 1916.

Kafka, Franz   *The Trial.* New York: Modern Library, 1956.
Kadare, Ismail   *The Three Arched Bridge.* New York: Vintage
                       International, 1998.
Karr, Mary   *The Liars Club.* New York: Viking, 1995.
                       (Memoir.)
King, Laurie   *The Beekeeper's Apprentice.* New York: St.
                       Martins, 1994.
Kingsolver, Barbara
                       The Bean Trees. New York: Harper, 1998.
Kennedy, Pagan   *The Exes.* New York: Simon & Schuster, 1998.
Kinkaid, Jamaica   *Annie John.* New York: Farrar, Strauss, Giroux,
                       1985.
Kollontai, Alexandra
                       *The Autobiography of a Sexually Emancipated
                       Communist Woman.* New York: Schocken, 1975.
                       (Memoir.)
Le Carre, John   *Single & Single.* New York: Scribner, 1999.
Leduc, Violette   *La Batarde.* New York: Farrar, Straus, Giroux.
                       1965. (Memoir.)
Lee, Tanith   *Lycanthia.* New York: Daw Books, 1981.
LeGuin, Ursula   *The Dispossessed.* New York: Avon, 1974.
Lem, Stanislau   *Solaris.* New York: Walker & Co., 1970.
Lessing, Doris   *The Golden Notebook.* New York: Simon &
                       Shuster, 1960.
                       Martha Quest. New York: New American
                       Library, 1964.
                       A Proper Marriage. New York: Harper Collins,
                       1964.
                       A Ripple from the Storm. New York: New
                       American Library, 1966.
Lethem, Jonathan   *As She Climbed Across the Table.* New York:
                       Doubleday, 1997.
                       Amnesia Moon. New York: Harcourt Brace,
                       1996.

Levi, Primo   *The Periodic Table*. (Stories). New York: Schocken Books, 1984.
If Not Now, When? New York: Penguin, 1985.
The Reawakening. New York: Collier Books, 1986. (Memoir.)
The Drowned and the Saved. New York: Simon & Schuster, 1988. (Memoir.)

London, Jack   *To Build a Fire and Other Stories*. New York: Bantam, 1990.

Matousek, Mark   *Sex, Death, Enlightenment*. New York: Riverhead Books, 1996.

McCourt, Frank   *Angela's Ashes*. New York: Touchstone, 1999. (Memoir.)

McCoy, Maureen   *Junebug*. Wellfleet: Leapfrog Press, 2004.

McInerney, Jay   *Story of My Life*. New York: Atlantic Monthly Press, 1988.

Melville, Herman   *Moby Dick*. New York: Macmillan, 1962.

Mailer, Norman   *Armies of the Night*. New York: New American Library, 1968.

Mitchell, Lauren Porosoff
Look at Me. Wellfleet; Leapfrog Press, 2000.

Morrison, Toni   *Sula*. New York: Knopf, 1973.
Song of Solomon. New York: Knopf, 1977.
Beloved. New York: Knopf, 1987.

Muhanji, Cherry   *Her: A Novel*. San Francisco: Aunt Lute Books, 1991.

Muller, Karin   *Hitchhiking Vietnam: A Woman's Solo Journey in an Elusive Land*. Guilford: Globe Pequot Press, 1998. (Memoir.)

Murdoch, Iris   *A Word Child*. New York: Viking Press, 1975.

Nabokov, Vladimir
Speak, Memory. New York: Putnam, 1966. (Memoir.)
Lolita. New York: Putnam, 1980.

Neruda, Pablo   *Memoirs*. New York: Farrar, Straus, Giroux, 1976.

Oates, Joyce Carol   *Blonde*. New York: Harper Ecco, 1999.

O'Brien, Edna. Storm
  In: A Fanatic Heart. New York: New American Library, 1985.
Paley, Grace *Enormous Changes at the Last Minute*. New York: Farrar, Straus, Giroux, 1974.
  Later the Same Day. New York: Farrar, Straus, Giroux, 1985.
Piercy, Marge *Small Changes*. New York: Doubleday, 1973.
  Woman on the Edge of Time. New York: Knopf, 1976.
  Braided Lives. New York: Summit, 1981.
  Parti-Colored Blocks for a Quilt. Ann Arbor: University of Michigan Press,   1983.
  Gone to Soldiers. New York: Summit, 1987.
  He, She & It. New York: Knopf, 1991.
  The Longings of Women. New York: Fawcett Columbine, 1994.
  City of Darkness, City of Light. New York: Fawcett Columbine, 1996.
  Three Women. New York: Morrow, 1999.
  Sleeping with Cats. New York: Morrow/Harper Collins, 2002. (Memoir.)
Piercy, Marge and Ira Wood
  Storm Tide. New York: Ballantine, 1998.
Power, Susan *Grass Dancer*. New York: Putnam, 1994.
Price, Richard *Clockers*. New York: Houghton Mifflin, 1992.
Pynchon, Thomas *V*. New York: Bantam Books, 1964.
  Vineland. New York: Little, Brown & Co., 1990.
Quindlen, Anna *One True Thing*. New York: Random House, 1994.
Raphael, Lev *The German Money*. Wellfleet: Leapfrog Press, 2003.
Rosenthal Richard *Rookie Cop*. Wellfleet: Leapfrog Press, 2000. (Memoir.)
Ross, Lillian *Portrait of Hemingway*. New York: Modern Library, 1999.

Roszak, Theodore.
    The Devil and Daniel Silverman. Wellfleet: Leapfrog Press, 2002.

Roth, Philip   *Portnoy's Complaint.* New York: Random House, 1969.
    Sabbath's Theater. New York: Houghton Mifflin, 1995.

Runyon, Damon   *Guys & Dolls: The Stories of Damon Runyon.* New York: Penguin, 1992.

Russ, Joanna   *The Female Man.* New York: Bantam Book, 1975.

Sarton, May   *Encore.* New York: W. W. Norton & Co., 1993. (Any of Sarton's many memoirs are recommended.) (Memoir.)

Scott, Melissa   *Trouble and Her Friends.* New York: TOR, 1994.

Sedaris, David   *Naked.* Boston: Back Bay Books, 1997.

Shreve, Anita   *The Weight of Water.* New York: Little, Brown, 1997.

Slouka, Mark   *Lost Lake.* New York: Knopf, 1998.

Smith, Zadie   *White Teeth.* New York: Random House, 2000.

Sobell, Morton.   *On Doing Time.* New York: Charles Scribner's Sons, 1974. (Memoir.)

Sophocles   *Oedipus Rex.* Mineola: Dover, 1993.

Sprigg, June   *Simple Gifts: A Memoir of a Shaker Village.* New York: Knopf, 1998 (Memoir.)

Tangherlini, Arne   *leo@fergusrules.com.* Wellfleet: Leapfrog Press, 1999.

Thomas, Elizabeth Marshall
    Reindeer Moon. New York: Pocket, 1991.

Thomas, Piri   *Seven Long Times.* Houston: Arte Publico Press, 1994.

Thompson, Hunter S.
    Fear and Loathing in Las Vegas: A Savage Journey to the Heart of the American Dream. New York: Vintage, 1998.

Thoreau, Henry   *Walden.* Princeton: Princeton University Press, 1989. (Memoir.)

Tolstoy, Leo   *War & Peace*. New York: Viking, 1982.
Traven, B.   *The Treasure of the Sierra Madre*. New York: Hill
                    & Wang, 1996.
Twain, Mark   *Huckleberry Finn*. New York: Penguin, 1986.
                    A Connecticut Yankee in King Arthur's Court.
                    New York: Bantam, 1994.
Vidal, Gore   *Palimpsest*. New York: Random House, 1995.
                    (Memoir.)
Voltaire. Candide   *New York*. Penguin, 1990.
Vonnegut, Kurt   *Slaughterhouse Five*. New York: Delta, 1999.
Wallace, David Foster
                    Infinite Jest. New York: Little, Brown & Co.,
                    1996.
Waugh, Evelyn   *Brideshead Revisited*. New York: Knopf, 1993.
Weldon, Fay   *Darcy's Utopia*. New York: Penguin Group, 1990.
Willis, Connie   *To Say Nothing of the Dog*. New York: Bantam,
                    1998.
Winterson, Jeanette
                    Oranges Are Not the Only Fruit. Boston: Atlantic
                    Monthly, 1987.
Woolf Virginia   *Mrs. Dalloway*. New York: Harcourt Brace &
                    Co, 1925.
Wood, Ann.   *Bolt Risk*. Wellfleet: Leapfrog Press, 2005.
Wood, Ira   *The Kitchen Man*. Wellfleet: Leapfrog Press,
                    1998.
                    Going Public. Cambridge: Zoland Books, 1991.
Woods, Teri   *True to the Game*. New York: Teri Woods
                    Publishing, 1999.
X, Malcolm with Alex Haley
                    The Autobiography of Malcolm X. New York:
                    Grove Press, 1964. (Memoir.)
Yurick, Sol   *The Warriors*. New York: Dell, 1979.
Zenophon   *The Anabasis*. Cambridge: Harvard University
                    Press, 1999.
Zinsser, William, editor
                    Inventing the Truth: The Art and Craft of Memoir.
                    Boston: Houghton Mifflin, 1987.

Also of use:

Deval, Jacqueline   *Publicize Your Book!.* New York: Perigee, 2003.
Jassin, Lloyd J. and Schecter, Steven C.
                     The Copyright Permission and Libel Handbook:
                     A Step by Step Guide for Writers, Editors and
                     Publishers. New York: Wiley, 1998.
Kirkpatrick, David D.
                     Report to the Author Guild Midlist Books Study
                     Committee. Available from:
                     http://www.authorsguild.org/miscfiles/
                     midlist.pdf
Levine, Mark L.   *Negotiating a Book Contract: A Guide for Authors,*
                     Agents and Lawyers. Wakefield: Moyer Bell,
                     1994.

Index

M

N

O

Q

R

S

U

V

W

Y

Z

Acknowledgments of Excerpts

Used in the Text by Page Number

Page 29   from *Look At Me* by Lauren Porosoff Mitchell. Wellfleet: Leapfrog Press, 2000. © 2000 by Lauren Porosoff Mitchell.

Page 30,   from *Storm Tide* by Marge Piercy and Ira Wood. New York: Fawcett/Ballantine, <u>1998</u>. © 1998 by Middlemarsh, Inc.

Page 33   from *He, She and It* by Marge Piercy. New York: Fawcett/Ballantine, <u>1993</u>. © 1991 by Middlemarsh, Inc.

Page 34   from *Gone To Soldiers* by Marge Piercy. New York: Fawcett/Ballantine,1988. © 1987 Middlemarsh, Inc.

Page 35   from *The Kitchen Man* by Ira Wood. Wellfleet: Leapfrog Press, 1998. ©1986 by Middlemarsh, Inc.

Page 38   from *Rookie Cop* by Richard Rosenthal. Wellfleet: Leapfrog Press, 2000. © 1999 by Richard Rosenthal.

Page 40   from *Sleeping With Cats* by Marge Piercy. New York: William Morrow & Company, 2002. © 2001 by Middlemarsh, Inc.

Page 53   from *Junebug* by Maureen McCoy. Wellfleet: Leapfrog Press, 2004. © 2004 by Maureen McCoy

Page 81   from *Storm Tide* by Marge Piercy and Ira Wood. New York: Fawcett/Ballantine, <u>1998</u>. © 1998 by Middlemarsh, Inc.

Page 84   from *Woman on the Edge of Time* by Marge Piercy. New York: Fawcett/Ballantine, 1997. © 1986 by Middlemarsh, Inc.

Page 87   from *Three Women* by Marge Piercy. New York: William Morrow, 1999; Harper/Torch, 2000. © 1999, by Middlemarsh, Inc.

Page 89   from *Three Women* by Marge Piercy. New York: William Morrow, 1999; Harper/Torch, 2000. © 1999, by Middlemarsh, Inc.

Page 90   from *Waiting for Elvis* by Toni Graham. Wellfleet: Leapfrog Press, 2005. © 2005 by Toni Graham.

Page 101   from "Thoughts on *Adult Education* Many Years Later: The Afterword to the 20th Anniversary Edition," *Adult Education* by Annette Williams Jaffee. Wellfleet: Leapfrog Press, 2000. © 1981 by Annette Williams Jaffee.

Page 135   from *Look At Me* by Lauren Porosoff Mitchell. Wellfleet: Leapfrog Press, 2000. © 2000 by Lauren Porosoff Mitchell.

Page 141   from *Small Changes* by Marge Piercy. New York: Fawcett/Ballantine, 1997. © 1986 by Middlemarsh, Inc.

Page 142   from *City of Darkness, City of Light* by Marge Piercy. New York: Fawcett/Ballantine, 1996. © 1996 by Middlemarsh, Inc.

Page 143   from *The Kitchen Man* by Ira Wood. Wellfleet: Leapfrog Press, 1998. © 1986 by Middlemarsh, Inc.

Page 144   from *Storm Tide* by Marge Piercy and Ira Wood. New York: Fawcett/Ballantine, 1998. © 1998 by Middlemarsh, Inc.

Page 146   from *City of Darkness, City of Light* by Marge Piercy. New York: Fawcett/Ballantine, 1996. © 1996 by Middlemarsh, Inc.

Page 147   from *Three Women* by Marge Piercy. New York: William Morrow, 1999; Harper/Torch, 2000. © 1999, by Middlemarsh, Inc.

Page 148   from *leo@fergusrules.com* by Arne Tangherlini. Wellfleet: Leapfrog Press, 1999. © 1999 by Gina Apostol-Tangherlini.

Page 165   from *He, She and It* by Marge Piercy. New York: Fawcett/Ballantine, 1993. © 1991 by Middlemarsh, Inc.

Page 205   from *The Kitchen Man* by Ira Wood. Wellfleet: Leapfrog Press, 1998.© 1986 by Middlemarsh, Inc.

Page 207   from The Devil and Daniel Silverman by Theodore Roszak. Wellfleet: Leapfrog Press, 2003.© 2003 by Theodore Roszak.

Page 211-13   from *The Kitchen Man* by Ira Wood. Wellfleet: Leapfrog Press, 1998.© 1986 by Middlemarsh, Inc.

A Note About The Authors

Marge Piercy is the author of seventeen novels including *The New York Times* bestseller *Gone To Soldiers*; the national bestseller, *The Longings of Women* and the classic, *Woman on the Edge of Time*; sixteen volumes of poetry, and a critically acclaimed memoir, *Sleeping with Cats*. The compact disk recording of her political poems, *LOUDER: We Can't Hear You Yet!* was named the Best Poetry AudioBook of the Year by *Library Journal*. Born in center city Detroit, educated at the University of Michigan, the recipient of four honorary doctorates, she has been a key player in many of the major progressive movements of our time, including civil rights, anti-Vietnam war, feminism, and the resistance to the war in Iraq. A popular speaker on college campuses, she has been a featured guest on Bill Moyers' PBS Specials, Garrison Keillor's *Prairie Home Companion*, Terri Gross's *Fresh Air*, the *Today Show*, and many radio programs nationwide. Praised as one of the few American writers who is an accomplished poet as well as a novelist, she is also the master of many genres: historical novels, science fiction (for which she won the Arthur C. Clarke Award for the Best Science Fiction Novel in the United Kingdom), novels of social comment and contemporary entertainments. She has taught, lectured and/or performed her work at more than 400 universities around the world. A great deal of information about Marge Piercy is available on her website, www.margepiercy.com.

Ira Wood is the author of two novels, *The Kitchen Man* and *Going Public,* and the co-author (with Marge Piercy) of the erotic thriller, *Storm Tide*. He has crafted stage plays and interactive fiction for children, as well as screenplays. Ira's work emphasizes humor, autobiographical material and the family. He and Piercy travel all over the country to give workshops in fiction and the personal narrative, which stress the importance of the writer's craft and overcoming the inner and outer barriers to creativity. In 1996, he and Piercy created Leapfrog Press, a small publishing company specializing in poetry, memoir and literary fiction. Find out more about Leapfrog at www.leapfrogpress.com.

Are you ready to take the next step and get feedback on your work?

Are you ready to sign up for a workshop?

You can learn a great deal from this book but nothing replaces the feedback you can take away from a writing class; not only from the comments of experienced working writers and teachers; not only from the observations of other writers in the class; but from the editor inside yourself. Sharing your writing with other serious writers, and at the same time hearing others' work, enables you to judge whether your intentions are successful or if they fall short. And if they fall short, why? What can you do about it? How can you change it to make it work?

Moreover, a workshop, like a publication deadline, requires that you actually finish something to share rather than simply thinking about it.

A workshop is a risk, no doubt about it. It may shake your illusions or your complacency. You might discover that not all, but certain parts of your project are weak; or that the work is actually very good and speaks to others. You may decide that it is time to revise your work with the aim of submitting it for publication.

Ultimately the decision rests upon how serious you are about your writing. Are you ready to take the next step and get feedback on your work? Are you ready to sign up for a workshop?
Find the complete schedule of the So You Want to Write Workshops, as well as a detailed description at www.leapfrogpress.com.